DECODING IRAN'S FOREIGN POLICY

DECODING IRAN'S FOREIGN POLICY

Strategic interests, power, and influence

Ross Harrison

I.B. TAURIS
LONDON • NEW YORK • OXFORD • NEW DELHI • SYDNEY

I.B. TAURIS
Bloomsbury Publishing Plc
50 Bedford Square, London, WC1B 3DP, UK
1385 Broadway, New York, NY 10018, USA
29 Earlsfort Terrace, Dublin 2, Ireland

BLOOMSBURY, I.B. TAURIS and the I.B. Tauris logo are trademarks of
Bloomsbury Publishing Plc

First published in Great Britain 2025

Copyright © Ross Harrison, 2025

Ross Harrison has asserted his rights under the Copyright, Designs and Patents Act, 1988, to be identified as Author of this work.

For legal purposes the Acknowledgments on p. xiv constitute an extension of this copyright page.

Series design by Charlotte Daniels
Cover image © Hossein Fatemi/Panos Picture

All rights reserved. No part of this publication may be reproduced or transmitted in any form or by any means, electronic or mechanical, including photocopying, recording, or any information storage or retrieval system, without prior permission in writing from the publishers.

Bloomsbury Publishing Plc does not have any control over, or responsibility for, any third-party websites referred to or in this book. All internet addresses given in this book were correct at the time of going to press. The author and publisher regret any inconvenience caused if addresses have changed or sites have ceased to exist, but can accept no responsibility for any such changes.

A catalogue record for this book is available from the British Library.

A catalog record for this book is available from the Library of Congress.

ISBN: HB: 978-0-7556-4606-7
PB: 978-0-7556-4605-0
ePDF: 978-0-7556-4607-4
eBook: 978-0-7556-4608-1

Typeset by RefineCatch Limited, Bungay, Suffolk
Printed and bound in Great Britain

To find out more about our authors and books visit www.bloomsbury.com and sign up for our newsletters.

This book is dedicated to my loving wife, Mahnaz M. Harrison, whose love for Iran is infectious. It is also in memory of Richard W. Cottam, teacher, friend, and colleague, who first introduced me to the mysteries of Iran's foreign policy.

CONTENTS

Preface viii
Acknowledgments xiv

1 The Historical Present 1
2 Iran's View of the World 27
3 Iran's View of the Middle East 67
4 Iran's View of Itself 103
5 Assessing Iran's Capability 119
6 Unpacking Iran's Foreign Policy Strategy 141
7 Iran's Strategic Future 187
　　Conclusion 219

Notes 225
Bibliography 257
Index 261

PREFACE

There is some risk in writing about Iran's foreign policy. Controversy over Iran's actions in the Middle East has been intensified by political polarization in the United States, like with so many other domestic and foreign policy issues. Objectivity about Iran tends to be construed as an apologia for its actions by some. And for others, any analysis that is critical of Iran's actions in the region leads to the charge of bias against the Islamic Republic.

This book is an attempt to skirt this peril by trying to explain Iran's foreign policy, neither defending nor condemning it. Of course, for some the line between explanation, analysis, and defense is blurred. But by examining Iran using a strategic lens, hopefully the fair reader will see the value in looking at Iran's foreign policy as a strategic response to its current and past geopolitical environments, using the resources and capabilities it has at its disposal.

Arguing that Iran's strategy is adaptive to what it sees as a treacherous environment should not let it off the hook for its regional transgressions or repressive domestic behavior. Leaders of nations sometimes burst onto the scene in a spirit of nationalism, only later to transmogrify into ugly, repressive despots. Countries, too, can follow a regressive path over time. There is much to find unsavory about Iran's regional and domestic behavior. But even so, a cool, dispassionate look at Iran's foreign policy using its own lens, and not ours, is important.

This book is not intended to be an exposé. Rather, it is an attempt to decode Iran's foreign policy, with the hope of rendering it less mysterious. This is important at a time when Iran is becoming more challenging given the advances in its nuclear enrichment program, its fortified relationship with Russia since the Ukraine war, and when all regional powers, including Iran, are flexing their muscles vis-à-vis global powers. And, of course, this is important as Iran has been a central actor in the activation of its allied militias after Hamas invaded Israel on October 7, 2023, killing over 1,200 and kidnapping over 200 civilians, followed by

Israel's invasion of Gaza, killing tens of thousands of Palestinians. Looking at Iran using a strategic lens is also critical as it faces the reality that its edifice of militias has been compromised with Israeli actions in Lebanon that have degraded the capability of Hezbollah, and in Gaza where Hamas has been damaged. A strategic approach is also important as Iran faces the consequences of the toppling of the regime of President Bashar al-Assad of Syria in 2024, which could potentially translate into the loss of Iran's only regional state ally. Furthermore, direct attacks by both Israel and Iran on each other alter the strategic landscape in ways that deserve consideration.

Seeing Iran's foreign policy as the result of tension between how it views itself in the present and in the past is one of the pathways this book will take the reader on. It will also look at how it views the region amid a shifting global geopolitical landscape.

There are several arguments that will be advanced in this book. The core argument is that Iran's view of the world, the region, and its place within this context is a byproduct of specific challenges and opportunities it faced before and since the revolution, including intervention by great powers, the Iran-Iraq war, and the civil wars that broke out in the Middle East during and after the Arab Spring. While many of the drivers of Iran's behavior are rooted in challenges of the modern day, several have echoes in Iran's distant past. Another argument is that Iran's power projection success has been built on the failed policies and stumbles of other actors. One of Iran's power skills has been adaptation, deftly parlaying the blunders of others into strategic advantages for itself. Policy failures by the United States, missteps of Saudi Arabia, and failed governance in Iraq, Syria, Lebanon, and Yemen have provided the canvas upon which Iran's foreign policy has been drawn. This is not to say that Iran's gains have been gifts provided by others. The missteps were owned by others, but Iran deftly took advantage of these and constructed an integrated strategy around them.

The other part of the argument that courses through this book is that Iran has built its alliance system, strategic doctrines, capabilities, and institutions in response to a world that evolved after the Cold War ended. It was built on a backdrop of failed states, civil wars, and the collapse of regional order. Iran has done a skillful job of adapting to a changing region and world, perhaps better than its rivals in the Middle East.

The question the book leaves the reader with is whether Iran is wedded to the status quo and only wins if the region remains in its current troubled state? Or, given its current leadership, capabilities, and worldviews, can it transform its narrow security capabilities into a broader spectrum of economic, social, and political capabilities that can redound to the benefit of the next generation of Iranians? And can it successfully navigate through the realities of a region shaken by and potentially reshaped by what happened after October 7, 2023?

The book will show that Iran's foreign policy entails multiple paradoxes, defying a linear treatment. We will see both continuities and discontinuities when looking at Iran's pre-revolutionary and post-revolutionary foreign policies. There is a tendency to treat Iran's post-revolutionary behavior as a paradigm shift and stark departure from the past. Certainly, there is plenty of evidence to suggest this is the case. Iran's behavior relative to the United States, Israel, and the Arab world changed dramatically after the revolution. Friends became enemies and enemies became friends. But when it comes to the major strategic challenges Iran has faced, many of them carry over from Iran's distant past, albeit interpreted through a different ideological lens and worldview. While the discontinuities receive the most press, the continuities are important to look at in helping us think about how Iran's foreign policy may evolve in the future, and what policy might be appropriate in terms of responding to those changes.

Henry Kissinger once said that "Iran must decide whether it is a country or a cause," meaning that Iranian leaders must choose between their revolutionary ideological views and the country's hard core realpolitik national interests.[1] This book shows that this is an oversimplification and false dichotomy. Iran's foreign policy is a blend of hardcore realpolitik considerations from the present and rigid ideological political biases and grievances from the past. As a mid-sized power in a tough neighborhood, it can't afford to completely abandon realpolitik principles in favor of an ideological foreign policy rooted solely in the past.

There are some limitations to analyzing Iran's foreign policy using a strategic lens. What if Iran doesn't really have an overarching grand strategy for dealing with its challenges, but merely responds tactically to these? And how can we speak about a single strategy when there are so many fits and starts and institutional inputs into Iran's foreign policy behavior?

The book doesn't presuppose that a single overarching strategy drives Iran's foreign policy behavior. In many ways, Iran has been a master at adaptation to changes and events outside its control. But a careful look suggests that there isn't necessarily inconsistency between Iran's tactical adaptation to events and the appearance of broad strategic patterns. The reader will see that while Iran's foreign policy has mostly been adaptive to changing circumstances, it has consolidated the incremental successes it has achieved along the way into what appears to be a more integrated strategy.

What we will see is that Iran made some early decisions about its priorities shortly after the revolution, such as in 1982 to support the formation of Hezbollah, and that this early decision was scaled up when opportunities opened decades later for Iran to expand its capabilities into Iraq, Yemen, and Syria. What started as a couple of ideologically supported tactical decisions in the 1980s morphed into a broader strategic direction later. We will also see how seminal the Iran-Iraq war of 1980–88 was in setting Iran on its current path.

The question the book ends with is will Iran need to rebalance its capabilities and strategic priorities in a post-October 7 environment? The October 7, 2023 attacks by Hamas on Israel, Israel's response in Gaza, and the direct attacks Iran and Israel have volleyed since then have undermined the delicate region-wide system of deterrence that had evolved in previous decades. Prior to 2023, Iran viewed its support for militias like Hezbollah and Hamas as serving its need to deter the United States and Israel. But in the new environment, Iran's support for groups like these could undermine rather than create deterrence. And the potential loss of Syria as an ally could undermine Iran's capacity to work with and coordinate efforts with already weakened Hamas and Hezbollah.

Iran has proven to be a master adapter. But now that the taboo on direct conflict with Israel has been broken with the back-and-forth attacks of 2024, and Iran's asymmetric capabilities through its militias have been compromised, will it be able to maintain its regional influence using more conventional means? Iran previously was able to generate regional power from the shadows of failed states using militias like Hamas and Hezbollah. But now that these militias have been compromised, the Assad regime in Syria has fallen, and Iran has engaged in open conflict with Israel, will Tehran continue to be able to wield significant regional influence? Will doubts about Iran's deterrence translate into it shifting the emphasis of its foreign policy to favor more conventional diplomacy? Or, will it lead to a mad dash for a nuclear weapon? While it is unlikely that Iran will give up on the system of militias it has built over the past decades, it may feel pressure from regional actors and global actors, including China, to recalibrate its policies toward more conventional military, economic, and political means.

The book doesn't presuppose that Iranian decision-makers hold consistent views or speak with one voice about foreign policy. When we analyze Iran's regional and international context, we will look at the views that prevailed to form Iran's policy over time, neither assuming that these are the only views nor that there is consensus across the regime. We are more interested in the patterns that make up Iran's foreign policy than the intra-regime push-and-pull across different voices.

The book draws on several different layers of research. Over the course of the years it has taken, I have had privileged access to senior Iranian leaders, including two sitting presidents, including the current President Masoud Pezeshkian, three foreign ministers, two UN special representatives to the United Nations, deputy foreign ministers, and many Iranian scholars in Iran and in the diaspora, as well as some lower-level government officials. I have also interviewed individuals close to the inner circle of Supreme Leader Ali Khamenei. For Iran's relations with surrounding Arab countries, I drew on meetings with a former Iraqi prime minister, several senior placed Saudis, and Lebanese. I also drew from secondary sources to help fill out the picture of the patterns of Iran's foreign policy. When appropriate and possible, these primary and secondary sources are clearly cited in the end-of-book chapter notes.

Each of the chapters in the book is designed to provide an angle into Iran's foreign policy strategy. Chapter 1 looks at how Iran's history, going back to the Safavid Dynasty, is relevant to Iran's foreign policy today. In Chapter 2, we examine how Iran's prevailing worldview was formed and how Iranian policy-makers analyze the changing global political and economic system. We will peer into how Iranian leaders evaluate power distribution in the global system today and the trends they see for the future. Chapter 3 will then do the same kind of analysis but scoping down to the Middle East region. We will see that the United States, both a regional and global actor, looms large in Chapters 2 and 3. Chapter 4 will look at how Iran views itself, including the assumptions it makes about its interests, role, motivation, and strategy in the policy formulation process. Chapter 5 will examine Iran's strategic capabilities and constraints, leaving the reader with questions about whether its current set of capabilities can be adapted to changes that might occur in the region in the ensuing years. Chapter 6 tells several stories about Iran's strategy that hopefully will give us an idea as to how Iran has been able to show success (and some failures) as it navigates its environment. And finally, Chapter 7 will tackle Iran's strategic future. It won't predict what the future of Iran's foreign policy will look like, but rather will consider different scenarios.

Chapter 7 will perhaps audaciously look at the case of Vietnam as a possible best-case scenario of how Iran might develop in the coming decades. There are plenty of reasons why Iran won't likely make the transformation away from being an outlier in the regional and global system, as Vietnam did in the 1990s. But it will lay out some of the conditions that might be conducive to such a turnaround. I am aware that this is tricky as it may open me up to charges of idealism or naivete. I am willing to take this risk as I think it is important to examine examples from outside the Middle East for clues as to how Iran might develop in the future. It wouldn't be unreasonable to argue that the most likely scenario is Iran remaining stubbornly on its current course. But also, Iran wouldn't be the first state to take the path toward transformation.

Iranian foreign policy embodies a dialectic. The country on the one hand has a history of a glorious and victorious ancient past, with roots extending back thousands of years to the Persian Empire. But on the other hand, modern-day Iran represents only a small portion of what had been ancient Persia, due to old and current challenges and threats. Iranians have immense pride in their past, but also are burdened by insecurities about their present and their future.

This book hopes to do Iran's foreign policy challenges justice in a way that considers the dialectic between ambitions of greatness and the challenges that frustrate this in such a way as to help policy-makers and analysts come to proper judgments. The United States has failed to interpret and deal with Iran effectively. If this book helps in some small way, then I have done my job.

ACKNOWLEDGMENTS

No book is written in an intellectual vacuum. This work was done with encouragement and support from the Middle East Institute in Washington, DC, my intellectual home for more than a decade. My colleagues, particularly my dear friend Paul Salem, its president until 2024, deserve much credit for providing the intellectual feedback for my good and bad ideas. I also want to thank another dear friend, Alex Vatanka, for serving as a sounding board on matters related to Iran. Alex and I have written several articles together over the years, which stimulated my interest in the topic of this book. I also want to thank Randa Slim, who ran the Track 1.5 and Track 2 initiatives at MEI, for giving me the opportunity to meet so many current and former decision-makers in the region, including from Iran, Saudi Arabia, Turkey, and the United Arab Emirates. And a special thanks to Dr. Shahrokh Fardoust, former Director of Strategy and Operations, Development Economics at the World Bank, for helping me through the section on Iran's economic capability.

I also want to thank Sophie Rudland, publisher and commissioning editor at Bloomsbury, I.B. Tauris in London for giving invaluable feedback, helping me stay on track and for giving me the encouragement I needed to finish this book. The book wouldn't have been written without her help and support.

Also, I would be remiss if I didn't mention the capable research assistants I had during the long process of researching and writing this book. Gaden James, who was at the University of Pennsylvania, worked very closely with me for a long stretch of this book, providing incisive analysis, research, and feedback. He also helped with the meetings with senior leaders and influencers, taking notes and later synthesizing what we learned from the various interviewees. He was also a great sounding board and was intensely motivated by a thirst for an understanding of Iran. Reily Christian, Dara Hadighi, Arshia (Ash) Alguneh, and Hannah Gursoy were also immensely helpful in doing deep dives on topics, freeing me up to keep up with the demands of writing.

Also, Alistair Taylor, Managing Director and Editor-in-Chief of the Middle East Institute's Policy Center was always ready to add assistance at the prospectus, review, and manuscript stages of this project. I am deeply indebted to all who helped along the way with this project. Their contributions were many, while any failings are solely my own.

1 THE HISTORICAL PRESENT

A country's foreign policy always has a tense relationship with the past. Leaders tend to tout their policies as modern and forged out of a vision for the future, rather than products of the past.

Revolutionary leaders almost inevitably change the arc of a country's foreign policy. Aside from the propulsive domestic dynamics of a revolution that catapult a country into new foreign policy directions, geostrategic factors also lead to profound foreign policy shifts. Revolution in one country can change the strategic calculations of neighboring states, transforming erstwhile allies into adversaries, and turning previously hostile states into allies. In other words, the spillover effects of revolution can lead to regional changes that render obsolete the policies of the old pre-revolutionary regime.

But alongside the inevitable discontinuities, there are likely to be inescapable threads of continuity. Revolutionaries may confront the stubborn realities of the tyranny of prior decisions that limit their range of options. They also will face vital interests that endure despite revolution, geographic realities that impose themselves, as well omnipresent threats from historical enemies. These dynamics can be like anchors that make clean breaks from the past difficult.

The threads of continuity and discontinuity from the past appear in the case of post-revolutionary Iran. To this day, Iranian leaders take pride in claims of having broken free of its pre-revolutionary history. The Iranian revolution embodied a populist ideology that promised change from the policies of the ancien régime of Mohammed Reza Shah Pahlavi.

This chapter will focus on how the past is relevant to the foreign policy-making of Iran today. It will address the continuities with the past, while later chapters will highlight the discontinuities and idiosyncratic nature of Iran's post-revolutionary foreign policies. Looking at some of the patterns of continuity in this chapter will help us depersonalize our look at Iran's foreign policy, perhaps giving us a wider and more analytic view of the patterns in Iran's decision-making today.

This will give us a broader perspective on current challenges of the country and perhaps even the motivational drivers of Iran's leaders. This exercise can also help us better understand how decisions made today could potentially impose themselves on future Iranian decision-makers.

In the process of researching this book, the author grappled with the question of where in Iran's history to start when striving for relevance of the past. In this chapter, we will go back 500 years to the Safavid dynasty. With a country whose roots go back over 2,500 years to Cyrus the Great, why commence 500 years ago when looking at the past to gain an understanding of the policy-making options and decisions made today? The reason to start our story with the Safavid period is that several challenges of today have roots in this and subsequent dynasties, such as the Qajar and Pahlavi.

Questions such as the connection between ideology and realpolitik pragmatism go back to this period, as does the issue of how internal domestic cohesion relates to the latitude leaders have to conduct independent foreign policies. In addition, questions related to the challenges of dealing with multiple great powers have roots in this era, including how to cope with betrayal by greater powers who prioritize relations with each other over matters related to Iran.

This is not to suggest that more ancient periods have no relevance. For many Iranians, the full expanse of the Persian Empire going back to Cyrus and the halcyon days of Persepolis echo in their own identities. But in terms of the geopolitical challenges faced by Iran, the Safavid era seems a reasonable and critical starting point.

The Historical Present

Asserting causality or even relevance between the foreign policy decisions of the past and the present is always a tricky business. The further back one goes in time, the more attenuated are the links between past events and present-day foreign policy behaviors.

It is much easier to link the relatively recent past to the foreign policy exigencies of today. The more immediate past can impose itself on current foreign policy in several ways that become more difficult the further back in time we go. Actions and decisions taken in the more recent past can impose themselves on the present by narrowing the range of options of governmental leaders of today. This is because decisions taken in the more recent past may have enduring legacies such as the reactions of adversaries and allies, and because prior decisions can either open opportunities or engender threats that have their own momentum and stubborn logic. In other words, prior decisions create path dependencies that are lines of causality between events of the past and the policy challenges of today.

But going back 500 years, the cause-effect relationship is a bit more strained and tenuous. Unlike with more recent decisions, it is hard to identify clear drivers. Instead, we can look for repeating patterns that clearly aren't coincidental and don't seem to attenuate or weaken as history marches on. Rather than identifying clear drivers or lines of causality, we look for *influencing factors* that are adduced to explain patterns of continuity or broader trends.[1] In other words, we are looking for events or even structural factors, such as geography, that impose themselves consistently over time.

There are several ways to think about the influence of Iran's remote past on today. The first is "historical memory," which means how decision-makers, and even mass publics, interpret the present considering the past. Iranians are both aware and proud of their country's Persian past, engendering a perception of superiority over the newer, Arab, countries of the Persian Gulf. This chauvinism can even today spill over into the country's foreign policy attitudes about and behaviors toward Saudi Arabia and other Arab neighbors.

The late Ayatollah Ruhollah Khomeini often linked the present to the past by harkening back to an earlier pre-nationalist age, when Islam was the primary organizing principle of Persia's foreign policy.[2] While the notion of *vilayat-e faqih* (Islamic jurisprudence or governance) is a relatively new phenomenon, Khomeini drew from earlier Islamic periods where the boundaries between the state and religion were blurred and even blended.[3]

What is most important isn't whether the present is built on an accurate representation of the past, but rather how it is remembered, interpreted, and instrumentalized for public consumption. Halcyon days are never as glorious as their overly simplified and popular depictions, but what is more important than the facts is the meaning assigned to earlier days by leaders.

Both the previous Iranian regime of Mohammed Reza Shah Pahlavi and the post-revolutionary government led by Ayatollah Ruhollah Khomeini have their own halcyon days as reference points of historic memory. While the shah and large slices of the Iranian population tended to go back to the early days of the Persian Empire for their landmark glory days and political sensibilities, the regime led by Ayatollah Khomeini used symbols of Islam and earlier days of Islamic empires for its historic anchoring. Until the Iranian regime started weaponizing these Islamic symbols against the Iranian people with the imposition of Islamic dress strictures on women, these different views of the glory days somehow coexisted in the collage of historical memory of the Iranian people.

But what if policy-makers have no official narrative or memory of past events? Even in the absence of an explicit reference to historical events by policy-makers, historical parallels between the past and present may be discovered by the observant analyst. Or policy-makers sometimes resurrect a dormant trend or series of past events to explain current events.

For example, one of the most significant events in Iran's recent past that has shaped its national security doctrine was the eight-year Iran-Iraq war that started with an Iraqi invasion in 1980. In many ways, it could be argued that the conflict originated from the megalomaniacal tendencies of Saddam Hussein. While certainly factually true, Iranians interpreted the war through a much broader historical and geopolitical lens. This war was seen as fitting a pattern of earlier invasions from outside powers, such as from Turkey, Russia, and Great Britain that go back centuries. And the fact that the United States and Soviet Union both backed Iraq during the war reinforced an historical pattern of rival great powers conspiring to keep Iran under their thumb. In other words, the invasion from Iraq and the behavior of great powers that ensued are seen in the context of Iran's history of great power intrusions.[4]

A pattern of consistent threats over time from neighboring countries or "historical enemies" can also become a structural driver of foreign policy that is carried forward for decades and even centuries. But it is also important to not become overly deterministic when it comes to geopolitical factors, as there can be and often are political and social factors that can override a purely geographic or geopolitical explanation. Large neighbors, hostile in the past, may or may not be persistent threats or foes. Ottoman Turkey posed an existential threat to the Persian Empire in the sixteenth century, but Turkey today is considered no more than a regional rival.

Russia, too, was a major threat in the nineteenth and twentieth centuries. The specter of possible betrayal by Russia in recent years harkens back to these earlier times. Shortly after Iran granted Russia use of its Hamadan military base on Iranian territory in 2016 to launch air missions into Syria, it revoked that privilege once it was made public, due to sensitivities about historical betrayals by Russia. The Iranian leadership was worried about the optics once the secrecy surrounding the arrangement was exposed.[5] While Iranians are often wary of Russia today, the magnitude of the perceived threat has attenuated over time and is less than from the more geographically remote United States.[6] Despite the historical pattern of Russian interference, Iran and Russia have become allies since the Russian invasion of Ukraine in 2022.

Strategic doctrines can also be a vital link between the present and the distant past. While Iranian leaders today may not be aware of the individual decisions made by leaders in the country's remote past, they are likely to have internalized some of the strategic concepts embedded in policies from earlier ages into doctrines that have relevance today. The "third power principle" of Iran, which involves aligning with a third major neutral power to counteract the effects of two other intervening powers, emerged during the Qajar and Pahlavi dynasties. While Iran currently is aligned with Russia and China against the United States, which in a way is a reverse third power policy of aligning with two against one, the idea of using an alliance to hedge against an intruding or hostile actor has roots in the geostrategic challenges of Iran's past.[7]

Irredentist movements are also threads connecting the past, the present, and a desired future. Memories and narratives about lost territories or prior empires have animated foreign policy decisions. For example, Iran's perception of past Persian greatness and grievances about how external powers, such as the Arabs with their invasion and occupation of Persia in the seventh century, help us better understand some of Iran's foreign policy decisional dilemmas of today.[8]

The rest of this chapter will take readers on a journey, starting with the Safavid dynasty in the 1500s and continuing through the Iranian revolution of 1979. We will look at the degree to which Iranian leaders had the latitude to make independent foreign policy decisions. For much of Iran's history, the country was constrained in terms of its decisional latitude by the overbearing nature of its external environment. But at other times, Iran was able to marshal the strength required to take reasonably independent foreign policies in its region and even on the global stage.

We will also examine the degree to which the country pursued a pragmatic, realpolitik foreign policy versus an overly ambitious, ideologically based foreign policy. In some circles, there is a bias that Iran's current foreign policy is an ideologically driven attempt to create a Shi'i arc across the region, while the regional ambitions of the last shah are seen as more of a realpolitik response to events. During Iran's history, we can see the tension between religiopolitical ideas on the one hand, and realpolitik strategic considerations on the other. In fact, there has been a mixture of both ideological and practical motivations evident in Iran's foreign policy. It is the interaction of these variables over time that give us a window onto Iran's foreign policy of the past, the present, and even perhaps a window onto the future.

Another theme from the Safavid dynasty forward is the connection between the exigency of internal domestic cohesion and the need for a robust foreign policy. We will see how, throughout the ages, Persian and Iranian leaders have tried to create internal cohesion to marshal external power. At times they were successful in this regard, and other times much less so. Perhaps before its time, the Constitutional Revolution of 1906 tried to use nationalism as a unifying factor, only to be undermined by Britain and Russia.

How does this help the policy-maker of today? Highlighting the continuities helps us get a better picture of how ingrained some of these patterns might be, and how resistant to change they are, regardless of attempts by the United States to do so. It could be considered as an admonition to western powers of the unintended consequences of trying to squeeze Iran, which may have great tactical effect, but are likely to stymie longer-term strategic ambitions and plans. While there is a danger that this could be construed as an apologia and excuse for Iran's aggressive behavior, the benefits far outweigh the risks. The purpose isn't to give Iran a pass for its behavior, but rather to understand how some of the themes of Iran's foreign policy have been constant over time.

Early Threads: The Safavid Dynasty

In June of 1980, Ayatollah Ruhollah Khomeini said:

> The will of almighty God, may He be praised, decreed the release of the oppressed nation from the yoke of the tyranny and crimes of the

satanical regime and from the yoke of the domination of oppressive powers ... It is our duty to stand up to the superpowers and we have the ability to stand up against them, provided that our intellectuals give up their fascination with Westernization or Easternization and follow the straight path of Islam and nationalism.[9]

While Khomeini spoke these words about the scourge of outside power intervention, and the power of Islam and the nation to resist, in the twentieth century, we see the origins of this reaching back 500 years to the Safavid dynasty. The themes from this earlier period haunt Iranian domestic and international politics to this day.

Several factors from this period shaped Iran's behavior in the years that followed. First, the boundaries of the state, which were in flux during earlier dynastic periods, were stabilized by the Safavids starting around 1722. Later in the 1800s, during the Qajar period, Iran lost Afghanistan to the British, and Georgia and Azerbaijan to the Russians. But it was the gains made during the Safavid period and later losses of these gains to the British and Russians that set up the geopolitical challenges of today.

Second, it was during the Safavid era that Iran became officially a Shi'i state. When Shah Ismail took over Persia in 1501, the empire had not regained the stride it had lost with the Arab invasion during the seventh century, which put Persia under a two-century Arab suzerainty and brought Sunni Islam to a people proudly embracing and defined by the ancient practices of Zoroastrianism.[10]

Shah Ismail burst onto the scene as a young monarch sporting both Shi'i Islamic religious fervor and a nationalist imperial ambition, the confluence of which would define Iran for the coming centuries. It was under the banner of a distinctly Persian flavor of Shi'ism that Iran tried to claim lands lost to the Persian Empire in the preceding centuries. In other words, Shah Ismail gave the empire a distinctly Persian rendition of Islam with the transition to Shi'ism. Shi'ism seemed to fit with Persian national sensibilities of being distinct from the Ottomans and Arabs.[11] This distinctiveness is in evidence today, as it was during the Safavids. At the time the tension and hostilities that arose were between Persia and the Ottomans, while today it is between Iran and Saudi Arabia.

The strategic significance of the move to Shi'ism is it played to the geopolitical interests of the Persian Empire at the time. It gave Iran a distinctiveness relative to the Ottoman Empire, which was a Sunni-dominated state. It was also useful in liberating the area of Khorasan from Sunni control. Lore has it that Ismail I personally killed the Uzbek king in the process. He then purportedly set the king's skull in gold and reportedly had it sent to the Ottoman sultan to send a menacing message about Safavid (and Shi'i) power.[12]

The other strategic parallel spanning the ages is how Persian Shi'ism created real – or at least perceived – leverage over its rivals by tapping into the sentiments of their populations. During the Safavid era, the Ottomans felt threatened by the specter of Shi'i Persia possibly gaining popularity and support among Ottoman populations. In other words, the potential messianic religious appeal of Shah Ismail spooked the sultan in Constantinople, prompting a war.[13] To be fair, it was the insecurity of the Ottoman Sultan, related to possible internal sectarian-driven troubles, that led him to attack Iran.

Today in a similar dynamic, Saudi Arabia sees its sizable Shi'i minority as a potential fifth column, more loyal to Shi'i Tehran and Qom than to predominantly Sunni Riyadh. A similar dynamic exists today in Bahrain, with the Sunni minority-dominated government seeing its majority Shi'i population as representing more the interests of Iran than their own country. In Iraq, the same themes haunt leaders. During the Iran-Iraq war, Saddam Hussein was concerned that his own Shi'i majority population would be more loyal to Tehran than Baghdad.

Moreover, Ismail used Shi'ism to consolidate control and create renewal in what had been a declining empire since the Arab invasions of the eighth century.[14] This was similar to how Khomeini saw his mission as renewal of a country that in his view had languished, strategically and morally, under the US-supported reign of the shah. For him and other revolutionaries, the prior several decades evinced a decline, not necessarily economically, but in terms of culture, values, and independence. For them the intruders weren't the Turks or the Russians of the Safavid era, but American penetration of the state and society, something they called "west-toxification".[15]

But we should be cautious about making a reductionist argument that all conflict then or today can be attributed to sectarian differences. The relationship between the Safavid Persians and the Ottomans took on a more complicated flavor than first meets the eye. Even then, alongside the fissures over religious sectarian differences were tensions based on geopolitics and territory. This was particularly true under Shah Abbas during the latter part of the sixteenth century, after much of the frenzy over religion had calmed down. Wars then were fought principally to regain Iranian territory lost to the Ottomans.[16]

Today, as during the latter Safavid era, conflict is less based on doctrinal differences between Sunni and Shi'i and more over a struggle over which state will have dominant regional leadership and which will have legitimacy in the broader Islamic community. And layered on top of the sectarian divide and the drive for regional influence is the struggle between Iranian and Arab nationalist identity. During the Safavid era the issue was territorial, while today the tensions revolve around regional influence and competing nationalisms.

The struggle for power

We have discussed the role internal cohesion under a Shi'i identity played in creating external power for the Safavid Persians. But the reverse was also true. During the Safavid era, like today, external enemies helped foster internal unity and cohesion. The need to instrumentalize external threats to create internal unity, which in turn invited foreign aggression, was a dilemma faced by Shah Ismail. Persia was fragmented in terms of governance, and Ismail used Shi'ism as a cudgel for consolidating internal control. Similarly, Ayatollah Khomeini and his minions used the fervor of the revolution to consolidate internal control. But he also used external conflict to help consolidate control and mobilize the Iranian population. This was evident during the Iran-Iraq war, and during the hostage crisis involving US diplomats.[17]

The use of external conflict to mobilize populations and consolidate control created quandaries and strategic trade-offs for the Safavids as it does for the Islamic Republic today. Shah Ismail's sectarian battle with the predominantly Sunni Ottoman Empire helped him consolidate internal control, but it came at a price of a loss of territory.

Ismail's use of external challenges to consolidate internal control narrowed his range of options of prosecuting an independent foreign policy. What we see during this period is how Persia vacillated between having a modicum of latitude in foreign policy and being denied that room for maneuver by outside powers. Shah Ismail had ambitions to expand even beyond Persia's prior Sassanid dynastic borders but was denied as such by a defeat by the Ottomans at the Battle of Chaldiran in 1514, which limited Persia's range of options, and during it which it lost much of what is today northern Iraq and Anatolia.[18]

While modern-day Iran hasn't lost any significant territory, notwithstanding disputes with the UAE over the islands of Greater Tunb,

Lesser Tunb, and Abu Musa, the notion of using a foreign threat to consolidate internal control has parallels with the Safavids. While for Khomeini it was the hostility toward the United States that helped the Islamists to consolidate control, for the Safavids it was Ottoman Turkey. The US hostage crisis, which lasted from 1979 until 1981, enabled Khomeini and his minions to navigate the treacherous political landscape following the revolution.[19] But like the trade-offs faced by the Safavids, Khomeini's antagonistic foreign policy came at a significant price of a reduction in maneuverability due to the imposition of US financial sanctions. And in the post-October 7, 2023 environment, whether Iran's "axis of resistance" creates more risk than deterrence is an open question.

One of the questions for today is how Iran could operate in the absence of demonization of the United States. Some historians have claimed that in the decades following Shah Ismail, when there was an absence of conflict with the Ottomans, Iran experienced internal decay.[20] Some of the debates in Iran to this day center around the question of what releasing the country from enmity with the United States would do to the Islamic Republic. Would integration with the global economy lead to internal decay, or to renewal? This question is taken up in part in Chapter 7.

Religion and the state

What Iran experienced after its 1979 revolution was a fusion between "church" and state, with the consolidation of governmental power by the Islamists at the expense of the other groups, including socialists, socialist Islamists, as well as more liberally minded secularist nationalist groups. We see the issue of the relationship between religion and the state today, with the enforcement of the hijab mandate for women that culminated in the death of Mahsa Amini in 2022 and the protests that followed. For the population, the issue is about freedom of individual choice and the rights of women. For the state, it is largely about power. In the coming decades, this question about the proper relationship between religion and the state will likely drive both domestic and international politics for Iran.

This melding of Shi'ism into the nature of the state has a precedent during the Safavid era. Then, Shah Ismail I made the claim that he was the agent of God on earth. While we know that he used this to try to restore lost lands of the Persian Empire, an inherently nationalistic mission, he did it by bringing the strands of nation, religion, and the state together.[21]

This tension between the interests of the state, the nation, and Islam became even more pronounced later in the Safavid period. While earlier, under Ismail, the empire's nascent Shi'ism eclipsed everything else, later in the dynasty Persian rulers had to balance its religious identity with the interests of the monarchy and the state, which came under attack by the Ottomans and Russians.

The notion today of *vilayat-e faqih* (Islamic jurisprudence) establishing the role of Iran's Supreme Leader Ayatollah Ali Khamenei as Shi'i religious authority and head of state, has parallels with the Safavid era. In addition to the deification of Shah Ismail, there were other manifestations of the melding of religion and the state. It was the cleric Mullah Mohammed Bagher Majlesi of Isfahan who, in the seventeenth century, promulgated ideas about Islamic rule called "Islam of the Law." This embodied some of the same ideas about the role the Shi'i clergy should play in matters of the state as later became embodied in Khomeini's *vilayat-e faqih*. This gives us the needed perspective that Khomeini's notion of the role of Islam in matters of the state wasn't new and in fact had an historical basis.[22]

Persian transitions

While the Safavids started out in 1501 with Shah Ismail as the ruler and a Shi'i theocratic state as the basis for authority, by the time of Shah Abbas in 1588, the logic of monarchical authority eclipsed everything else. Even though Shi'ism was still the official religion, Abbas made capture of lost territory to Turkey something that overshadowed many of the religious and sectarian concerns of previous decades.[23] Shi'i Islam remained as the legitimizing logic of the state, but not the governing logic.

The struggle of how far to push an ideological mission while not compromising the power of the state in a challenging international environment clearly existed throughout the Safavid dynasty and redounds to today.[24] One strategic question that hangs over from the Safavid period is whether geopolitical interests are advanced or undermined by following ideological or irredentist impulses. Holy wars launched by Ismail, later attempts by Shah Abbas, and then by Nader Shah Afshar during the later Afsharid dynasty, to regain territories put the country in the crosshairs of Turkey and later Russia, oftentimes leading to wars, and sometimes partition, lasting into the twentieth century.[25]

The modern-day question the rest of this book will address that has roots in the Safavid era is how will Iran balance its foreign policy? Will

Iran's use of its militias be the dominant feature of its foreign policy, or will Iran pivot to a more conventional state-based foreign policy? Iran's support for militias in the Arab heartlands of the region are rooted in Iran's legitimate security concerns and a need for deterrence. But there is also an ideological tinge to this as well, since most (but not all) of Iran's militias are cut from the Shi'i cloth and Iran is using its presence in Iraq, Syria, and Lebanon to strengthen Shi'i institutions. Will Iran be able to continue to support this part of its foreign policy, which takes place mostly in the shadows, and still maintain its security interests? The Hamas attacks on Israel on October 7, 2023, and Israel's punishing attacks on Gaza, prompted an activation of almost all of Iran's militias, which culminated in direct attacks by Iran and Israel on one another in 2024. Going forward, Iran will need to make sure that it balances the interests of the state with ideological considerations. With the degradation of the capability of Hamas and Hezbollah, and the fall of the Assad regime, all part of Iran's "axis of resistance," Tehran will face some of the same issues and dilemmas as Safavid rulers did over five hundred years ago.

The treachery of the international political arena

One of the issues Iran faces today that has roots in the Safavid era is the challenge of balancing one external power against another. Peace treaties with European states provided the backdrop for Ottoman Sultan Selim to wage an attack on Persia in the early 1500s. To try to stave off the Ottomans, the Safavids sent a delegation to Hungary and Poland, imploring them to invade the Ottomans, a request that was denied.[26] Toward the end of the Safavid dynasty, the Persians were sought out by the European powers which were fighting the Ottomans from the west, imploring the shah to weaken Constantinople from the east. Smartly the shah declined lest Persian independence be put at risk.[27] While it must have been tempting to join the Europeans against a hostile Ottoman Empire, fear of betrayal by Europe must have animated Persian decision-making. Distrusting the global considerations of outside powers at the expense of Iran is a theme that resonates still to this day. Distrust of Europe still prevails among Iranian decision-makers, particularly since none of the European signatories to the Joint Comprehensive Plan of Action (JCPOA), or Iran nuclear agreement, really came to Iran's rescue once the Trump administration withdrew.

The Safavid era is strategically important as it demonstrates the limitations of an ideologically aggressive foreign policy when faced with multiple hostile powers.[28] The modern parallel was the Iran-Iraq war of the 1980s. While Iraq was the aggressor, Saddam Hussein did feel threatened by the jingoistic language used by Khomeini urging the Iraqi Shi'i to rise in revolt. Aside from a belief that Iran was weakened by revolution and could be overrun, Saddam also was motivated to attack by the specter of what he saw as a Shi'i menace next door and at home. As with the Safavids, war tended to temper the ambitions for an ideologically laden foreign policy. After the Iran-Iraq war ended in 1988, Iran's foreign policy moved much more into the realm of pragmatism and realpolitik under the late President Akbar Hashemi Rafsanjani and his successor former President Mohammed Khatami.

In summary

The lessons of the Safavids have worked themselves into the narratives of key Iranian decision-makers. Former Foreign Minister Javad Zarif has said many times that Iran has had to deal with outside challenges in the past and that it will prevail in the future. While there are seldom specific references to the Safavids, it shows that Iranian leaders have an appreciation for the historical perspective, and long-term strategic horizon. It is no coincidence that after the revolution of 1979, the field of Safavid studies flourished in Iran, indicating that the parallels were not lost on decision-makers.[29]

These parallels speak not only to the power of a Shi'i-first foreign policy but also its limitations. Ideology can be a powerful foreign policy motivator, but it also can create the risk of over-extension, as we witnessed with the Safavid's relationship with the Ottomans. The Safavid period seared into the Iranian consciousness the inherent risks of trying to balance one great power against another. The track record of Iranian monarchs during the Safavid dynasty was a mixed one in this regard. The risks of relying on outside powers to compensate for a mismatch between means and ends was a lesson learned in some cases too late by the Safavids.[30] Iran's current approach to foreign policy of using militias in the shadows of the region rather than relying on overt military aggression against its adversaries is an indication that this historical lesson has been internalized and learned. How the direct attacks on Israel in 2024 play out in this regard remains to be seen.

Lessons of Geopolitics: The Qajar Period

The Qajar period has a record of both foreign policy successes and failures. The lessons from this period, however, that have been seared into Iran's historical narrative and political consciousness, mostly stem from the challenges endured rather than any victories that may have been achieved.

For sure the dynasty that started in 1789 ended on a low note in 1925. Because of a combination of leadership mismanagement, corruption, and insuperable obstacles put in place by multiple external actors, much of this period was defined by an egregious mismatch between means and desired ends. The period also featured foreign occupation by multiple external powers, which alternately were both rivals and partners in keeping Persia in a state of dependence. It is a story of betrayal by each of the external powers, particularly when they decided that relations with one another took precedence over any interests in a comparatively weak Iran. And it was during this period that outside actors, namely Russia and Britain, occupied Iran and worked to quash its nascent constitutional democracy. For Iranians today, the machinations of Britain and Russia during the Qajar period link up with what they see as later betrayals during the Pahlavi dynasty when the Americans undermined Iranian democracy with the coup against Prime Minister Mohammed Mossadegh.

The contrast between the Qajar and Safavid eras is stark. The Safavid era foreign policy was shaped by ideological fervor, irredentist claims on lost territories, and internal frenzy due to Shi'i revivalism. The Qajar period was defined by more secular issues, such as coping with interventions by multiple outside powers, namely Russia, Britain, and France. During much of this period, Persian leaders had little real decisional latitude in foreign affairs and few good options for maximizing power. The Qajar shahs launched irredentist battles to reclaim lost territory, but with little regard for the means with which to wage such battles successfully.

Some of the most profound cases from the Qajar period where ends and means don't align provide lessons for today. By the time of the Qajar dynasty, the primary challenge was from Russia, not the Ottoman Empire. During this period, Iran fought two wars with Russia to regain lost territories. The first was from 1804 to 1813, which was disastrous for the

Iranians as it entailed the loss of much of the Caucuses, including parts of Georgia, Azerbaijan, and Dagestan. The defeat became enshrined in the infamous Treaty of Gulistan. The second defining war, initiated by Persia, was from 1826 to 1828, which ended in a similar outcome with Iran losing even more of the Caucuses. This war ended disastrously with the Treaty of Turkmenchay.

But Iran didn't suffer just at the hands of Russia. The defeats by Russia were augmented with betrayal by Britain, which had an alliance with Iran starting in 1801, promising support if Persia was attacked. When in 1804 Iran called on the British to counter Russian ambitions, London demurred, which made the humiliating treaties of Gulistan and Turkmenchay that much more searing.

These two devastating and humiliating defeats at the hands of Imperial Russia and betrayal by Britain embodied several themes, all relevant today. The first is over-extension, meaning Iran embarked on foreign policy adventures without careful calibration of capabilities and goals.[31] The seeming inattentiveness to this very basic strategic principle of ensuring that there is an intrinsic capability to fight a larger power is not lost on decision-makers today, particularly as Iran faces a US-backed Israel.

But the second theme that redounds to today is an intense distrust of Russia due to its dark history of swallowing Persian territory. Related to this is the theme of great powers selling out Iran for broader interests. France had an alliance with Persia in 1807 to deal with Russia, consummated in the Treaty of Finckenstein. But when France's relations with Russia improved, it terminated its alliance with Persia.[32] From the Persian perspective, the alliance with France was motivated by a desire to regain Georgia from Russia, a mission France had pledged to earlier undertake. But broader considerations with Russia and issues with Britain weakened Paris's resolve, cementing in a pattern of betrayal at the hands of great powers. One could argue that the French promise and betrayal whetted Iran's appetite further to recover Georgia, motivating it to re-engage militarily with Russia in the disastrous war of 1826–28, culminating in a second devastating defeat at the hands of Russia and the humiliating Treaty of Turkmenchay. Persia also had made agreements with Britain but after conflicts arose between Persia and Russia, the relationship atrophied and fell by the wayside.

These betrayals resonate with the circumstances of today. Prior to the invasion of Ukraine by Russia in 2022, some quarters in Tehran feared that Russia might sell it out, prioritizing relations with Europe and the United States over relations with Iran. Russia being ostracized by the west because of the war has allayed some of that concern. But the theme of Iran being wary of and circumspect with regards to alliances goes back to the Qajar period and is still a strategic consideration today.

The Qajar period is also instructive about both the limits and opportunities for Iran to wield power. Today, Iranian leaders face issues of how to deal with competing global powers, using Russia and China as hedges against the United States and its regional allies, particularly Israel. There are also important parallels in terms of the risks associated with engaging with global powers. As we will cover in subsequent chapters, post-revolutionary Iranian decision-makers viewed the two Cold War superpowers who competed with one another as being part of a new "great game." In other words, global powers may compete with one another, but when their bilateral interests become threatened, they often band together to betray Iran. The mantra after the Iranian revolution of 1979 was "neither east, nor west," which reflected the view that neither superpower is trustworthy and that in effect they are part of the same hegemonic structure. This view has roots in the Qajar period, with France, Britain, and Russia as the protagonists. When each of the European powers strikes deals with Iran for common defense, circumstances intervene to have them recant on their commitments to Iran and conspire with their fellow great powers.

Recent history has added to the litany of cases where Iran hasn't been able to count on great powers to keep their end of the bargain. For Iranians steeped in their country's history, these cases are echoes from the Qajar period. The ineffective response by the Europeans after the US peremptorily withdrew from the JCPOA in 2018 can also be seen in this light. Even though Iran hewed to the nuclear deal, the European signatories to the JCPOA – Britain, France, and Germany – were unable to neutralize the punishing effects of sanctions imposed by the United States under the Trump administration's campaign of maximum pressure. While the Europeans tried to circumvent US trade restrictions and sanctions with Iran through its Instrument of Support of Trade Exchanges (INSTEX), it translated into only a trickle of trade. The specter of secondary sanctions threatened by the Trump administration discouraged European companies worried about being shut out of the lucrative US market if they conducted business with Iran. The perception this left the Iranians with was that at best the Europeans were ineffective, and at worst duplicitous.

The issue of Iran having to contend with multiple great powers in the Qajar era extended beyond geopolitics to include domestic politics. Russia and Britain, though rivals, acted as co-conspirators in subjugating the Iranian political process and undermining the green shoots of Iranian democracy. When their mutual interests in Persia were threatened by a more open process and energized population, as was the case during the 1906 Constitutional Revolution, both Russia and Britain acted against the interests of Iran.[33] And they signed what was known as the Anglo-Russian Convention of 1907.

For the first few years following the 1906 revolution, which established a parliament, it appeared that Iran's nascent nationalist movement would deliver for the country the internal transparency and external freedom that it fought for. But the treaty between Britain and Russia meant that despite having competing interests, the two great powers also had common underlying interests in keeping Iran internally weak. While nationalism was strong enough at this stage to engender a revolution against the absolute monarchical rule of the Qajar shahs, it wasn't powerful enough to withstand the joint efforts of two external powerful actors.[34]

As part of this conspiracy, the new constitution was undermined and the Majlis parliament was disbanded. In an effort to keep Iran both weak domestically and internationally, Britain and Russia essentially split the country into two parts, with Russia occupying the north and Britain the south. This severely reduced Iran's foreign policy decisional latitude. While prior to this period Iran was able to use Britain as a hedge against Russia, this ended with the Anglo-Russian Convention of 1907. It was Russian actions that had the most profound effect on Iran, as they showed a determination to squash the reality of a constitutional monarchy and kill the constitutionalists.[35]

One might argue that currying favor with the British represented a clear breach and repudiation of Iranian nationalism. But this would be a misreading of the complexity of both the Iranian political psyche and power politics at the time. For some, like Fath-Ali Shah, the second Qajar king, Britain was seen as a hedge against Russian intentions to swallow Iran. While no committed nationalist would ever sing the praises of British imperialism, the reality of Russia next door loomed large in the Iranian political consciousness at the time. Understanding that Britain itself had imperial designs, but also seeing that London could be useful in frustrating Russia's even more ambitious designs on Iran, added complexity to the strategic calculation of Iranians.[36] Because of this, the imperative of working with outside powers became part of the reality Iranian leaders were forced to contend with.[37]

It was against the backdrop of the complex interactions between Britain and Russia that Iran developed the third power principle, which entailed counterbalancing the influence of the two great powers with a third power. What is ironic given the current state of US-Iran relations is how the United States at an earlier time was idealized as a possible third power that could counter and offset the power of Russia and Britain. This idealization started with Morgan Shuster, who became the Treasurer General of Persia in 1911 to put Iran's finances in order so that it could maximize its foreign policy strength. In addition to helping Iran internally, he also was quite vocal in the imprecations and scorn he heaped on the encroaching British and Russians. This in addition to US President Woodrow Wilson's doctrine of self-determination gave Iranians a sense that the United States could serve to mitigate the effects of London and Moscow's stronghold over Iran. As history shows us, this idealized view of the United States didn't survive the Cold War, a topic of a later section.

The inability for Iran to marshal sufficient power to thwart the conspiring interests of great powers led to disastrous foreign policy outcomes during the Qajar period. Particularly vis-à-vis Russia, Iran's irredentist ambitions exceeded its capacity, with the wars waged by Persia during this period failing abysmally to regain lost territory.[38] In the aftermath of the Constitutional Revolution of 1906, the battle was between the nationalist ambitions of the Iranian population and the imperial interests of Britain and Russia. But rather than delivering to Iran a sustainable constitutional monarchy, the revolution in many ways pushed Iran further into the grasp of the two imperial powers. The lesson from this was that while the Iranian people were increasingly nationalistic, without a more modern and powerful state this wouldn't translate into a capacity to thwart the ambitions of the imperial powers.[39] This would have to wait seventy years when in 1979 the Iranian revolution overthrew the shah and ended an era of American influence in the country.

But the question for Iran today is whether the lessons of the Qajar era have any bearing on the strategic challenges the country faces. With poor relations with the United States and open hostility with Israel, how will Iran navigate its regional and global environments to maintain its room for maneuverability? At the time of this writing, Iran's ability to project influence into the region has been compromised by the degradation of the militias it has supported, such as Hamas and Hezbollah. It may be calculating that it can lean on regional powers, such as Saudi Arabia, with which it re-established relations in 2023, and global powers like Russia and China. But whether they will back Iran at a moment of ultimate vulnerability is doubtful. Like their Qajar ancestors, the Iranian leaders of today will face dilemmas and painful choices about how to deal with multiple external actors.

Consolidation of the State: Reza Shah Pahlavi, 1925-1941

In contrast to the Qajar rulers, Reza Shah Pahlavi in the 1920s helped build a state apparatus that would eventually support a nationalist foreign policy. While during the Qajar period both constitutionalism and nationalism failed due to cracks in the capacity of the system to resist foreign powers, Reza Shah corrected some of the cracks and prepared Iran to enter the modern day.

When Reza Khan emerged as the tour de force of Persia in 1921, presaging the end of the Qajar dynasty a few years later, the main protagonists on the international stage were Great Britain and the Soviet Union. Reza was a Persian colonel who had become Minister of War and then Prime Minister under the Qajar shah, but his power continued to grow until he was able to oust the last Qajar shah and enthrone himself in 1925.[40]

Reza Shah was important for Iran's slow and uneven march toward an independent foreign policy for several reasons. One was that he fashioned his ruling style after Kemal Ataturk of Turkey, who had imposed a form of dictatorship that hurtled the country toward modernity. Reza saw a couple of impediments to Iran becoming sufficiently independent and went about rectifying them. One was embarking on a campaign to modernize Iran's infrastructure. In an attempt to unite the country, he built highways and railroads. He also embarked on a modernization campaign within the military, to redress the gaps in Iran's strategic capabilities that had hobbled it in prior years. He also launched a ruthless campaign to weaken the provincial governors and tribal leaders. Reza, like Ataturk, believed that centralization was the key factor in both internal and external power generation.

Iranian nationalism didn't start with Reza Khan. As we saw, nationalist and democratic sentiments were the dominant forces behind the

Constitutional Revolution that had taken place nearly two decades before. While the Constitutional Revolution of 1906 created a professional foreign policy class and elite, it wasn't until Reza Shah that the state was strengthened and consolidated internally.[41]

What Reza Khan did was meld nationalism with realism, a combo missing in the policies of the Qajar kings of the nineteenth and early twentieth centuries. While earlier under the Qajars there was a mismatch between Iran's ambition and its means, Reza Shah went about trying to correct this imbalance. In essence, Reza Shah's consolidation of the state gave Iranians something they coveted, but that had remained elusive: improved conditions for independence. Albeit brutally, he insisted on a high degree of regimentation and order, which prepared Iran for a more independent foreign policy. This involved brutally subduing the tribes, creating a financial state capability, and professionalizing the military.

Another factor during the period of Reza Shah was using industrialization as a form of resistance against the economic dependence on Russia. While not a perfect parallel with today, the formation of a resistance economy against US-imposed economic sanctions is a similar reflex. The difference is that in the post-1979 revolutionary period, industrialization was largely done by the Revolutionary Guards, strengthening the military gendarme of the state.

But there were limitations in how Reza Shah prepared Iran for more autonomy on the international stage. A fervent nationalist himself, he didn't transfer this sentiment to the people through popular mobilization, which itself was a limiting factor in Iran moving toward a more independent foreign policy.[42]

On the geopolitical stage, remember that Iran had been in constant pursuit of the third power principle, which involved offsetting the dominance of two contending powers, such as the Soviet Union and Britain, with a more neutral third power. Originally the Americans were seen as this third power, which could help protect Iran from the two main powers that were the Soviet Union and Britain. The United States wasn't just seen as a geopolitical counterbalance, but also instrumental in having Iran develop its own economic and administrative capabilities from within. The work of the American Arthur Millspaugh, who built on the earlier work of Morgan Shuster, helped organize Iran's finances. While this started before Reza Shah rose to power, he continued to support this modernization initiative by the Americans until 1927.[43]

But during the Second World War, the third power became Hitler's Germany, the common enemy of both Britain and the Soviet Union. Unfortunately for Reza Shah and Iran, this led to the joint occupation of Iran by Britain and the Soviet Union, signaling the end of Iran's ability to conduct an independent foreign policy. While this didn't destroy Reza Shah's ultimate legacy, it did come at a considerable cost to him personally. He was toppled after the British and Soviet invasion of 1941. In his stead, the two powers installed Reza's young and more pliable son, Mohammed.

For Iranians, the Reza Shah era was a mixed bag. Iran was able to modernize and develop the fundamentals of a strong, independent state. He was a seminal and transitional figure in Iran's long march to modernity, helping transform the old Persia to the new Iran. And he was a true Iranian nationalist and is revered by many nationalists to this day.

But misapplying the third power principle, he led to his own demise and the occupation of Iran. The knock-on effects of the toppling of Reza Shah were considerable. His son and successor, Mohammed Reza Shah, was more pliable externally and more vulnerable internally than his more authoritarian father. Because his "origin story" involved being installed by outside powers, he had an intrinsic legitimacy problem. This problem with domestic legitimacy was exacerbated in 1953 when he became complicit in the overthrow of Prime Minister Mossadegh at the hands of the United States and Britain. Mossadegh was immensely popular, a dedicated and fervent Iranian nationalist, and had been chosen democratically.

The relevance of the era of Reza Shah to the current day are the perils of the third power principle. While the parallels aren't exact due to the lack of a world war today, the question of how to deal with three powers is still as relevant today as it was one hundred years ago. While today it is Iran aligning with two global powers, Russia and China, against the United States, the question of Iran not overplaying its hand and choosing the wrong partner as Reza Shah did with Germany is still germane. A close alignment with Russia after its invasion of Ukraine in 2022 has invited international opprobrium and further isolation, particularly from Europe. At the time of the writing of this book, Iran is feeling less isolated due to its shared pariah status with Moscow, and because of Russia's dependence on Iran for drones in its war in Ukraine.[44] But should Russia, in an act of desperation, do something rash, like explode a nuclear weapon or commit even more egregious atrocities in Ukraine, it is possible that the leverage Iran believes it derives from Russia could dissipate and the relationship could become a liability. And should China distance itself from the Ukraine war, this could add stresses to the strategic relationship Iran has with Beijing. Also, if Iran's actions in the region in the post-October 7, 2023 environment create economic and political instability, international support from China may dissipate and aggressive actions by the United States and Europe could increase.

Mohammed Reza Shah: The Last Shah of Iran, 1941–79

Generally, there is a correlation between the robustness of a country's foreign policy and the domestic legitimacy of its leadership. Egyptian President Gamal Abdel Nasser's star rose after Egypt nationalized the Suez Canal and withstood an invasion in 1956 from France, Britain, and Israel. This success redounded to his skyrocketing popularity in Egypt and across the Arab world.

The curious thing about the case of Mohammed Reza Shah is that in the years before the revolution, he had started to embark on a relatively independent foreign policy, but he received very little credit for this. His critics, the loudest of which was Ayatollah Ruhollah Khomeini, portrayed him as an American puppet.

Throughout the 1950s and into the 1960s, the shah did in fact take his foreign policy cues from Washington. When a pro-Soviet, pan-Arab regime took hold in Iraq after its 1958 revolution, Iran followed a pro-western foreign policy of conducting a subversive strategy of inciting the Iraqi Kurds against the new government. And he backed Lebanese Shi'i groups to break the perceived pan-Arab phalanx led by Egyptian President Gamal Abdel Nasser. The idea was that collectively these actions would deal a blow to the Soviet Union, which backed both Egypt and Iraq.[45]

The shah was criticized by the opposition in Iran, but also felt pressure from its benefactor, the United States. When the Kennedy administration came to office in 1961, it demonstrated a bias toward reform-minded leaders in contrast to Eisenhower's more comfortable relations with monarchs. Because of this more progressive bent, the Kennedy administration had a good relationship with Iranian Prime Minister Ali Amini, who was encouraging the monarch to move in a more transparent and reformist direction. Reports were that the shah kept Amini on until 1962 and launched his White Revolution in 1963 partially to placate Washington.

The problem was that these moves toward reform didn't have the intended effect of building legitimacy for the shah and his government. Rather, it gave ammunition to the clerical opposition of Ayatollah Ruhollah Khomeini, who painted these moves as reflecting western rather than Iranian values.[46] This perception was amplified by the hangover effect of the US role in overthrowing Prime Minister Mohammed Mossadegh in 1953. The fact that, after the coup, the shah was repatriated and re-enthroned by the United States was considered his "original sin" in the eyes of the Iranian opposition.

But the caricature of the shah as a hapless leader manipulated by the grand puppeteer of the United States wasn't really accurate. While he was authentically concerned about the Soviet Union given Russia's historically intrusive role in Iranian affairs, he also used the Soviet specter to get the United States under the administration of President John F. Kennedy to overlook domestic abuses and demand more foreign aid. And he also used the possibility of coddling the Soviets as a way to keep his leverage with Washington.[47]

Starting in 1973, the shah struck out and pursued a more robust and independent foreign policy. Spiking oil prices due to the Arab embargo against the United States gave him the power to do this. He intervened in Arab politics and developed a better relationship with Moscow. He waded into the civil war in Oman in 1972 when insurgents from Dhofar threatened to topple the sultan. During the period, Iran became a formidable naval power and a strident voice within OPEC. And the shah saw himself as a regional leader with policies that extended from Pakistan in the east to Lebanon in the west. But he got scant recognition of this from his people, who still saw him as a leader beholden to the United States.

To be balanced, part of the problem rested with the shah himself. Not having connected to his population and further alienating them with the repressive measures of his US-trained SAVAK security service, his foreign policy didn't connect with the Iranian population. His legitimacy issue was intrinsic to his rule and not related to specific policies. In fact, his policies were almost beside the point. Even though they may have hewed to Iranian strategic interests, this didn't matter given that the regime itself was considered illegitimate. In fact, his foreign policy and White Revolution exacerbated his legitimacy problem, as the opposition framed the White Revolution as an attempt to westernize Iran.[48]

How is this period strategically important for today? It represents a line of causality between the coup against Mossadegh in 1953 and the

Iranian revolution of 1979. It also instructs us about the unintended consequences of an overly adventurist US foreign policy. It would be foolhardy to suggest that absent the 1953 coup against Mossadegh, the Iranian revolution would have been averted. Revolutions as sociopolitical human phenomena are mysterious and defy a simple, singular theory of causality.

But what we can say is that Mossadegh's overthrow created a political legitimacy vacuum. The shah was denied legitimacy because of his association with the coup, becoming a symbolic focal point for the opposition. As the 1970s unfolded, even those who during an earlier age would have been counted as Mossadegh supporters threw their support behind Khomeini. For Khomeini, beauty was in the eyes of the beholder. Islamists projected their hopes for an Islamic society onto him, and even secular nationalists saw him as an iconic figure that could unite the country. They saw this aged religious figure as more of a symbol than a ruler and were taken by surprise when the revolutionary government purged the secular groups that had supported the Khomeini movement and turned Iran into a theocracy.

For Iran's strategic narrative, the coup against Mossadegh is just the midpoint in a continuum of betrayals at the hands of outside powers, linking Iran's pre- and post-revolutionary periods. Starting with betrayals at the hands of the British and French in the nineteenth century, Russia and Britain in the early twentieth century, the coup orchestrated by the United States and Britain fit a pattern of great power perfidy for many Iranians. The 2018 decision by the Trump administration to renounce the JCPOA nuclear deal is just the latest example of betrayal at the hands of the United States and its European allies. While it was a shock to other signatories of the JCPOA, it was less surprising to Iranians inured to great powers not keeping their end of the bargain.

Conclusion

One way of thinking about the revolution of 1979 is that it was a culmination of a pattern that commenced with the Safavid dynasty. Of course, there is the thread of Shi'i Islam connecting the Safavids to the present day. But more profoundly the connections with this earlier dynastic period have to do with the issue of the generation of internal and external political power.

A major theme connecting the various periods in Iran's long history since the Safavids is the calibration between Iran's large foreign policy ambitions and more limited means required for their achievement. The Safavids were successful in gaining back territories lost during earlier periods. But excessive zeal also led to confrontations with the Ottoman Empire that exposed some of the vulnerabilities and weaknesses of the Persians. Later during the Qajar period, the Persians fought wars with Russia in a bid to reclaim lost territory, only to experience defeat and the signing of two humiliating treaties. Iran during this period also learned the importance of internal cohesion in successful external power projection.

The Persian Empire had languished, lacking proper financial institutions and discipline, a condition that facilitated penetration by Russia and Britain. The reign of Reza Shah, during which Persia was renamed Iran, represented a break from the patterns of the past. It was during this period that Iran developed modern infrastructure and national coherence that would enable it to deal more successfully with its foreign policy challenges. But even Reza Shah faced the problems inherent in dealing with multiple great powers. In a bid to resist interference by the British and Russians, Reza Shah aligned with Germany, a move that counterproductively led to occupation by Britain and the Soviet Union for the duration of the Second World War. While it appears that multiple great powers give Iran choices in terms of playing one power against the other, history shows that this oftentimes backfires.

But notwithstanding the flawed strategy of aligning with Germany, Reza Shah's accomplishments in forcing Iran into modernity shouldn't be trivialized. His son, Mohammed Reza Shah Pahlavi, built on the successes of his father, launching economic, social, and cultural development programs that brought prosperity and military might to Iran. Unfortunately, these accomplishments were portrayed by the opposition as promoting "west-toxification" and as serving the interests of the United States, ultimately leading to the shah's demise.

The patterns starting with the Safavids serve as a backdrop for the foreign policy of the Islamic Republic of today. In many ways, its foreign policy is an attempt to deal with the power generation problems that have bedeviled Iran since the Safavid era. The mantra of the revolution, "neither east, nor west," represented an acknowledgement that if Iran falls into the orbit of a great power, it is likely to lose its independence. Despite the bravado of Iran's "axis of resistance" concept, it is a recognition of the challenges of generating geopolitical power. Iranian leaders have acknowledged that they can't compete with the United States and its allies using conventional means. Iran's network of militias and strategy of operating in the shadows of the region is itself a response to and recognition of the limits of its conventional power. Iran believes that it can only compete using asymmetric unconventional means.

We will see in the following pages how Iran has tried to avoid repeating the strategic missteps of earlier periods by maneuvering and adapting to the seismic events that have rocked the region. We will see how Iran has had to adapt to the collapse of the Soviet Union, an unbridled America after 9/11, and collapse of several states in the region following the Arab Spring. Through this process Iran has built a foreign policy that has given it regional influence, but that hasn't benefited the Iranian people.

The test of whether Iran has truly internalized the lessons from the past will come in the wake of the attacks by Hamas on Israel in 2023 and the brutal war in Gaza that ensued. In the early days of this war, it appeared that Iran's star in the region had brightened with the impressive display of coordination of its network of militias. But with the 2024 degradation of the capabilities of Hamas and Hezbollah by Israel, and the direct military conflicts with Israel, Iran's power projection capabilities will be tested and put under stress. Time will tell if it uses some of the lessons accumulated over the 500 years since the Safavid era to manage the risks of confronting a wounded yet emboldened Israel and possibly a hostile United States and Europe.[49]

2 IRAN'S VIEW OF THE WORLD

Those of us who came of age in the United States during the Cold War tend to think of foreign policy decision-making as tied to a grand strategic logic. This was understandable given that the strategy of Soviet containment dominated the policy-making process for nearly half a century and bound together different US administrations. While there was variance in the approaches taken by different presidents, there was remarkable coherence in how the United States marshalled the available instruments of military, economic, and political power to weaken the grip of the Soviet Union and advance US vital national interests.

This coherence was largely a product of a shared worldview that helped US policy-makers make sense of the rush of events that challenged them over the expanse of the Cold War. The focus of this chapter is on Iran's worldviews. In other words, it is about how Iran sees and interprets the world and makes sense of challenging events. The story that will unfold is how Iranian policy-makers frame, simplify, and assign meaning to the deluge of facts that come their way.

The facts facing Iranian decision-makers seldom speak for themselves—they must be interpreted. We will look at the interpretative worldviews used by Iranian policy-makers to deal with the inevitable complexities, contradictions, and ambiguities in their international environment. Worldviews help policy-makers simplify complexity to facilitate decision-making. Sometimes policy-makers are conscious of the worldviews or interpretive lenses they use and sometimes they are not. Some worldviews are ideological, while others are analytic. And sometimes worldviews are hybrids, combining ideological biases with analytic assumptions.[1]

Worldviews can be both useful and dangerous. They can serve as blinders for policy-makers, blotting out key bits of information. But they can also provide insight, help interpret events, and provide a window into how the world works.² They can also fill in where there are gaps in known facts and can create meaning out of disparate, contradictory facts. For Iran, a focus on worldviews is particularly important in the post-Cold War era, where there is more ambiguity in the strategic environment than ever before.

Building on the previous chapter, this section will show how Iran's worldview, as revolutionary, self-justifying, and other worldish as it appears to us in the west, emerged out of Iran's historical challenges of generating power. While Iran imbues its foreign policy narratives with ideological references, at the core it reflects a realpolitik worldview and interpretation of how power is distributed within the international system.

Is it possible that the worldviews held by leaders of great powers like the United States and middle powers like Iran are characteristically different? The answer is that of course it depends on the country and the individual leaders. But an overall observation is that global powers are prone to ask fewer deep interpretative questions than are regional powers like Iran. Disproportionately large power gives a greater margin for error, oftentimes obviating the need to ask deeper questions. Or perhaps more accurately it lulls policy-makers to falsely assume they don't have to dig deeper for greater understanding.

This was witnessed during the age of European imperialism in the Middle East where questions about the political developments and nuances of the colonized country were seldom asked by the occupying powers. Even the anthropological studies done on Egyptians by British scholars treated them as children and objects to be studied rather than as dynamic political beings.³ They saw the populations in the occupied countries in very simplified, stereotypical terms, oftentimes filtering out inconvenient facts such as growing nationalist sentiment, something that would have required a more complex perceptual frame.⁴ This resulted in the British not properly seeing the challenge nationalism posed to their continued dominance over Egypt.

Obliviousness to the political dynamic nuances in Egypt in the nineteenth and twentieth centuries was reasonably cost-free for the British up to a point. But once political modernization took hold and the power disparity between ruler and subject narrowed, the lack of a clear interpretive lens had costly consequences for British occupiers caught off guard by the power of nationalist movements. It turned out that the nationalist leaders fighting for their independence had a clearer analytic hold on the situation than the far more powerful occupying forces. The lack of an accurate situational lens on the part of the British leveled the playing field with their nationalist adversaries, rendering obsolete traditional power-based, realist theories that no longer had predictive and analytic power.[5]

Small and even middle powers like Iran have a smaller margin for error than great powers. Therefore, the imperative for an interpretative framework that helps leaders evaluate the motivations, capabilities, and strategies of other actors is even stronger. Smaller powers also need to accurately assess the distribution of power in their regional and international environments. Because of a lower margin for error, they need to dig deeper to more fully comprehend the threats they confront. The interpretative lens as a roadmap for strategic decision-making can mean the difference between life and death for decision-makers, as Saddam Hussein of Iraq discovered in 2003. Arguably, his interpretations of reality were one-dimensional and only allowed the most convenient facts to enter the decision-making process.[6]

This chapter will look at the interpretative lenses Iranian decision-makers used to make sense of their rapidly changing world. Our purpose is to neither validate nor discredit any of Iran's worldview frameworks. Rather, it is to try to create some understanding of the interpretative lenses used, and then in later chapters evaluate whether they provided Iran with a reasonably accurate strategic roadmap.

Based on interviews and a close reading of policy statements, both public and private, of present and former key Iranian decision-makers, this chapter will lay out the picture of the international system that dominates the Iranian decision-making process. It will also lay out the more particular dominant views about key actors in the international system, namely the United States, Russia, and China.

We will look at three different periods in the evolution of how Iran saw the international system. The first will be the Cold War, including the early days of the Iranian revolution before the Soviet Union collapsed. Here we will look at how Iranian decision-makers interpreted the actions of the two superpowers, particularly during the Iran-Iraq war. It will show that the war affirmed the revolutionary worldview about the conspiratorial nature of superpowers. The second will be the post-Cold War period when the United States had no global competitor to oppose its actions in the Middle East. Here we will look at how Iran interpreted the power, motivation, and strategy of the United States during this fleeting unipolar moment. While this period of an unbridled America posed threats to Iran, gross miscalculations on the part of the United States and other regional actors also created opportunities.

We will also look at the current moment and see how Iran's worldview encompasses what it sees as a trend toward a shift in the distribution of power in the international system, away from the west and towards the east. What we will see is that Iran's views of the United States are more fixed and stereotypical than the views it holds of Russia, which have evolved over time from the simplified imagery of the Soviet Union to the more complex imagery of Russia today.[7] Stereotypical views seem to be perpetuated when there is irregular or no contact, such as is the case with the United States. But stereotypical views can be softened and morph into greater complexity under the dint of more regular contact, such as is the case with Russia and China.

It will be argued that while Iran's worldviews reflected the ideological views of Ayatollah Ruhollah Khomeini, Iran's first Supreme Leader, they were reinforced by events such as the Iran-Iraq war.[8] The chapter will argue that the themes and lessons forged during the 1980–88 war became hardwired into the strategic thinking of decision-makers and prevail to this day.

This is not to suggest that there has been unanimity among decision-makers on all dimensions of Iran's worldview. As with most countries, in Iran there is a significant variance of views across the leadership structure. What it does suggest, however, is that there is agreement on certain principles and, notwithstanding variance of views among decision-makers, certain views have become dominant and institutionalized. In some cases, this could be a worldview that gained dominance and prevailed among all other competing worldviews. In other cases, it could be a consensus view that emerged from different bureaucratic voices. In other cases, it could be a view that has become institutionalized, embedded, and unquestioned since or even before the Iranian revolution of 1979. Worldviews can transcend the perceptions of individual decision-makers and become part of the ethos of the foreign policy establishment. And pieces of worldview can inhere in the institutional norms and implicit assumptions that guide foreign policy outside the realm of individual leader perceptions, misperceptions, or psychologies.[9]

To some degree, Iran's view of the world is largely a projection of how Iran sees itself. It is based on how Iran has experienced and observed the world. As we saw in the previous chapter, for much of Iran's history it has been the recipient of, rather than a direct contributor to, international politics. Because of the degree to which it has been penetrated, it has been forced to interpret the international community in ways that more powerful actors aren't compelled to do. This fact has become an important part of the Iranian political psyche, stemming from a sense that Iran shaped the world during the early days of the Persian Empire, then lost that shaping capacity over several different dynastic periods. Questions about Iran's ambition for regional influence today need to be nested in the context of Iran's historical struggle to shape its own destiny.[10]

Iran's Interpretative Lens as Worldview

One might say that the way the world is organized is observable on the surface. It consists of clearly demarcated sovereign states, international institutions, and treaty organizations. But while these are the formal structures that define the international political order, what lies beneath the surface is more ambiguous and open to interpretation and analysis. A sole focus on the structures we can see fails to ask questions about changes in power dynamics in the international system. It also fails to answer critical questions about the strengths, weaknesses, and motivations of key international actors. Answers to these questions are more subjective and open to interpretation than might initially meet the eye. And in the case of Iran, the answers are informed by the country's unique historical experiences.

This is where the importance of worldview comes into play. Iran's worldviews have evolved within the context of interactions with the west, and therefore deal explicitly with questions of political power. But there is also an ideological tinge to Iran's worldview. Ayatollah Ali Khamenei has said that there is no inconsistency between Iran's ideological values and its realpolitik concerns, arguing that Islamic values and Iran's interests are inseparable and compatible. In other words, his belief is that decisions concerning the national interest need to be made within the conception of Iran's Islamic values.[11] Within his worldview construct, the west has violated both Iran's Islamic values <u>and</u> its national interests.

There are significant differences in the worldviews held by Iranian and American decision-makers. Understanding this helps explain tensions between the two countries.¹² The United States has a mechanical view of the world, defined by formalized power structures. Iran has more of a hermeneutic interpretative view that sees power in less formal, structural terms.¹³

There are also stark differences between the dominant worldviews in Iran before and after the revolution. For Reza Shah Pahlavi, the penultimate shah, and his son and last shah, Mohammed Reza Shah Pahlavi, Islamic ideology and parochial tribalism had weakened the country, keeping it in the dark ages. According to them, the backwardness that ensued led Iran down a path of penetration by external powers in the nineteenth and twentieth centuries.¹⁴ They believed that Iranian nationalism, with roots in the country's pre-Islamic past, could be marshalled as a source of strength and national renewal.

Khomeini's worldview turned the Pahlavi view on its head. His view was that secular nationalism, a western construct, had weakened Iran, while the authenticity of Islam could generate political power and pull Iran out of its state of dependence. In essence, the worldview debate was about the nature of political power and which ideology could generate the most.

Iran's worldview involves several concentric circles. Spreading out from Iran is a region defined by a struggle between a US alliance system and an Iranian-led "axis of resistance." It is a battle between the status quo powers and an Iran-led revisionist bloc. The second concentric circle extends beyond the region to the international system consisting of a struggle between the United States and the more revisionist powers of Russia and China. So, in a way, there is some symmetry between the region and the international system, both defined by tensions between status quo and revisionist powers. Iran, while not a superpower, sees itself as part of the revisionist club.

Iran's view of the world is intertwined with its view of itself. Iran has struggled with its grandiose view of its past but its subsequent vulnerabilities in the international system. Paradoxically, the United States has reinforced both sides of this dialectic. After the collapse of the Soviet Union, Iran occupied a bigger place in the foreign policy psyche of American policy-makers than its middle power size dictated, in a way replacing Moscow as its primary nemesis. In some ways, this amplified Iran's sense of its worth in the world, but also its vulnerability as being alone against an unbridled superpower. In a strange way, US actions have added to Iran's perception of grandeur but also vulnerability.

Iranian Worldviews During the Cold War

Most of us who grew up in the west during the peak of the Cold War saw the primary geopolitical cleavage to be between the United States and Soviet Union, between capitalism and democracy on one pole and communism and autocracy on the other. The prevailing worldview in the west was of a bipolar world split into east-west axes. We saw the struggle as an existential, zero-sum battle between the United States and Soviet Union.

Part of this worldview extended deep into the Middle East and the rest of what we then called the third world. Countries like Israel, Turkey, Iran (until 1979), Jordan, and Saudi Arabia were on the American side of the divide, while Syria, Iraq, Egypt (until 1978), and Libya were on the Soviet side.

Imagine the shock of analyzing Ayatollah Khomeini's alternative worldview, something I did as a young graduate student after the Iranian revolution of 1979. It turned the Cold War worldview I had internalized directly on its head. His portrayal was that the two superpowers were joint hegemons, bound by a common interest of suppressing the Muslim masses through their support of oppressive, authoritarian leaders, like the Shah of Iran.

In Khomeini's own words he spoke about what he saw as collaboration by the superpowers:

> The fact is that the imperialist governments from the East and West, especially America and the Soviet Union, have politically divided the world into two sections, namely politically free and quarantined sections. In the free section of the world, these are the superpowers which observe no bounds and laws, and they consider as essential and completely justified the launching of aggression against others' interests, and colonization, exploitation, and enslaving of nations.[15]

This worldview that has influenced Iranian foreign policy since the revolution of 1979 is something that westerners might find bizarre, other-worldish, perhaps even delusional. Even to regional leaders, like Egypt's Anwar Sadat, Khomeini's musings on world politics seemed crazy.[16]

Through a set of western eyes, the natural response was to dispute the facts by clearly demonstrating that the United States and Soviet Union were in fact rivals, pointing to skirmishes in Berlin, elsewhere in Europe, in Asia, and of course the global nuclear standoff. But in many ways, this misses the point, which is not the seemingly incontrovertible facts, but rather different outlooks on the meaning of the facts around this Cold War competition and rivalry.

As crazy as the worldview may have sounded to Americans and others in the Middle East, several of the events that occurred before and after the revolution reinforced the perceptions articulated by Khomeini, making them more mainstream among Iranian policy-makers.

Deep-dive discussions with Iranian policy-makers reveal that there isn't complete incompatibility between the American and Iranian worldviews. Khomeini didn't necessarily dispute that the two superpowers were rivals and driven by a desire to best one another. But what the Khomeini worldview focused on was the underlying structure of the game both superpowers played to avoid direct conflict. The view was that Moscow and Washington pushed hostilities down into the developing world to avoid a direct nuclear exchange. The more sophisticated version of this I have heard from Iranians doesn't claim there was an active conspiracy between the superpowers, but rather that there was a tacit agreement on the rules of the game. For them, even this tacit abidance of the rules of the game created a structure of dominance that felt like conscious joint oppression to those in the region.

In other words, Khomeini asserted that there was an imperialist logic that bound together the uncommon bedfellows of the United States and the Soviet Union. His "neither east, nor west" mantra was built on an assumption that while the United States and the Soviet Union might see each other as intense rivals, in fact they had a common stake in perpetuating the inequitable rules of the game.[17] He believed the superpowers froze their direct conflict to avoid the risk of a nuclear exchange by pushing their conflict down into the region.

While Khomeini's worldview seemed shocking and revolutionary, it really wasn't completely sui generis. Earlier Islamic thinkers too had adopted a Manichean worldview, extolling the virtues of Islam versus the perfidy of Christian Europe.[18] Jamal al-Din al-Afghani in the nineteenth century and Sayyid Qutb in the twentieth century developed their ideological chops against the backdrop of European imperialism and the struggle for countries like Egypt to assert power.[19] In those days, the two "co-oppressors" were France and Great Britain, both of which competed and collaborated in perpetuating the institution of colonialism.

The notion that competing global powers could also collaborate was part of the Middle Eastern experience. For Iran it was Russia and Britain and for much of the Arab world it was Britain and France. In both cases, great powers competed for influence but also conspired against the interests of the countries in the region.

Khomeini's worldview went a lot farther than merely analyzing the international system. His view was that Islam held the power to push back against this collaborative tendency of great powers. He saw Iran as part of a drama of a civilizational attack on Muslims by the decadent and exploitive superpowers. The golden key to unleashing sufficient power to resist exploitation by the superpowers was political Islam. Islam, in contrast to nationalism, could extract the passion, commitment, and power of the Iranian people and Muslim populations needed to resist western encroachment.

Khomeini, in addition to drawing from the writings of earlier Muslim thinkers, such as Afghani and Qutb, was able to draw on specific historical experiences of Iran to give context to his worldview. In fact, given the context of Iran's historical experiences with great powers, his thinking wasn't revolutionary at all but rather built on empirical observations about their behavior. The experience of dealing with great powers which on the surface are rivals but ultimately collaborate, is part of Iran's history.[20]

The betrayals and manipulations that followed these collaborations reinforced the worldview that great powers can't be trusted as they will ultimately betray Iran. Collaboration between the United States and Britain in the 1953 coup against Prime Minister Mohammed Mossadegh was one of the most egregious examples of this. Cold War fears rode roughshod over any benevolence the United States may have shown to Iran in earlier, simpler times. Also, oil interests and American relations with Britain, apoplectic over Premier Mohammed Mossadegh's nationalization of the Anglo-Iranian oil company, were contributing factors in the collaboration.

Ayatollah Khomeini believed that regardless of intermittent expressions of goodwill, great powers would eventually turn on smaller powers like Iran. Intrinsic to his view is a convergence between ideology and historical record, the combination of which made for a powerful narrative that survived him.[21]

Khomeini believed he understood how the world worked, and he crystallized his worldview into the "neither east, nor west" mantra of the revolution. This became not just a slogan; it also guided Iran's foreign policy after 1979.[22]

In Chapter 6 we will see how Iran built its strategic responses to the challenges it faced within this worldview. But we will next examine how events after the revolution reinforced Iran's worldview, embedding it further into the country's foreign policy strategic ethos.

Cold War worldview shaping events: The Iran-Iraq war

The events that ensued after Iran's momentous 1979 revolution provided Iranian leaders with plenty of evidence to support Khomeini's worldview biases that the United States and Soviet Union were on the same side of a global game.[23] The seminal event that cemented that worldview, not just for Khomeini but for the mainstream foreign policy establishment, was the Iran-Iraq war of 1980–88 when almost the entire world, including the two superpowers, diverted its gaze after Iraq invaded. And then when Iran gained the initiative in 1982, both superpowers and all Arab states except Syria tilted toward Iraq in its bid to defeat Iran.

In terms of how international politics played into Iranian leader worldviews at the time, the primary emphasis was on the motivations and actions of the United States. The war which had started in September 1980 with an Iraqi attack on Iran played out against the drama of the hostage crisis involving the captivity of fifty-two American diplomats starting in November of 1979. Ayatollah Khomeini believed that the United States gave Saddam Hussein of Iraq a green light to wage war on Iran. He saw this as America's payback for the detainment of the American hostages, saying the war waged was, "the U.S. hand emerging from Saddam's sleeve."[24] This view was reinforced further when towards the end of the war, the United States gave Iraq targeting information that was used to wage chemical attacks on Iran.[25]

But the piece of the worldview that was most heavily reinforced by the war was that the superpowers, even at the height of the Cold War, would collaborate to preserve their dominance over the Middle East.[26] The suspicion felt by the Iranians was that both superpowers saw the Iranian revolution as potentially disruptive to the Cold War status quo structure, and therefore a threat to both of their interests. The view was that collectively the superpowers had an interest in preventing Iran from keeping its promise of exporting its revolution, which could upend the

Cold War system of alliances that each of them had so assiduously built after the Second World War.

Soviet and American actions confirmed Khomeini's suspicions about the mutual interests of the two superpowers. While the United States didn't formally tilt toward Iraq until 1982, from the beginning of the war the Iranians suspected Washington's "hidden hands." But by 1983 Khomeini also showed his suspicions and disdain for the Soviet Union by expelling eighteen Soviet diplomats and banning the communist Tudeh party.[27]

The joint-hegemon view was perpetuated by the actions of the superpowers later in the war as well. When Iran disrupted shipping through the straits of Hormuz and the wider Persian Gulf in 1987, both the United States and Soviet Union worked with Kuwait to reflag Kuwaiti tankers as a deterrent to Iranian attacks.[28] While it was the United States that ultimately reflagged the tankers, both it and the Soviet Union helped patrol the Persian Gulf. Also, Kuwait chartered Soviet tankers as a form of protection against an attack.[29] Adding insult to injury for the Iranians, when the United States gave targeting information to the Iraqis used to wage chemical warfare, the Soviet Union remained mum. The Soviets also supplied Frog SSM's and Scud-B missiles to Iraq, which subsequently landed on Iranian territory.[30]

The war was the crucible that solidified the worldview that the superpower rivals were bound by a set of unspoken yet common interests. This affirmation of the worldview can be seen in the statements of leaders who were part of the ruling clique during the war. In 1987, Ayatollah Hussein-Ali Montazeri, who was at the time Khomeini's successor before being sidelined later to make way for Ali Khamenei, said:

> Today any blow that is dealt at this fledgling {Islamic} republic emanates either from Western imperialism, the U.S. ... or from the East [the Soviet Union] by means of such advanced weapons as the MIG, Soviet missiles ...[31]

Former Iranian President Abol Hassan Bani-Sadr said something similar reflecting the belief of superpower collusion:

> I was already convinced that neither the Soviets nor the Americans would permit an Iranian victory, and that since their rapprochement on November 21, 1985, in Geneva, they had decided to act jointly.[32]

Ali Khamenei, who in 1987 was president of Iran, said the following at the UN, conveying the notions of both strategic loneliness and collaboration by the superpowers against Iran:

> I would like to ask that big question from this podium. A good number of governments know for sure that the Iraqi regime started this war and carried out this invasion, but the question is, why do these governments keep silent in the face of this great crime and this international sin? ... The key to solving this puzzle may lie in familiarity with the state of political relations in the modern world and the flawed geometry which has been created in global relations by the hegemony of the superpowers, and this is not hidden from our nation.[33]

It wasn't lost on Khomeini that in addition to superpower collaboration, the entire world, apart from Syria, lined up against Iran and in support of Saddam Hussein.[34]

This worldview was seared into the political consciousness of the ruling elites at the time, extended out to include international institutions. In a 1987 letter to the UN Secretary General, Iranian Foreign Minister Ali Velayati said:

> The UN Security Council and other similar world bodies are nothing but tools at the disposal of the arrogant powers (i.e., the superpowers). UN Resolution 598, calling for both sides to commence a ceasefire to bring to close the then seven-year-old Iran-Iraq War leaves no doubt in anyone's mind as to the Council being manipulated by the arrogant powers ...[35]

Iranian perceptions of the superpowers being animated by a common interest aside, the reality behind both superpowers tilting toward Iraq was more complex. Paradoxically, it was the logic of Cold War rivalry that caused Washington and Moscow to both tilt toward Iraq. The United States was concerned that if Iran prevailed, it would be empowered to fulfill its promise to export the revolution. If it did this, the most vulnerable countries were US allies like Saudi Arabia and Jordan, which if they fell would give the Soviet Union a strategic advantage. The Soviets were concerned that the demise of its ally Iraq would be a clear win for the United States and its allies. Moscow was also concerned that a clear Iranian advance would give the US a pretext for launching military action in the Gulf, something that was certainly against Soviet interests.

Notwithstanding the vitriolic rhetoric of equivalency about the two superpowers, Iranian leaders did make clear distinctions between them. The view of the United States was visceral, emotional, and intense. The imagery of the United States as the "Great Satan" was fresher, and more immediate given the recent support the US had given the shah and the earlier US role in the overthrow of Mossadegh. It wasn't just the behavior of the United States, but also the ideas and culture it propagated that Khomeini found anathema. He also saw threat coming from western universities, which he believed to be progenitors of "west-toxification."[36] While Russia potentially could be the more credible threat due to the proximity of its border, the ideological core of the revolution painted the United States as the "Great Satan."

What we saw during the Iran-Iraq war that is true today is more flexibility and less vitriol about Russia than the United States. The views of the United States are more fixed and entrenched than the views about Russia. In the early days of the war, the Soviets professed neutrality, which rankled the Iranian government. But this paled in comparison to the intensely negative comments by Washington. Also, for practical reasons Iran kept its dispute with Moscow at a low boil during the hostage crisis, to avoid confronting the ire of the two superpowers simultaneously. Even with the issue of Soviet arms sales to Iraq and Iran's opposition to the Soviet invasion of Afghanistan, there was more flexibility in the views of the Soviets than of the Americans.[37]

The war was an inflection point in convincing the revolutionary regime in power that Iran was alone in the international system. Of course, the central piece of this was that Washington and Moscow would close ranks to oppose and suppress any disruption to the status quo that benefited them both.[38] But the fact that almost no country supported Iran, even though Iraq had been the aggressor, reinforced a view of strategic loneliness, something that wouldn't be lost on Iranian decision-makers going forward.

The other thing that was reinforced during the Iran-Iraq war was Ayatollah Khomeini's belief that it was the power of Islam that was decisive in fending off the Iraqis, particularly in the early days of the war.[39] The number of young people clutching symbols of "keys-to-heaven" as they ran to their certain deaths over the minefields laid by the Iraqis was ample indication to Khomeini of the power of revolutionary Islam.

While the overall view of the power of Islam is still embedded in Iranian strategic culture, confidence in the ability of the regime to extract sacrifice from the Iranian people has declined in the decades since the war. The protests in 2018 specifically aimed at Iran's involvement in the Syrian civil war were a pretty good reinforcement of this reduced confidence.[40]

Another part of Iran's worldview that was reinforced by the Iran-Iraq war was the conflation between the international and regional systems. Accompanying Ayatollah Khomeini's agreement to end the war with Iraq was a statement calling for the removal of US and European forces from the region. US refusal indicated to Iran that as Soviet power was ebbing, the United States would use its power to penetrate the region, erasing any semblance of distinction between the regional and international systems.[41]

The Iraqi invasion and the responses of the United States and Soviet Union spawned the strategic doctrine of forward defense. Iran claimed that to prevent future attacks and protect the homeland, it needed to create a strategic buffer zone around Iran. The creation of Hezbollah in 1982 in Lebanon was a piece of what later became part of Iran's forward defense doctrine.

While the war reinforced the ideological biases of the revolution, it also injected a cold, hard realpolitik pragmatism in Iran's foreign policy. As a result of the war, Iran became willing to deal with either of the superpowers when and if it satisfied their interests. The Iran-Contra affair was an example of this, with Tehran holding furtive talks with the United States starting in 1985 to procure arms. While this initiative fell apart over differences among the ruling elite in Tehran and because of the scandal it spawned in the United States, it did show the regime's emerging pragmatic streak.

Iran's foreign policy became less ideological and more pragmatic after the war. President Rafsanjani sought to rebuild ties with the Arab world and focused heavily on reconstruction and economic growth. He also tried to reduce tensions with the United States.[42] In some ways, this pragmatism survives to the current day. Iran's receptivity to the talks that culminated in the JCPOA Iran nuclear deal in 2015, can be seen as a realpolitik trend that was afoot in Iran, starting with the end of the Iran-Iraq war.

How this pragmatism fares in the post-October 7, 2023 changed geopolitical climate, will be something to keep watch for. Russia and China, Iran's allies, have played low-profile roles since the Hamas attacks, while Washington is on full alert for future Iranian regional activities.

How Iran calibrates and perhaps even rebalances its foreign policy to minimize the risk of isolation will be the key to knowing whether the pragmatism that emerged from the Iran-Iraq war is still a dominant feature of Iran's foreign policy.[43]

Cold War worldview shaping events: The hostage crisis

In terms of Iranian perceptions, the hostage crisis and Iran-Iraq war are inextricably linked. The American hostages were taken November 4, 1979, and Iraq invaded Iran in September of 1980. In the interim, there was a failed US rescue attempt to free the hostages in April of 1980. The belief in Tehran was that the invasion by Iraq was instigated by the United States as payback for the hostage crisis. Khomeini's imagery of "cut off the U.S. hand that has come out of Saddam's sleeve" demonstrates how he and his coterie of advisors saw the connection between Iran's battle with Washington and the onslaught from Iraq.[44] Even later in 1985 after all the hostages had returned and as Iraqi planes dropped bombs on Tehran, there were shouts of "Death to America", an indication of how closely tied were the perceptions of the US with perceptions of Iraqi aggression.[45]

The hostage crisis in many ways reflected how Iranian leaders saw the capability of Iran after the revolution. And it gave us a window as to how they saw US capability relative to the revolution.

The hostage crisis served the hardliners in the revolutionary regime in their successful struggle to outmaneuver other factions. There are plenty of studies that focus on the domestic and bureaucratic dynamics behind the storming of the American embassy and the holding of the hostages. This analysis focuses more on how the crisis fits into the Iranian political psyche, its view of the world and even Iran's strategic calculus.[46] From all the available evidence, Ayatollah Khomeini had no foreknowledge of the storming of the American embassy. But he certainly used it to his political advantage once it started, rendering any quick resolution of the crisis virtually impossible.[47]

One of the most stunning findings is that some regime figures at the time claimed that the holding of the hostages fit into a strategy of trying to alter the worldview of the United States. Richard Cottam, one of the world's foremost experts on Iran, recounted several phone conversations and a visit to Tehran to meet with then Iranian Foreign Minister Sadegh

Ghotbzadeh. What Ghotbzadeh told Cottam was that Khomeini believed the United States needed shocks to shake it out of its current worldview of a US-centric world. The perpetuation of the hostage crisis was to be that shock. If true, this is a striking attempt to shift the direction of US foreign policy through a shift in worldviews.[48] In other words, Khomeini believed that his audacious act of violating and piercing the veil of the diplomatic immunity of the hostages would shake the United States out of its anachronistic, imperial worldview, and create an understanding that international power dynamics had changed.[49]

There is other evidence to suggest that the Iranians were aiming to alter US worldviews. On April 8, 1980, Ayatollah Khomeini said that the US breaking relations with Iran the day before was a good omen, as it indicated that Washington had given up hope in being able to control Iran.[50] There was a belief that the Iranian revolution represented a sea change in world politics, from a global power-dominated system to a political system where Muslims and other oppressed peoples have agency and a voice. Khomeini's successor, Ayatollah Ali Khamenei, in 2017 stated that Iran's revolution (and the hostage crisis) altered the structure of a world dominated by the United States.[51] This was an extension of the thinking that prevailed during the hostage crisis. The view was that Iran had the potential to change the global structure, or at least break the psychological bonds that supported the old structure.

Cold War worldview shaping events: Gulf War I

One could convincingly argue that prior to the Gulf War commencing in August of 1990, events reinforced a worldview of the United States as a paper tiger. The hostage crisis from 1979 to 1981, and then the peremptory evacuation of US troops from Lebanon after the 1983 explosion that killed 241 American soldiers, gave Iran fodder to support its view that Washington's day as an impresario of the region had passed. Khomeini saw this as a pattern of a weakened and unsteady America that began with the US entanglement in Vietnam.[52]

But the Gulf War, which started after the 1990 Iraqi invasion of Kuwait, prompted a reconsideration of the view that the United States lacked the capacity and the desire to impose its will on the region.[53] While the war constrained Iran's nemesis, Saddam's Iraq, the invasion also showed Iran that Washington still could impose red lines on the region. Even further it demonstrated that as the Cold War was winding down, through Washington's assemblage of an impressive coalition to fight Saddam, it had the capacity and will to impose a Pax Americana upon the region.

The views about what response to the war best served Iranian interests were not unanimous across the Iranian foreign policy establishment. Some, like then President Rafsanjani and newly minted Supreme Leader Ali Khamenei, declared Iran as a neutral party in the dispute. Given that Iran's long and bloody war with Iraq had ended just two years before, this stance of neutrality showed a clear-eyed view of risk and restraint on the part of the Iranians. Siding with the Americans against Iraq, as emotionally tempting as that might be, would have been politically unthinkable. Actively opposing the American-led coalition of thirty countries to support Saddam would have been suicidal. It also would have ignored that Iraq's invasion of Kuwait showed that Saddam's aggressive bloodlust knew no bounds. A victory in Kuwait could be a harbinger of future threats to Iran.[54]

But restraint and the policy of neutrality weren't supported unanimously across the regime, even if they reflected official policy. More radical voices, including Ayatollah Ali Khamenei's younger brother Hadi Khamenei, advocated looking beyond Iran's own bloody war with Iraq to support Saddam Hussein. The logic was that Kuwait was a western lackey, deserving of its fate. And he and others were sympathetic to Saddam's threats to Israel during the war, a blood enemy of the Islamic Republic.[55] It appeared that Saddam Hussein believed that supportive voices in Iran would prevail. He sent a hundred Iraqi jets to Iran during the war to keep them out of range of the US coalition force, perhaps in a spate of both naivete and desperation.

What is important to note is that Rafsanjani and Khamenei held the same worldview as those with the more radical voices like Hadi. Their consensus view was that the United States was setting a dangerous precedent by treading on the Middle East, with the possibility of ultimately trampling on Iranian sovereignty, and eventually feeling emboldened enough to act upon a long-held goal of regime change in Iran. The differences weren't in their worldviews, but rather in how they saw Iran's capacity to manage risk and cope in a world where Iraq was contained but the Americans became more empowered.

The period following the Gulf War was one of the most formative in shaping Iranian impressions and views. Because the Gulf War in 1990–91 came on the heels of the Iran-Iraq war, the lessons from the two wars became intertwined. With Iran needing to consider the dual threats from Iraq and the United States, its threat environment became eminently more complex. Since the Americans didn't deliver a fatal blow to Saddam or his regime, there still was a residual threat from Saddam, notwithstanding the US-enforced no-fly zones that attenuated the threat. But this attenuation of threat from Iraq was counterbalanced with threats and risks from a United States fresh from victory. There was a growing sense that while the Gulf War and its aftermath rendered a blow to Iran's primary nemesis, Iraq, it meant that the United States now had the will and capacity to impose a Pax Americana on the region, something that could threaten Iran's range of options.

This was a critical perception, as it was Iran's war with Iraq that led to changes in Iran's security doctrine. Now the US war with Iraq threatened to circumscribe Iranian attempts to create the strategic depth and buffer zone it became committed to after its own war with Iraq. While the mandate for this came from a lingering distrust and hatred of Saddam Hussein, now Tehran had to face the possibility of an American permanent presence in the region. And it had to face the fact that while the forward defense doctrine might create sufficient strategic depth to protect it from regional actors like Iraq, it couldn't protect it from a global actor like the United States. It was just a few years later that US President Bill Clinton's dual containment concept aimed at both Iraq and Iran proved that in fact the United States would turn its sights on Iran.

The other factor related to the Gulf War that shaped Iran's threat perceptions and worldview was the collapse of the Soviet Union in December of 1991, less than a year after the war's conclusion. The view at the time was that the end of the Cold War was a mixed bag for Iran. Without the Soviet Union to counterbalance American power, Washington's regional ambitions could go unchecked. Moreover, the collapse of the Soviet Union changed Iran's geostrategic reality, with newly independent countries in neighboring central Asia craving close bonds with the United States, thus creating a new type of encirclement.[56] But on the other hand, the loss of the Soviet Union meant that America had lost its strategic north star. The Iranians saw that a rudderless Washington could create threats but also that the Islamic Republic could deftly navigate around American overreach and missteps.

This was a seminal and transitional moment in terms of Iranian perceptions. Now Tehran had to weigh and possibly balance regional threats with international threats. During the Iran-Iraq war, most of the world's powerbrokers were tilted toward Iraq and had abandoned Iran. But by 1990 Tehran discerned that the United States saw Iraq as the primary threat to regional security. The Iranians had to calculate what it meant strategically that Iraq had been circumscribed by the United States. They had to weigh the obvious benefits of this against the risk created by a longer-term military commitment to the region by Washington.

The hostage crisis had been perpetuated by a perception by Iranian leaders that the United States was operating according to anachronistic calculations of American power. But the Gulf War and the end of the Cold War signaled to the Iranians that their assumption of American decline may have been premature. What was clear was that despite the shock value of the revolution and the hostage crisis, the US still had the will and now the fresh capacity to intervene in the Middle East.

Iran's Worldview in the Post-Cold War Period

To give context to how Iran sees the international system today, it is important to track the evolution of how it was perceived after the 1991 collapse of the Soviet Union. First and foremost, Iran faced the specter of the United States running unopposed in the Middle East. After the first Gulf War, which ended less than a year before the Soviet collapse, there were several initiatives and trends that signaled to the Iranians that a new Pax-Americana might be afoot. The Oslo Accord that laid the foundational steps for a two-state solution between Israel and Palestine was signed on the lawn of the Clinton White House in 1993. A short time later, Iran's only Arab ally, Syria engaged in short-lived US-sponsored negotiations with Israel. Reinforcing the trend of US propensity to intervene was the dual containment doctrine articulated in 1993 by the Clinton administration, designed to circumscribe the regional ambitions of both Iran and Iraq. A doctrine that purported to contain Iran, a former US ally, and Iraq, an erstwhile Soviet ally, would have been unthinkable during the Cold War. This was a clear indication to the Iranians that the United States had both the intention and capacity to play a formidable role in the Middle East.

As worrisome as the actions of the Clinton administration had been, the events that occurred on September 11, 2001 under US President

George W. Bush changed Iranian perceptions of Washington considerably. What had been a soft-pedaled unipolarity during the Clinton period became a more aggressive variant after 9/11. The invasions of Afghanistan in 2001 and of Iraq in 2003 rang alarm bells in Tehran.

But eventually Tehran saw a paradox about American power that survives to the present day: at a moment of peak power projection in the Middle East, Washington would become increasingly prone to missteps and miscalculations. Handled adeptly, these stumbles could create opportunities for Iran to advance its interests. The downside risk was that Iran, squeezed between US forces on its eastern border in Afghanistan and western border in Iraq, would have little room for maneuver. But the opportunity was that the collapse of Saddam's regime in Iraq gave Iran the capacity to create the strategic depth it had believed it needed since the end of the Iran-Iraq war.

This opportunity wasn't a gift to Iran. Tehran had to navigate around the multiple risks it faced in projecting influence into Iraq under American military occupation, something which required careful policy calibration. On the one hand, the US invasion of Iraq rid Iran of its worrisome rival, Saddam Hussein. On the other hand, the Iranians faced the reality that the mania that beset Washington following 9/11 could mean that they might be next on the target list.[57]

Iran had seen the ups and downs of managing risk of a post-9/11 United States with the earlier 2001 Afghan invasion. Iran believed it mitigated its risk of being targeted by Washington somewhat by expressing condolences to the victims of the 9/11 attacks and offering the use of Iranian territory for rescue missions in Afghanistan. This belief proved short-lived when President Bush at the State of the Union in 2002, clustered Iran alongside Iraq and North Korea as part of an "axis of evil."[58]

But even after it was clear to Iranians that Washington retained hostility toward them despite the goodwill they had shown after 9/11, threat perceptions were attenuated somewhat by the absence of a clear US winning strategy for Afghanistan and later for Iraq. Despite attempts by Washington to impose its will on the Middle East, Iran was a witness to the dual insurgencies in Afghanistan and Iraq weakening the US posture in the region. The Iranians came to believe that once again Washington was forced to confront the limits of its power. The belief that by overreaching in Afghanistan and Iraq, the United States had lost any strategic benefit it had gained from the collapse of the Soviet Union.

Discussions with Iranian leaders reveal how closely their perceptions of the current moment represent an extension of the views that were forged after the US invasions of Iraq and Afghanistan over two decades ago.[59] The belief still lingers that despite the use of overwhelming military power in the region, the United States has experienced strategic setbacks and decline.

They see the US withdrawal from the JCPOA nuclear deal in 2018 by Donald Trump as a relatively recent misstep that inadvertently strengthened the hand of Moscow and Beijing in the Middle East. What I heard from Iranian leaders in 2022 and 2023 is that this move by Washington pushed Iran to strengthen its ties with the east, culminating in strategic deals with both Russia and China and Iran joining the Shanghai Cooperation Organization in 2023. In other words, the Iranians believe that the US withdrawal from the nuclear deal, while it contributed to their own economic woes, redounded to the benefit of both Russia and China to the detriment of the United States.

Post-Cold War worldview shaping events: Dual containment

It was 1993 in the early days of the post-Cold war era that Martin Indyk, special advisor to President Bill Clinton, conceived of dual containment as a policy for dealing with the twin challenges of ultra-nationalism in Iraq and extremist Islam in Iran. For the Americans, the Iranian triggers of dual containment were support for Hamas, opposition to US Middle East peace plans, alleged support for terrorism, its ballistic missile program, and concerns about weapons of mass destruction (WMD).[60] American concerns with Iraq stemmed from what was seen as the unextinguished ambitions of Saddam Hussein to disrupt the regional status quo after his failed bid to annex Kuwait a couple of years earlier.

The Iranian view saw dual containment as aimed at populist leaders who threatened to undermine the Pax Americana Washington intended to impose on the Middle East after the Cold War. It is unclear whether the Iranians saw the lack of strategic coherence of the dual containment approach. Aside from the intrinsic flaw of combining two countries with very different leadership structures and regional ambitions under one containment umbrella, there were the risks of calibration. The theory was that US military power in the region would deter and contain both Iranian and Iraqi expansionism. Iraq had proven to be territorially expansionist in the Iran-Iraq and Iraq-Kuwait wars. But Iran's growing influence was of a different, less conventional variety. Iran's power was projected into the region through proxy militias like Hezbollah of Lebanon and Iran's "power skill" of operating in the shadowy, subterranean world of fragile states. Because Iranian power was diffused throughout the region rather than concentrated like Iraq's, it defied the traditional concept of containment. How dual containment would simultaneously contain the conventional threat of Iraq, and the less orthodox threat of Iran was unclear.[61] Moreover, a one-size-fits-all approach for two very different strategic challenges was inherently problematic. In terms of calibration, what if US power contained one of the two regional powers more successfully than the other? Would this lead to a power asymmetry that would unwittingly invite rather than deter aggression by one or both countries?

While the Iranians said little publicly about the US doctrine itself, we do know how they coped with the specific policies that flowed from dual containment. We know that what wasn't lost on the Iranians was that Iran and Iraq, both still reeling from their eight-year war with each other, were in effect counterbalancing one another. We also know that in 1995 the American oil company Conoco had struck a $1 billion deal with Iran to develop two offshore oil and gas fields. The deal was peremptorily denounced and scuttled by the Clinton administration on the grounds that it was inconsistent with the efforts to contain Iran. As part of the US response, Secretary of State Warren Christopher threatened to further tighten an overall trade ban on Iran.[62]

US Senator Alfonso D'Amato launched the attack on the deal in the Senate, but reports were that the American Israel Public Affairs Committee (AIPAC) had helped craft the anti-Iran legislation.[63] The Iranians commented little on a possible Israeli contribution to the scuttling of the deal. They clearly knew that Iran's efforts to undermine the Oslo peace process was one reason for dual containment. But unlike the future Ahmadinejad and Raisi administrations, neither Rafsanjani nor his successor Mohammed Khatami used anti-Zionist rhetoric in response.[64]

Iranian President Rafsanjani seldom granted interviews to western journalists, but on the heels of the cancellation of the Conoco deal, he sat in 1997 with Mike Wallace of the program *60 Minutes* and expressed his frustration and perplexity at the US rebuff. Rafsanjani claimed that the deal was awarded to the American company Conoco, rather than its French competitor Total, to mend ties with Washington, not antagonize it.[65] He saw the scuttling of the Conoco deal as a missed opportunity on the part of the United States to rehabilitate its relationship with Iran.[66] The Iranians believed that despite what they saw as their good faith efforts, Washington either ignored or misinterpreted the signals. Toward the end of his administration and with the election of reformist Iranian President Mohammed Khatami in 1997, Clinton warmed up to the idea of improved relations with Iran, but by then there was little time for making progress.

In terms of further Iranian perceptions, we know that officials believed the unspoken goal of dual containment was regime change in Iran. As prima facie evidence, they pointed to $20 million in US funding for covert operations against Iran.[67] Rafsanjani believed the Americans thought that economic pressure and isolation would mobilize the Iranian people against the regime. The Iranians suspected that dual containment could be interpreted as a euphemism for "dual-regime change." They saw the scuttled Conoco deal in this light.

Initially Iran saw the election of George W. Bush as an opportunity, citing the fact that Vice President Dick Cheney's ties with Halliburton might make pragmatic oil interests a priority.[68] They also believed that the Bush administration might be less beholden to Israel's AIPAC than the Clinton administration and that it might be less ideological and more realpolitik in its orientation. But US actions after 9/11 disabused Iranian leaders of this notion.[69]

Post-Cold War worldview shaping events: 9/11

With the benefit of hindsight provided by the events of 9/11, for the Iranians the era of dual containment turned out to be a transitional moment. While the policy of dual containment may have pointed to ultimate American ambitions in the Middle East, it didn't involve active US military action and didn't ultimately change the regional distribution of power. That was reserved for the post 9/11 period which upended the regional status quo, with US military interventions in Afghanistan and Iraq profoundly altering the strategic calculus of Iran.

Douglas Jay Feith was US Undersecretary of Defense for Policy on 9/11. This put him at the center of US conduct for the Afghan and Iraq wars that were launched in 2001 and 2003 respectively. When he was a colleague of the author in 2006 at Georgetown University, Feith related conversations that had taken place at the highest levels of the Bush administration. Feith had been overseas when the 9/11 attacks occurred but returned to Washington with others on a US military transport. He recounted conversations on the plane about how the red lines of the United States had changed with the attacks on New York and Washington. While before 9/11 the United States was willing to accept some ambiguity and risk, after that event any country that actively opposed the US could be a target. According to Feith, the attacks on the United States shook off any complacency about threats from the Middle East.[70]

9/11 also led to changes in Iranian perceptions.[71] The US invasion of Afghanistan, which came just a month after the terrorist attacks, created strategic ambiguity for the Iranians. Initially, Iran saw an alignment of interests with Washington in the toppling of the Taliban. But this was followed very quickly with concerns that a wounded and unbridled United Sates might turn its sights next to Tehran. It signaled that the period of restrained unipolarity of the Clinton era dual containment approach was over.

The responses from the Iranian government right after 9/11 were noticeably mixed. President Khatami made an unqualified condolence statement, but Supreme Leader Ali Khamenei's message of condolence was more ambiguous, laced with admonishment about a possible US military response in Afghanistan.[72] These views represented the duality of a perceived need to avoid unnecessary provocation of a potentially aggressive United States, but also a belief that the attacks on 9/11 had roots in US misguided actions in the Middle East.

Despite Khamenei's warnings about US military action, Iran tried to work with the United States in confronting the Taliban in Afghanistan. Among other forms of cooperation, it offered to help rescue downed US coalition pilots. These efforts proved short-lived given the American rebuff of being grouped with Iraq and North Korea as part of an "axis of evil" in President George W. Bush's State of the Union address in January of 2002.[73]

After the US invasion of Iraq in 2003, the strategic ambiguity of the Iranians became even more pronounced. Tehran abhorred the idea of the Americans being on Iran's eastern and now western borders. Given perceptions of threat, the Iranians didn't offer to cooperate with the Americans in the Iraq operation. To the contrary, Iran committed itself to trying to frustrate the success of the Americans. The expeditionary

Iranian Quds force of Iran's Islamic Revolutionary Guards Corps (IRGC) headed by the now late Major General Qassim Soleimani took advantage of the chaos that ensued in Iraq by strengthening contacts it had with Shi'i leaders inside the country, becoming the early-stage efforts by Iran to insinuate itself into the political, security, and religious fabric of the country. And Iran under Soleimani planted improvised explosive devices (IEDs) to slow down and inflict casualties on US personnel.[74]

But over time Iran's worldview shifted from seeing threat toward perceiving opportunity. With the US invasion of Iraq in 2003, Iran's worldview became less dominated by imagery of the United States as a calculating hegemon, and more by images of it being a feckless, lumbering, and self-defeating giant. Missteps, such as the dismantling of Iraq's military and the Baath Party, helped plunge the country into civil war, undermining the interests and plans of the United States. Perceptions of American flat-footedness formed during the American presence in Iraq survive to this very day.

While the Iranians never fully let their guard down with the specter of possible American aggression, they believed that Washington's struggles in Iraq gave them room to maneuver and caused general bullishness that they could weather the storm. They came to believe that they could project political power into the Shi'i-dominated post-Saddam government, something the American military could do little to counter. Iran was quite brazen in its projection of political power into Iraq. Major General Qassim Soleimani, the head of Iran's Quds force, texted to US General David Petraeus that he controlled Iran's policy for Iraq, as well as Afghanistan, Lebanon, Syria, and Gaza.[75] The belief was that the growing Iranian political swagger in Iraq would compel the Americans to face the reality of Iran's interests in Iraq and more broadly in the region.[76]

The view at the time was that the United States could be dangerous militarily, but that Iran had the upper hand in the murkier political terrain of Iraq. The corollary to this was that if Tehran's time horizon was long-term, it could take advantage of Washington's limited understanding of the subterranean reality of Iraqi politics.

This gave the Iranians a heightened awareness of their own competitive advantage. A combination of strategic patience and an extension of Iranian tentacles into the political, cultural, economic, and religious structures of Iraq, gave Iran the sense of a winning formula that later would be used in its substate strategies in Syria and Yemen. This will be expounded on in Chapter 6.

A key takeaway of the post-9/11 period was the counterintuitive insight that the closer the United States came to the region, the greater was the opportunity to challenge it. In the first decade of the post-Cold War era, the United States used offshore balancing to project power and contain Iran by employing its allies, Israel and Saudi Arabia. With the invasions of Afghanistan and Iraq came the reality that now the United States was not just a global power, but also a regional power. The Iranian belief was it was easier to challenge the United States closeup than from afar. US heavy-handedness in its role as a regional power paradoxically gave the Iranians strategic room to maneuver.[77]

The US invasions of Iraq and Afghanistan after 9/11 reinforced the insight that while the United States was a global military superpower, as a regional power its ability to shape the politics of the region was limited. It could act as a spoiler and disrupter by militarily toppling regimes, but it couldn't operate effectively in the regional and local political landscapes. While Iran had few competitive advantages vis-à-vis the United States on the global stage, on its home turf of the region it had many.

The Arab Spring and civil wars

The Arab Spring protests that commenced in Tunisia in December 2010 and then spread to Egypt, Yemen, and Syria caught everyone by surprise. Iran responded initially with dubious claims that these revolts against the sclerotic Arab regimes were a knock-on effect of the Iranian revolution.[78] As the Arab Spring unfolded, it was clear that more was at stake for Iran than just the primacy of its brand as the region's only authentic revolutionary movement. Over time, as protests led to violence and civil war, Iran's strategic interests were threatened with the teetering of the Assad regime in Syria, its only Arab state ally. Now that the Assad regime has collapsed, Iran has lost a key longstanding ally, but also potentially its supply lines to Hezbollah in Lebanon could be disrupted.

As the Arab political order collapsed with civil wars in Syria and Yemen, and state weakness rendered Lebanon and Iraq unstable, Iran developed a "whole-of-region" view that allowed it to launch a multipronged response to Washington's growing role as a regional power. The near simultaneous collapse of Syria and Yemen gave Iran the opportunity to scale up operations and leverage the assets it had established in Lebanon in the 1980s with Hezbollah. It also impelled the

Iranians to expand on the methods it had developed and tested in Iraq after the 2003 US invasion. At the center of Iran's expansion of its regional capacity was Major General Qassim Soleimani, who as head of the Quds force was a master in insinuating Iran into the political and paramilitary fabric of neighboring countries. Alongside its regional portfolio of Hezbollah in Lebanon, Hamas and Palestine Islamic Jihad (PIJ) in Gaza, and the Hashd al-Sha'bi in Iraq, Iran was able to add militias in Syria and Yemen to its Arab portfolio.

The Iranians believed that the presence of these various militias across the region gave them a retaliatory capability against a possible attack by Israel and the United States. They also believed that this regional strategy of distributing and diffusing its security assets widely across the region made Iran more impervious to US containment efforts.

The Iranians were also confident that their wide regional footprint translated into negotiating power in the 2015 nuclear negotiations that culminated in the Joint Comprehensive Plan of Action (JCPOA). While Iran's regional activities were not part of the file discussed during the nuclear negotiations, the belief was that the potential for Iran to retaliate if either the United States or Israel attacked Iran's nuclear assets created a sense of urgency among the global powers to use diplomacy and not military force to rein in Iran's program.

The Iranians exhibited considerable pride regarding their record of turning what started out as menacing circumstances into opportunities. One area the Iranians are particularly proud of came in its ability to respond effectively to the ISIS capture of large swaths of Iraq and Syria in 2014. The rapid appearance of an expansionist, brutal Sunni proto state gobbling up two countries critical to Iran's national security, Iraq and Syria, was alarming.[79] But Iran was able to nimbly form new anti-ISIS militias in Iraq under what became the Hashd al-Sha'bi, many of which fell under the direct command of Iran's Quds Force, and some which were more closely tied to the Iraqi military. While all territorial holdings of ISIS have been liberated since 2017, many of the Hashd al-Sha'bi militias in Iraq remain loyal to Iran, cementing Tehran's hold on Iraq.

What is fascinating about this is how many American and Iranian interests intersected in Iraq during the anti-ISIS campaigns, though acknowledgement of this would be considered heresy in some circles in Washington and even in Tehran. While they didn't formally cooperate, the two countries operated parallel efforts in Iraq to defeat the Islamic State. The United States focused on training the Iraqi military and helping them get ready for the 2016–17 liberation of Mosul, while the Iranians were helping organize the militia forces required to keep ISIS away from Baghdad, the Shi'i areas of the south, and even some of the Sunni areas of the north.

But the intersection of interests proved more tactical than strategic. There was little change in the mutual suspicion with which the US and Iran held each other. And suspicion between the United States and Iran only intensified after the US pulled out of the JCPOA nuclear deal in 2018, and then again in the aftermath of the October 7, 2023 attacks by Hamas on Israel.

The post-Cold War period for the Iranians was defined by growing threats but also opportunities. The perceived threats were mostly centered on the United States and its allies in the Middle East, particularly in the period following the terrorist attacks of 9/11. But given the US missteps and vulnerabilities in Afghanistan and Iraq after the invasions of each of these countries, Iran saw an opportunity to project power into these areas and create long-coveted strategic depth.

The question for the future is whether Iran's axis of militias will continue to create strategic strength or lead to more vulnerability for Tehran? At the time of writing, the degradation of both Hamas and Hezbollah by Israel has created a risk of lost deterrence for Iran. Also, Tehran will likely be held increasingly accountable by Israel for the actions of its network of regional militias. Given the direct attacks both Israel and Iran perpetrated on each other, this risk that the actions of the militias could lead to direct attacks on Iran by Israel could rise in the future. This risk and Iran's options for a strategic response to this will be covered in more detail in Chapter 7.

Dominant Worldview: Global Powers

As covered in Chapter 1, Iran's history is replete with situations where it has faced the need to balance between multiple global powers, seldom successfully. Therefore, any treatment of how Iranian leaders view the international system today needs to include how they see the three main powers of the United States, Russia, and China.

The views of each of these three global powers are interconnected. When the United States withdrew from the JCPOA nuclear deal in 2018, the isolation it intended on imposing on Iran was diluted by Tehran's pivot to Russia and China. While Iran has perennially harbored suspicions about the reliability of any global power, it now shares a common bond of hostility to Washington with Russia and China.[80]

As the weakest member of the troika with China and Russia, Iran must navigate cautiously. Iranian leaders today take solace in the fact that since its invasion of Ukraine, Russia shares pariah status with Iran. They also feel more confident given Iran's status as a critical arms supplier to Russia. But China could prove trickier for Iran. While Beijing has strong relations with Tehran, their interests don't completely align. While China has an interest in thwarting the United States, it doesn't want to burn its bridges with Europe or harm the global economic system it relies on for trade and economic growth. Iran therefore must navigate cautiously, lest it find itself once again disappointed by a global power that accords greater primacy to its global interests than to Iran.

The other key belief of Iranian leaders is that they can ride the trend of global economic and political power shifting east to China and away from the west. But how it navigates this transition will be critical for its future. While long term, it may be able to ride the wave of this eastern trend through its membership in the Shanghai Cooperation Organization and other Asian affiliations, in the short to medium term it will likely face the need to mend its relationship with the west to meet the economic needs of its population. This long-term trend versus short-term exigencies will likely weigh on the government of President Masoud Pezeshkian, elected in 2024.

Iranian views of Russia

In 2016, at the height of Russia's air campaign in Syria to prevent the toppling of President Assad at the hands of a powerful insurgency, an unusual request was made by the Kremlin to Iran. It was to give the Russians access to the Iranian Nojeh airbase, near Hamedan (a former American base) to conduct operations in Syria. Reportedly the Iranians agreed, given how committed they too were to keeping Assad in power. But they had a condition: Russia would keep news of the agreement out of the press due to sensitivities from the past. Purportedly Russia agreed but news still leaked out, unleashing a firestorm in Iran against the defense ministry which had negotiated the deal. Ali Larijani, the speaker of the parliament or Majlis, and several media outlets railed against the deal.[81] The response from Iranian Defense Minister Hossein Dehghan is instructive in how Russia is situated in Iran's worldview:

> We most definitely did not provide them [the Russians] with a military base. There was never a written agreement, rather it was just operational cooperation. Naturally the Russians have an interest in presenting themselves as a superpower ... The news [by the Russians] was a kind of showing off and disloyalty.[82]

Another incident that lays bare the fundamental distrust of Russia is the visit on June 8, 2022, by senior Iranian officials, including several top generals, to the Russian embassy on "Russia Day." Photos showed Iranian generals standing in line to shake the hands of the Russian Ambassador Levan Dzhagaryan. This created a media firestorm in Iran, where Iranian officials were criticized for appearing subservient to the Russian Ambassador.[83] What is instructive about this incident is the optics of Iranian officials following otherwise normal diplomatic protocol bumping up against a worldview of Russia as an imperious power.

Both stories show the sensitivity about Russia that still lingers in the Iranian psyche. The history is long and tortuous. Russia was the major power that cut the Persian Empire down to its current size. The Treaties of Gulistan and Turkmenchay, which ended wars between the two countries in the nineteenth century, were humiliating defeats for Iran with significant territorial losses, including what today are the countries of Georgia, Armenia, and Azerbaijan.

Less than a hundred years later, Russia and Britain, after settling their differences conspired to split up Persia into spheres of influence with the 1907 Anglo-Russian Convention. Later, between 1908 and 1911, they worked to undermine the democratic and nationalist gains made in the Constitutional Revolution of 1906. It was an American, Morgan Shuster, sent to Iran to become Treasurer General of Iran from 1911 to 1912, who sided with Iran in its "dispute" with Moscow and London. Then during the Second World War, Russia and Britain invaded Iran to deny the Germans a strategic foothold. After the war, Russia on its withdrawal from Iran, stopped short of the border under the pretense of supporting an Iranian Azerbaijani separatist movement. It only relented under pressure from the United States. Then after the revolution, Moscow continued its support for Iraq, even after it invaded Iran in 1980.[84]

There have been more recent transgressions. If one looks closely at the celebratory photograph taken after the signing of the JCPOA nuclear deal in Vienna in 2015, you will see that Russian Foreign Minister Sergey Lavrov is conspicuously absent. From an interview with former Iranian Foreign Minister Javad Zarif released in 2021, it seemed clear that there were two actors opposed to the nuclear deal. One was Qassim Soleimani, the head of the Iran's Quds Force. The other, according to Zarif, was Russia, presumably over concerns about the deal leading to rapprochement between Iran and the west. Apparently Lavrov wasn't in a celebratory mood and left before the photo could be taken.[85]

Given this history, why have Iran-Russia relations been less fraught than Iran-US relations? There are several reasons for this. One is that the American betrayal of Iran followed a period when the United States had been placed on a pedestal as a possible third power against Russia and Britain. The overthrow of Mossadegh in 1953 came after an earlier period of goodwill, and occurred as Iran was transitioning from a traditional elite society to a mass-based society. Because it occurred at this inflection point of modernity, its imprint on Iran's political consciousness is more indelible.

While Russia's depredations with Iran go back centuries, they took place before Iran had modernized politically. Iranians haven't forgotten or forgiven Russia for its transgressions, but they are remembered in more of an historical rather than a contemporary context.

Also, Russia's geographic propinquity and a full range of intersecting interests contribute to Iran having a more complex and nuanced view of Russia. It's not that there aren't friction points between Iran and Russia on energy, security, and trade. They compete for markets for their oil and gas sectors, particularly since Russia joined Iran in the club of countries subject to economic sanctions by the United States and Europe due to the Ukraine war.

But from the Iranian perspective, disagreements with Russia are issue-based and nothing outside the boundaries of normal diplomatic discourse. The conflict with the United States in contrast is more visceral, emotional, and ideological. Iran can work through its differences with Russia, while Iranians see bad relations with the United States as almost congenital.

Also, the relationship between Russia and Iran has evolved and is nourished through continual contact, preventing more stereotypical views from congealing. In contrast, the absence of diplomatic relations between Iran and the United States means there is almost no day-to-day interaction, allowing toxic stereotypes to accrue and be sustained.

Iranian leaders believe that their relationship with Russia today is driven more by naked necessity than warm desire. This attitude came through during meetings I had with the late President Ibrahim Raisi of Iran in 2022 and 2023, during which he stated that Iran wanted positive relations with all great powers, but that hostility from the United States has made this untenable.[86] He cited the Trump withdrawal from the JCPOA nuclear deal in 2018 and the punishing sanctions that followed as leaving Tehran with few good options other than tilting toward Russia and China.

Besides Iranian leaders believing the alliance with Russia is one of necessity, the two countries do share a worldview. Both countries perceive the United States as a hegemonic power that must be rebuffed. Iranian leaders worry less about betrayal by Russia because of what they see as this strong common bond and interest.[87]

Moreover, notwithstanding a history of Russia and Iran harboring mutual suspicions that the other could trade their relationship for better relations with the United States, this fear has abated somewhat with the Russian invasion of Ukraine. President Raisi told me directly in 2022 that he believed that Iran's leverage with Russia has improved since the war, mitigating the risks of betrayal. While he didn't specifically cite Iran's critical role in supplying drones to Russia for the Ukraine war, the enhanced military relationship between the two countries has made the Iranians more confident in their relationship with Russia.

Furthermore, Iran doesn't see Moscow's pariah status in the west ending anytime soon, another factor that in the eyes of Iranian leaders mitigates the risk of betrayal. Both states now seem chronically isolated from the west with no apparent path back to better relations with the United States. Iran doesn't seem to worry that an end of the Ukraine war will bring Russia back to the good graces of Washington. And Russia sees Iran in the post-October 7 environment remaining isolated from the United States over the long term.[88]

The Iranian view of enhanced leverage with Russia isn't mere rhetorical bravado. There was evidence of an Iranian willingness to take greater risks with respect to Russian interests, particularly in Syria before the Assad regime collapsed. Iran had stepped up its cultural and militia activities in Deir ez-Zour, Syria, presumably taking advantage of Russia being preoccupied and distracted by the Ukraine war.[89] Also, Russian President Vladimir Putin's highly publicized trip to Tehran in 2022, which happened to overlap with US President Joe Biden's trip to the Middle East, was interpreted by the Iranians as a sign of Iran's enhanced status and leverage with the Russians.

What is stunning is the shift in the Iranian worldview from seeing Russia as part of the superpower phalanx lined up against the Muslim world early in the post-revolutionary Khomeini era, to seeing Russia today as more reliably opposed to the current global preeminence of the United States and its allies. This is part of a broader shift of Iran seeing a north-south world order of superpower domination give way to today's east-west political order where the triple axis of Iran, Russia, and China is arrayed against the western powers of the United States and Europe.[90] As part of this, Iran doesn't see itself as preyed on by the east, but rather as an integral part of the east. Iran's membership in Asian regional institutions such as the Shanghai Cooperation Organization in 2023 and BRICS in 2024 needs to be considered in this context.[91]

What this adds up to is that Iran now sees Russia as a regional power in its near-abroad. Whether Iran can nimbly keep Russia in its camp on regional matters, whilst the wily Putin navigates the global environment, will be a major strategic question for Iran. Iran understands that Russia has regional interests beyond Iran, including with the Gulf Arab states and Israel. But the fact that Russia's current focus is more on Ukraine and less on the Middle East gives the Iranians a sense of confidence.[92]

Iran's view of China

Shortly before Iranian President Masoud Pezeshkian assumed office in July of 2024, he said the following about China:

> ... Iran values its traditional friendship with China and looks forward to collaborating more extensively with Beijing as we advance towards a new global order.[93]

Most of the press coverage about Iran's self-described "axis of resistance" portrays it as a regional alliance, comprised of Iran, Syria (before Assad fell), and militias in Palestine, Iraq, Lebanon, and Yemen. But what is implicit in Pezeshkian's statement is that Iran sees its regional resistance axis linking up with a global axis of resistance led by China (and Russia). In other words, Iran sees China as trying to do globally what Iran is doing regionally: to use power to thwart the agenda of the United States.[94]

Iran and China may seem like strange and unlikely bedfellows to western eyes. Iran is a middle power, and China is a global power. Iran is a theocracy, and China is an avowedly secular state. China suppresses its own Muslim populations and Iran rails against the suppression of Muslims in the Middle East.

But despite these differences, the two countries share some common characteristics. They both experienced spasms of revolution, for China the communist revolution and for Iran an Islamic revolution. Also, both countries are committed to defying the United States—Iran in the Middle East and China globally from East Asia.[95] In other words, they share an axis of resistance sensibility.

While it is important to point out that in the Iranian worldview China and Iran are part of a regional and global movement for challenging the existing political order dominated by Washington, it is also necessary to focus on the ambivalence in their relationship. China relies heavily on trade ties with the United States and Europe, and on the stability of global markets. For Iran this raises concerns that any alignment with China could prove fragile in the face of economic pressure from Washington. In other words, China may support Iran, but there are limits as to how far Beijing will go. It is unlikely to jeopardize its global economic interests to support Iran.

Iranian leaders nevertheless remain confident that shared worldviews with China will be enough to sustain the relationship. What is striking is that Tehran seems nonplussed about China's relationship with Iran's rivals. China has been clear that it intends to remain neutral on regional rivalries, something the Iranians have accepted and seem to appreciate. The benefits of China's position of neutrality showed themselves in 2023 when Beijing finally brokered the deal re-establishing diplomatic relations between Iran and Saudi Arabia, after seven years of broken diplomatic relations and intense hostility.[96] As a result, Iranians have a nuanced and sophisticated understanding of China's relationship with Saudi Arabia, trusting that the foundation is hardcore economic interests, not ideology.

This contrasts with how Tehran sees US alliances with Saudi Arabia and Israel in threatening terms. Iranians see that Washington, unlike Beijing, has weaponized its regional allies against Iran.

Of course, Iran would like to count on China being in its court on regional disputes. But in meetings with Iranian diplomats and Chinese foreign policy influencers, I saw first hand that Tehran saw China's regional neutrality in positive terms, as a direct repudiation of the US approach of taking sides and offshore balancing against Iran. In other words, while Tehran may want China to take its side, they seem to understand that its neutrality shines a light on the failures of US policy toward the Middle East, rendering it more acceptable to Tehran.[97]

The Iranians see China as a realpolitik actor motivated by economic interests, making it predictable. The Iranians believe that China is working with Tehran on behalf of its long-term economic interests while the United States is more impetuous and focused on containing Iran and possibly even pursuing regime change.[98]

Iran's worldview vis-à-vis China crystallized in the wake of the withdrawal by the United States from the JCPOA nuclear deal in 2018. Sanctioned by the United States and isolated from Europe, Iran believed its tilt toward Russia and China came from economic and political necessity. Iranian President Pezeshkian has implied that additionally Iran is playing the long game in cozying up to China, riding an ineluctable eastward shift in the regional and global political and economic order. Even Iranian hardliners wary of any integration with the west seem to accept integration into an Asian-driven economic system. Proof of this is Iran's signing of a 25-year trade deal with China in 2021, and its accession to the Shanghai Cooperation Organization and BRICS.[99]

While Iranian pragmatists have argued that Iran must eventually integrate into the western-dominated economic order to meet the needs of its people, hardliners see China as a safer and more reliable long-term gambit. Moreover, it is seen as an opportunity to counterbalance against the United States. While some might suggest this is delusional given the economic costs Iran incurs from its hostility to Washington, the Iranians see few alternatives given the conviction that negotiating with the United States is a diplomatic and economic dead-end.

The question is whether China will continue to tolerate Iran's militia strategy, considering the instability it has created since the attack by Hamas on Israel on October 7, 2023. China supports Iranian moves that challenge and potentially weaken the US position in the region. But it might become impatient if Iran takes actions that destabilize the region such that China's economic and political interests become compromised. China showed its preference for conventional regional diplomacy over the use of shadowy militias by helping broker Iran's normalization agreement with Saudi Arabia in 2023. Once the dust settles in the Gaza conflict, Iran may feel pressure to double down on regional diplomacy.

The pressure that will have the greatest influence will likely come from Beijing rather than Washington.

Iran's view of the United States

"America cannot do a damned thing against us" said the late Ayatollah Rohullah Khomeini during Iran's 1979 revolution.[100] This statement can be dismissed as revolutionary bravado, but it is both true and false at the same time. Since the day this statement was uttered by Iran's first Supreme Leader, the United States has imposed punishing sanctions that have harmed Iran's economy, marshalled the UN Security Council against it, and negotiated and later withdrew from a multilateral nuclear agreement. All of these have had profound effects on Iranian politics and society. But Iran has developed a system of militias and substate alliances that have frustrated US efforts to fundamentally change the behavior of the Islamic Republic. And Iran has successfully challenged and bedeviled US allies in the Middle East, including Israel and Saudi Arabia. While the US invasions of Afghanistan and Iraq after 9/11 were supposed to send a strong message to Iran about the risks of challenging US interests in the region, they had the opposite effect of empowering Iran.

Against this backdrop, the question addressed here is how is the United States viewed in Iran? Of course, there is not a singular universal view, but upon close inspection a composite picture emerges. For many in the regime, opposition to the United States is part of the DNA of the Iranian revolution, occupying a large part of their political psyche. These views relate to both the past and the present. One significant data point extending back prior to the revolution is the 1953 overthrow of the very popular Prime Minister Mohammed Mossadegh with the help of the United States (and Britain), and the subsequent re-enthronement of the shah.[101] And in the more contemporary period, US support for Israel and Saudi Arabia are interpreted as Washington's attempts to control the region. And the fact that the United States unilaterally withdrew from a nuclear deal the Iranians were complying with in 2018 is part of the narrative.

In the eyes of Iranian leaders, the United States is both a status quo and disruptive power. According to this worldview, US support for Israel maintains the status quo by perpetuating a repressive reality for millions of Palestinians in the West Bank and Gaza. Washington also continues to support repressive governments, such as Egypt and Saudi Arabia, throughout the region. But it has also been a disruptive force with its reckless toppling of regimes in Iraq and Afghanistan, and at times has suggested regime change in Iran.

This dialectical view of the United States is in many ways a legacy of the Cold War, when Ayatollah Khomeini saw both superpowers as wedded to the status quo. He witnessed the incendiary rhetoric Washington and Moscow leveled at one another, pushing rivalry and tensions to their peak. But he also saw that both superpowers supported the status quo by propping up authoritarian regimes in the Middle East. While Washington wrapped many of its foreign policy decisions in language for human rights, and Moscow defended its policies using revolutionary rhetoric, both these powers were seen through an Iranian revolutionary lens as joint stewards of oppression. While the Cold War seemed dynamic and fraught to the two superpowers, to the brooding revolutionaries in Iran, it underpinned a structural support of the status quo. While the United States saw rivalry with the Soviet Union, Iranian revolutionary leaders saw two co-hegemons trying to preserve an oppressive regional status quo.

This paradoxical view of the superpowers extends to how Iran sees the United States today. On the one hand, it sees the US as flat-footed, bereft of a clear strategy, and incapable of playing a constructive role in the region. But it also credits the United States as having a formidable conventional military capability that brought down Saddam Hussein in a matter of a few days, an outcome Iran couldn't achieve in eight years of war. Iran's foreign policy is designed to avoid tangling with the US military in an overall confrontation by operating in the shadows with its militias. While Iran knows that the United States could do damage if incited, it has learned from the American experiences in Iraq and Afghanistan that overwhelming military power alone can't bring Iran or the region to its knees.[102]

Since October 7, 2023, this belief is being challenged with Israel and Iran having attacked and counterattacked one another, and with the possibility of direct military entanglements between Iran and the United States. Iran wants at almost any cost to avoid a direct confrontation with the United States, as it knows that while it may be able to operate effectively in the shadowy world of militias, it can't win a conventional conflict with the Americans. With Hezbollah and Hamas degraded, Iran is more vulnerable to having to defend itself using conventional means, a battle it may not be prepared to win if it finds itself face-to-face with the United States.

Conclusion

Iran's glory days at the onset of the Persian Empire loom large in how it sees itself in the world.[103] Iran sees itself simultaneously as an influential and a vulnerable power, a difficult circle to square.[104] In terms of being an influential power, Iran has strong relations with great powers Russia and China and prides itself in outmaneuvering the United States. But it is also vulnerable with several of its allied militias weakened by Israel in 2024 and lacking a significant state ally in the Middle East, now that the Assad regime in Syria has collapsed.

How this influences Iran's foreign policy is complex. Iran has been a strong power in the regional context, but only a middle power on the global stage. The challenge for Iran is that its regional and international statures are inextricably linked. Its ability to be a truly influential regional player depends heavily on meeting the challenges it faces internationally. Iran's isolation within the international community to some degree circumscribes its ability to be competitive in the Middle East regional game.

One way of thinking about Iran's asymmetric, militia-based approach is that it is an attempt to square this circle, maximizing Iranian power in the region while deterring the United States. At the time of writing, Iran's "having its cake and eating it too" approach is being tested. It is unclear whether Iran will be able to maintain its posture of resistance using its militias in a way that enhances its security. The militia strategy it used to deter Israel and the United States is now doing the opposite by inviting attacks and creating risk of an all-out war.

All the other major players in the region, such as Israel and the Gulf Arab states, have thrived because of their integration into the global economic system. Iran can perhaps maintain its current influence using its militias in the failed states of the region for the time being. But in the long term it can't compete with its regional rivals directly without a healthier relationship with great powers. Iran's relations with Russia and China buy it time and give it the confidence to oppose the United States. But the Iranian people are unlikely to wait for a long-term payday to come, when the populations of surrounding states are thriving better now.

Also, as China becomes more powerful in the Middle East, it is possible that Iran's importance shrinks. The more China becomes a stakeholder in a stable and secure Middle East, the less patient it is likely to be with Iran's regional antics. We can see the early signs of this in how China is prioritizing diplomacy in the region, between Iran and Saudi Arabia in 2023, and Fatah and Hamas in 2024.[105] A wise Iran will likely see this as a sign of things to come.

What we have seen in the preceding pages is the evolution of Iran's worldview in response to changes in the international system. The Khomeini worldview of the superpowers being jointly oppressive seemed otherworld-like and extreme to westerners and even some Iranians in the lead-up to Iran's revolution. But this view became more mainstream during the Iran-Iraq war when both superpowers turned their backs on Iran to support Iraq.

The notion of joint hegemonic superpowers became less important when the Cold War ended, leaving Tehran to tangle with the United States alone. We saw in the preceding pages that Iran faced a far more confusing and ambiguous set of strategic realities at the end of the Cold War than during it. Particularly after the 9/11 attacks on New York and Washington by al-Qaeda, the US became an unrestrained power, initially rattling Tehran. But the Iranians also observed that the lack of a global rival made the United States sloppy and even reckless, giving them possible openings to take advantage of the fact that the US had become not just a global but also a regional power. Iran understood it couldn't challenge America the global actor, but that it could outmaneuver America in the regional game. Over time it increasingly saw the capacity to take advantage of the mistakes the United States and its allies were making. Whether the foreign policy it has constructed to do this can deliver to the Iranian people a better future is still indeterminate. Iran has been an astute observer of regional and global power trends. Whether it continues to do this effectively in a post-October 7 environment is the question.

3 IRAN'S VIEW OF THE MIDDLE EAST

The atmosphere on the Air France Boeing 747 that transported Ayatollah Ruhollah Khomeini from Paris to Tehran in February of 1979 was charged and exciting for those lucky enough to be on the plane. Less than two weeks before, the shah's reign of nearly forty years had come to an ignominious end with his departure and roving exile. Tempering the excitement somewhat was the concern that the plane might be shot down, taking with it Imam Khomeini, his coterie of key advisors, along with the members of the international press accompanying him on this historic journey.

Prior to landing, Imam Khomeini was interviewed by BBC journalist John Simpson, who accompanied him on this historic return to the country he had been exiled from for nearly fifteen years. The Imam was asked how he felt as he was about to land in Iran as the leader of a revolution that had captured the imagination of millions of Iranians. His response was "nothing."[1]

While this was consistent with his signature stoicism and ascetic demeanor, it also spoke to a bigger issue of how the founder of the Islamic Republic and his acolytes conceptualized the moment. Khomeini seemed to be suggesting that the revolution was more the result of divine will than of the nationalist aspirations of millions of Iranians. In other words, for Khomeini the revolution unfolding 30,000 feet beneath him was an Islamic revolution, not merely an Iranian revolution. While he might not have been moved by the national pride felt by the millions of his followers anxiously awaiting his arrival, his vision was that the revolution must extend beyond Iran's borders to the broader Middle East and Islamic world.

While the notion of nationalism may have been lost on Khomeini, what wasn't lost was that Iran could serve as the epicenter of a messianic expansion of the revolution. He said:

We should try hard to export our revolution to the world, and we should set aside the thought that we do not export our revolution, because Islam does not regard various Islamic countries differently and is the supporter of all the oppressed people of the world.[2]

This rhetoric shows Khomeini's partiality for revolution over regional stability. The question for today is how much of this revolutionary zeal still resides in the foreign policy outlook of the Islamic Republic? The exigencies of governing a large country encompassing multiple ethnic groups and nearly ninety million people have a way of injecting sobriety into the thinking of decision-makers. While today there are large pieces of the revolutionary ethos in Iran's foreign policy, the picture of how Iran conceptualizes the region is more complex than the simplified view of Khomeini at the start of the Iranian revolution.

This is not to suggest that Iran always chooses pragmatism and stability over ideology in its foreign policy. Iran's responses to the October 7, 2023 attacks on Israel by Hamas showed a penchant for believing it can benefit from regional instability. But what is being suggested is that Iran has had it both ways. How it conceptualizes the region sometimes takes it down the path of regional stabilizer, and at other times as regional disrupter. In other words, it can at times act as a responsible regional steward and stakeholder, and at other times as the region's worst nightmare. Simultaneously Iran is making peace with Saudi Arabia and supporting regional militias that potentially undermine diplomacy.

The contradictions inherent in this duality of Iran's foreign policy are rooted in how it perceives threat and opportunity in its regional and global security environments. Understanding how Iran sees the region can help us unlock an understanding of what drives a foreign policy that to westerners appears as schizophrenic. That is the purpose of this chapter.

Iran's View of the Region: A Split Screen Approach

It would be convenient if we could arrive at a clean and neat delineation of how Iran sees the region, but reality is more stubbornly complex than that. As with almost any sovereign state, Iran conceptualizes its foreign policy using multiple lenses and frames of reference.

This chapter will attempt to provide an understanding of Iran's regional frames of reference for its foreign policy. In the following pages, we will try to capture the various ways the regime looks at and interprets the broader Middle East. We will also try to draw a connection between Iranian views of the region writ large and views of the individual constituent states.

Ideology vs. realpolitik

As was stated in the preface, Henry Kissinger once said that Iran needs to decide whether it is a cause or a country, seeing ideology and realpolitik as inherently contradictory.[3] But in reality, this is a false binary as these two strands of Iran's foreign policy coexist and in fact are not contradictory.

This isn't unique to Iran, and in fact applies to American foreign policy as well. Washington has had strong ideological tendencies in its foreign policy. The administration of former President George W. Bush, for example, embodied a messianic neoconservative view of spreading democracy in its interventions in Afghanistan and Iraq. But the United States also follows a power-based realpolitik approach in its approach to Saudi Arabia, even though the current government in Riyadh has an authoritarian non-democratic bent.

There are vestiges of Islamic revolutionary thinking embedded in Iran's conception of the Middle East, and in its calculus of how it should operate within the region. Khomeini's comments about exporting the revolution give us one window onto this. But alongside this ideological view sits a realpolitik element in Iran's foreign policy. Iran's foreign policy today reflects a view of a region with looming threats, a perception that was heightened and forged with Iraq's invasion of Iran in 1980. It is this perception that drives Iran's core foreign policy security doctrine: forward defense, which contends that to secure the homeland, Iran needs to build strategic depth in the surrounding region.[4]

Skeptics will surely argue that this notion of forward defense is just a way for Iran to justify and sanctify its ideologically driven interventionist policies in the region. Reading Khomeini's incendiary statements about Saddam Hussein before Iraq attacked Iran seems to support the view that Iraq and the broader region were seen as a canvas for aggressively spreading his ideological revolution. He tried to incite the Iraqi Shi'i to revolt against Saddam Hussein as a first step in the export of the revolution to Iraq. There was a poster in Iran circulating in 1980 showing Saddam

Hussein as a dog on a leash emblazoned with both American and Soviet flags, implying that Saddam was doing the bidding of the superpowers. There was an image of a fist punching Saddam. The poster slogan was: "We [Iranians] will punch Saddam and the Baath Party so hard that they will never rise again."[5]

Even today, there is incontrovertible evidence that Iran's view of the region is not shorn of ideology. The anti-Zionist rhetoric of the regime in Tehran shows there is still strong ideological strains to how Iranian leaders see the region, even though the Palestinian issue is accorded less importance by most Iranian citizens.[6]

But looking at Iran's view of the region in ideological terms is part of, but not the entirety, of the story. There are more practical factors that drive Iran's activist role in the region, particularly a sense of threat from the United States and Israel. The risks Iranian leaders talk about from both Israel and the United States may in fact be self-inflicted, but they feel real to Iranian leaders.[7]

Another way of thinking about this is that ideological and realpolitik views of the region in fact are complementary. Iran's experience before and since the revolution of 1979 melded the two. The Manichean view of the world (and the region) as a struggle between good and evil forces has roots extending back centuries to Iran's Zoroastrian, pre-Islamic period.[8] Later, after the Arab invasions and Iran's conversion to Islam, political thought portrayed a civilizational struggle between the forces of Islam and the forces of western Christianity. This ideological view became embodied in Ayatollah Khomeini's ethos which said that "godless great powers" would collaborate to suppress Islamic masses.[9] These ideological ideas of good versus evil were reinforced after the 1979 revolution by the Iran-Iraq war, when both "godless powers," the United States and Soviet Union, sided with Iraq against Iran. What the Iran-Iraq war teaches us is that when threat perceptions are intense, ideology and realpolitik thinking become indistinguishable. The realities on the ground guided Iran's adaptation to events, while the ideology helped decision-makers make sense of and explain these events.

We see both the ideological and realpolitik strands in Iran's foreign policy today. The support Iran gave to the activities of its network of militias in the wake of the October 7 attacks on Israel by Hamas reflects Iran's ideological support for the Palestinians and its anti-Zionist proclivities. But alongside this ideologically driven, shadowy element of Iran's foreign policy, we see the improving relationships between Iran and

Saudi Arabia, the UAE, and Egypt, reflecting a more practical view and approach to the region.

The question going forward is what will the relationship be between these ideological and realpolitik tendencies? Prior to October 7, 2023, Iran could claim that there was nothing inherently contradictory between its ideological and realpolitik views and interests. Tehran argued that its support for Hamas, Hezbollah, and the Houthis, while ideologically compatible with Iran's revolutionary ethos, also generated regional power for Iran and established deterrence.

But this changed with the October 7 attacks, with Iran's support for Hamas and Hezbollah potentially undermining Iran's system of deterrence. This growing tension between the ideological and realpolitik strands of Iran's foreign policy could prompt a subtle recalibration of its foreign policy. Once the Gaza war winds down, we could see a shift toward and greater emphasis on Iran's relations with its Arab neighbors. No responsible scholar should be foolish enough to suggest that Iran would totally give up its support for its network of militias, even with the degradation of Hezbollah and Hamas at the hands of the Israelis in 2024, or to predict with any degree of certainty that a more subtle shift toward diplomacy will take place. But it is perfectly reasonable to point out the risks of Iran's militia strategy to its own security in the post-October 7 environment, and to suggest that there might be opportunity for some reassessment. It is possible that the cutting down to size of several of Iran's militias and the collapse of the regime of President Bashar al-Assad in Syria, Iran's only true regional state ally, could create the impetus for such a recalibration. The policy goal for the United States should be to support such a shift when possible, by working to bring hostilities in Gaza, Lebanon, and the broader region to an end.

Two Middle Eastern realities: Sovereign states and shadowy substates

Given the complexity of today's international politics, it should be no surprise that the foreign policies of most states are multitracked. The foreign policy of the United States has traditionally operated within a world of nation-states and international institutions. But since 9/11 it has had to open a new track of its foreign policy that puts international terror organizations like al-Qaeda and the Islamic State (ISIS) in its crosshairs.

Iran's foreign policy, too, operates in multiple tracks. But Iran's behavior seems almost schizophrenic to the casual observer, lurching between support for regional diplomacy *and* support for militias that gets in the way of diplomatic progress. It operates simultaneously as a traditional nation-state *and* as the head of a network of non-state militias. Of course, we can attribute the duality of Iran's foreign policy to ideological revolutionary peculiarities or even contradictory voices within Iran's foreign policy apparatus. While these may be explanatory factors, it is important to understand that more is going on here than meets the eye. The duality in Iran's foreign policy is also a function of how Iran sees the Middle East of today. Iran believes it operates not in one Middle Eastern reality but two. The split-screen feature of Iran's foreign policy reflects this belief.

The first Middle East reality Iran sees is a neighborhood populated by traditional states with recognized boundaries, such as Turkey, Saudi Arabia, Egypt, and Israel, among others. Within this terrestrial Middle Eastern context, state-to-state diplomacy and balance of power politics are the currency of foreign policy. But the second Middle East reality Iran sees looks nothing like the first. In this reality, the Middle East isn't a neighborhood of states, but rather a subterranean, borderless region consisting of the detritus of collapsed states, such as Lebanon, Iraq, Yemen, and Syria. Within this regional reality, foreign policy takes place in a murkier, more dangerous landscape of substate militias. Balance-of-power politics and diplomacy are useless in this subterranean Hobbesian world of failed states.

What should be striking to the observer is as starkly different as these two regional realities are, the foreign policies that take place in each are strategically connected. This makes decoding Iran's foreign policy difficult and at times confounding. But there is a strategic logic that connects the two. With an economy that is groaning under sanctions, corruption, and mismanagement, leaders in Tehran understand that Iran has few competitive advantages in the terrestrial world of states. At the time of writing, Iran can't compete with Turkey, Saudi Arabia, the UAE, and even Israel economically or militarily. Unlike Iran, all these other states derive benefits from being integrated to one degree or another into the global economy, giving them distinct advantages.

But the competitive landscape between Iran and its neighbors is turned on its head in the other Middle East of shadowy militias in weak and failed states. Within this boundaryless reality, Iran has insinuated itself into the political and economic systems of Lebanon, Iraq, and Syria, and to a lesser degree Yemen. Because the other strong states in the region can't really compete in this subterranean world, Iran has created an unmatched advantage that strikes fear in the hearts of its adversaries. In this world, Iran has developed a strategy of preclusion, preventing other states from projecting power by strong-arming the weak and vulnerable governments in Iraq, Syria, and Lebanon, and using militias to protect its advantages.

Iran's much vaunted regional influence is derived from this shadowy second Middle East reality, not from the first reality of sovereign states. The problem for other states in the region is that Iran has used its competitiveness in the substate world to punch through to create advantages in the terrestrial world of states. Iran's shadowy foreign policy enables it to compete with the strong Arab states by blocking their ability to trade with and influence Syria, Iraq, and Lebanon. In a perverse way, the substate reality has been a way for Iran to compete for regional influence.

Two Iranian scholars, Kayhan Barzegar and Abdolrasool Divsallar, depict the Iranian view on the strategic importance of Iran's substate reality to state-to-state competitiveness. They correctly analyze the limits Iran has in competing conventionally in the world of states and how instead it resorts to unconventional hybrid means in the shadowy substate realities of Syria, Iraq, Yemen, and Lebanon:

> ... the country [Iran] is not in a position to heavily engage in costly conventional operations and confrontations. Yet, due to its enormous unconventional military capability and powerful security apparatus, it has enough capacity to project its forces in rather low-cost environments. The combination of military power as a foreign policy resource and the strategic limits of a developing economy lead Iran to favor engagements with the lowest possible costs. Hybrid warfare suits these conditions best.[10]

There are several ways in which Iran views its expansion into the region's substate reality. In talking with Iranian officials, it became apparent that Iran sees a connective web between the various substate environments, linking together Lebanon, Syria, Iraq, Yemen, and Gaza into a seamless operational landscape. What has evolved, particularly with the influence wielded by the late Quds Force commander Major

General Qassim Soleimani, is the view of a borderless battlefield. Iran's use of Hezbollah in Syria and Yemen is emblematic of this integrated, single battlefield view. The events following the October 7, 2023 attacks by Hamas on Israel demonstrates the degree to which Iran takes a "whole-of-region" view of its substate militias network. The attack on Israel by Iran with drones and missiles on April 13, 2024, but also from allied militias across the region, show the degree to which Iran now sees the substate reality of the Middle East as fully integrated.

The question is which Middle Eastern reality will be predominant in the future, the sovereign state or the substate reality? When Iran has perceived intense threats, it has tilted more in the direction of a substate reality. In these circumstances, Iran tends to emphasize creating deterrence in the substate world at the expense of diplomacy in the world of states.[11] Also, when Iran is shut out of global markets, it further entrenches itself in the shadows of failed states to circumvent sanctions.

With Israel's degradation of Hamas in Gaza and Hezbollah in Lebanon in 2024, and Iran's uncertain future in Syria with the collapse of the Assad regime, Iran's integrated web of substate militias has been significantly compromised. How Iran adjusts its view of the region and its strategy going forward will need to play out in the future. Iran has proven to be highly responsive to geopolitical shifts, so it is likely that Iranian views of the region will adjust accordingly. But it is important to point out that as Iran considers its options going forward, the advantages it has garnered in the substate realities of the region are mostly in the security realm, with few benefits for the economic future of the Iranian people. Iran's substate approach has historically created deterrence but hasn't translated into economic or social benefit for the Iranian people. The shallowness of Iran's foreign policy has been reflected in the protests in 2018, which specifically opposed Iran's interventions in Syria.[12] The question will be whether Iran takes this domestic element into consideration as it accommodates regional shifts.

In this balance between state diplomacy versus substate militias, it was fascinating to watch how Iran managed the duality of the region at the joint Arab-Islamic meeting in Riyadh in November of 2023, in the weeks following the October 7 Hamas attacks on Israel. The meeting was a crucible for seeing how Iran navigated both realities. The late President Raisi wore the Palestinian keffiyeh as a symbol of supporting Hamas in the substate reality of the region, but also met with Saudi Crown Prince Mohammed bin Salman and was present when countries signed onto the declaration supporting a two-state solution.[13] At this meeting, Iran operated simultaneously in the two distinct but interconnected realities of the Middle East.

The October 7, 2023 offensive attacks on Israel by Hamas undermined the argument that Iran's subterranean operations are primarily about defense and deterrence. Through Iran's support for Hamas after the attacks and the escalation in activity against Israel by Hezbollah and the Houthis, it appeared that Iran chose to favor instability over stability. Iran currently has one leg in the terrestrial state-based reality of the Middle East with diplomatic relations with Saudi Arabia and other Arab states, and the other leg in the borderless substate reality of militias which attack Israel, US positions in Iraq and Syria, and shipping in the Red Sea. There will be tensions that may compel Iran to recalibrate its approach. With the degradation of Hezbollah, there will be pressure to rebuild the capacity of this and other militias, but also risk that this will attract Israeli aggression. The risk of leaning hard on the substate reality could pressure Iran to lean harder on state-to-state regional diplomacy. While we shouldn't bet on this happening, we shouldn't discount the possibility either.

Global chess board or regional neighborhood?

In the previous section, we saw that Iran has its feet planted in two different Middle East realities simultaneously. One foot is firmly planted in a reality of sovereign states, while the other foot is planted in the porous world of substates. In this section, we will address a different bifurcated reality that drives Iranian perceptions. One is the Middle East as a regional neighborhood with its own power dynamics, while the other is a Middle East so tied to the international system that the boundaries between the global and regional are blurred. For Iran, the common element between the regional and global is the United States.

There is a paradox here as with so much of Iran's foreign policy. The Middle East is undergoing a region-wide transformation driven by the rivalry between the major regional powers, namely Iran, Saudi Arabia, Turkey, and Israel. All these regional powers are acting more independently of global powers than ever before. The Ukraine war represents a case in point, with Israel and Saudi Arabia distancing themselves from the anti-

Russian policies of the United States, and Iran feeling it is on a more level playing field with Russia than at any time in the past.

Even though this is indicative of regional players acting according to their own political and regional logics, the degree to which Iranian decision-makers feel the tug of the United States is striking. Of course, Iran contributes to what it sees as its American problem with its behavior of animus toward Israel. And the Iranian regime draws benefits from using America as convenient foil to justify its domestic crackdowns and cover up rampant corruption. Notwithstanding the role Iran plays, security issues related to the United States and its allies overshadow regional priorities and blur the lines between the global and regional.

In many ways, this has a distortive effect on the politics of the region at a moment when regional actors are bursting with independence and autonomy. I saw this firsthand in two meetings with the late President of Iran, Ibrahim Raisi. When I asked a question pertaining to the state of Iran-Saudi relations in 2022, about six months prior to the resumption of diplomatic relations between the two countries (with the help of Beijing), he replied:

> Iran seeks to strengthen and develop relations with its neighbors and we have repeatedly emphasized that if outsiders do not interfere in regional issues, the countries of the region themselves have sufficient capacity to resolve the issues between each other.[14]

It was clear from his direct comments and from my discussion with key members of his senior national security team how prevalent was the view that the United States is a spoiler and disrupter of regional politics. What struck me when hearing this view from President Ibrahim Raisi and then again from President Masoud Pezeshkian in 2024 is that in many ways, a mirror image has developed between Washington and Tehran, both seeing the other as a regional disrupter, the effect of which distorts the politics of the region.[15] When the United States peers at Iran, it sees the disruptive effect of its militias and its anti-Israeli rhetoric and policies. When the Iranians see the United States, they see it as having created chaos in Iraq and Afghanistan and as having encouraged Saudi Arabia and other Gulf allies to eschew diplomatic engagement with Iran. The narrative is that without American machinations, regional rivals would be compelled to deal with each other.

When Iran envisions the future, which regional picture comes into the sharpest focus? Is it a region where bilateral relations with neighboring

Saudi Arabia, the UAE, and Turkey focus on neighborhood issues? Or will regional politics be overshadowed by global politics, particularly vis-à-vis the United States? Iranian leaders understand that their long-term future depends on operating in a more normalized region.[16] Climate change, water shortages, rejuvenation of the Persian Gulf waters spoiled by desalination, the specter of a re-emergent ISIS, and regional security concerns represent common threats and interests for all states in the region. Iranian leaders have expressed an interest in addressing these issues.[17]

But the strategic dilemma for Iran is that its current regional influence comes more from its unconventional activities in the failed states than from conventional advantages with strong states. In other words, Iran's real competitive advantages today are at the substate level where it can flex its muscles with the United States and Israel. When operating in the terrestrial world of sovereign states, Iran has fewer competitive advantages and less political muscle. Of course, Iran has many great fundamentals in terms of an educated cadre of professionals, and a reasonably diversified, albeit struggling economy, that could potentially be leveraged toward a strong competitive posture. But at the current moment these are underutilized assets, and Iran's real strength comes from the world beneath.

In a way, then, Iran contributes to and benefits from the vicious cycle of conflict with the United States. It has become more comfortable and competitive in creating deterrence, retaliatory capabilities, nuclear enrichment, and missile programs that provoke Washington than in competing directly for competitiveness with its Gulf Arab and Turkish neighbors. Iran's activities, and those of the United States and its allies, help perpetuate the vicious cycle of penetration of the Middle East by the United States and other great powers. This impedes any progress toward the region developing cooperative measures that could improve the security and economic outlook for the Middle East.

Whether Iran can break out of this cycle and pivot to create competitive advantages with other strong states in the region remains to be seen. Domestic and international pressure will build on Iran to prioritize regional stability over conflict with the United States. This is particularly true at the time of this writing when the capabilities of Hamas and Hezbollah have been degraded at the hands of the Israelis. But there may be counter-pressures pulling Iran in the opposite direction. And those pressures can come from more extremist voices within the regime, from the United States under a second Trump presidential term or from Israel.

Events like the killing of Hamas leader Ismail Haniyeh in Tehran while attending the inauguration festivities for President Masoud Pezeshkian, the gunning down of Hamas leader Yahya al-Sinwar in Gaza, and the killing of Hezbollah leader Hassan Nasrallah in Lebanon, could reinforce the international conflict model over the regional stakeholder model.

It is possible that the election of President Masoud Pezeshkian in 2024 will cut a path to a future where Iran puts greater emphasis on regional cooperation than on fostering conflict with Israel and the United States. Prior to his death, President Ibrahim Raisi was already working toward regional diplomacy, re-establishing diplomatic relations with Saudi Arabia and normalizing relations with Egypt. While the overall tenor of Iran's foreign policy will be largely decided by Supreme Leader Ali Khamenei and the Revolutionary Guards, a more reformist leader can help lower the temperature in Iran's foreign relations. And it is also possible that Supreme Leader Ali Khamenei uses the election of President Pezeshkian to give himself and the Revolutionary Guards some wiggle room. If he concludes that a doubling down on Iran's militia activities in the post-October 7 milieu creates unacceptable risk to his regime and the country, he could give Pezeshkian a longer leash with which to improve relations with the west. A reformist president could give Khamenei the ability to maintain a modicum of distance and even deniability from reformist measures that he himself may have approved behind the scenes. While it is unrealistic to think that Iran will give up its subterranean militia activities and assets, as this is the foundation of Iranian regional influence today, it isn't out of the realm of possibility that it will rebalance its foreign policy to tilt toward stronger state-to-state regional relations and a more conventional basis for competitive advantage. Whether the degradation of Hamas and Hezbollah by Israel pushes Iran toward more conventional means of diplomacy and competition or impels it to double down on rebuilding its militias, and perhaps make a dash to a nuclear weapon, remains to be seen at the time of writing.

In summary

Iranian views of the region are paradoxical. While Iran may lack today the fundamentals for competing economically and even militarily in the region using conventional means, it has stumbled on a way to deal with the lopsided asymmetry of power with the United States. Iran believes that its subterranean militia strategy has made it immune from efforts by the United States to use its considerable power advantages to harm Iran. In other words, the fear felt by Iranian decision-makers about the United States isn't what one would expect from a regional power confronting a superpower. Iranian decision-makers see the United States as a hostile power but believe that the substate system of deterrence they have erected has effectively made the perceived cost of waging aggression against Iran untenable for Washington and its allies. The belief is that Iran's alliances within the failed states of the region gave it sufficient deterrence and retaliatory capability to operate freely.[18]

This view has also firmed up within the national security establishment of the United States. A 2019 report by the US Defense Intelligence Agency (DIA) points to Iran having significant Anti-Access/Area Denial capabilities for blocking US efforts to contain Iran. The Iranians are aware that Washington has acknowledged Iranian capabilities, despite an asymmetry of US power, which increases their confidence.[19]

Iran's confidence in this regard was revealed following the attacks by Hamas on Israel on October 7, 2023. Even with heightened tensions that followed the Hamas attack, Iran rhetorically supported Houthi attacks on international shipping in the Red Sea and Hezbollah's actions on Israel's northern borders.[20] Of course, Iranians understand that support for its militias doesn't come cost-free, and that the April 1, 2024 attack by Israel on IRGC officials in Damascus was payback for Iran's support for these militias. But less than two weeks later, Iran broke through all previous red lines by attacking Israel with drones and missiles. It launched an even more audacious attack on Israel in October of 2024 after the spate of assassinations of Hamas and Hezbollah leaders by Israel. This shows that even though these militias no longer provide Iran the deterrence it once did, Iranian leaders believe there is greater risk of lost deterrence in not responding than responding. But it also shows a certain hubris that its substate support for militias still gives it significant regional and international power. Whether, after Israel's October 2024 attacks on Iran's missile program, Iranian leaders feel they must respond again is something we will need to wait and see.

In the pre-October 7 environment, Iran seemed to have had a winning approach by being able to balance regional diplomacy in the world of states with support for its militias in the subterranean world of substates. Whether in the current environment this buys Iran long-term regional influence depends on its own ability to read and adapt to its regional environment in a nuanced way, as well as how adeptly other regional and global actors read and react to Iran.

Stephen Walt's notion of "balance of threat" is relevant here. His claim is that what is more important than the actual balance of power dynamics between states is the balance of threat perceptions. This implies that what is as or more important than a state's actual power is how rival states perceive that power.[21] Iran has seen its support for militias in the shadows of the region as creating a wall of threat that heretofore has staved off any significant intrusions from international or regional powers. The Iranians believe that the United States will never abide a strong Iran, and that the only way forward is to use unconventional means to create deterrence.[22] The 2019 US Defense Intelligence Agency report cited above indicates that the United States does in fact see a balance of threat with Iran, even if there is an imbalance of conventional power. How Iran, Israel, and the United States see the "balance of threat" dynamics in the Middle East going forward will determine the direction of Iran's regional foreign policy as well as how the region will evolve.

Iranian Views: Strong States in the Region

Within Ayatollah Ruhollah Khomeini's worldview, Islam reigns supreme with scant regard for the sovereignty of the nation-state.[23] His promise and intent to export the Iranian revolution to neighboring sovereign states is evidence of this. Iran at various times has in fact tried to incite the Shi'i populations of Bahrain and Saudi Arabia in opposition to the state. And we know how blithely Iran crosses state boundaries to project power into Syria, Iraq, and Lebanon.

But Iran isn't casual at all about protecting its own boundaries, enshrining this interest in its forward defense doctrine. The paradoxical logic of defending its own boundaries while casually disregarding the sovereignty of other states means Iran has no real regional states as allies, now that Assad has been deposed in Syria. Some states like Oman, Kuwait, Qatar, and even the UAE have complex, yet functional relations with Iran, but they are not allies. Iran's only real regional allies are substate militias, which are seen as menacing and threatening by the stronger states in the region, like Israel, Saudi Arabia, and Turkey. Of course, on the global scene Iran has close relationships with Russia and China, but it is telling that Iran is bereft of allies in the Middle East itself.

The question addressed in this chapter is how Iran sees other states in the region. In this section, we will address how it sees the strong states, like Saudi Arabia, Turkey, and Israel.

We will see that how Iran perceives other regional states hinges on two factors. The first is the degree to which other states are seen by Iran to be doing the bidding of the United States. The second is its portfolio of interests with that country. Paradoxically, Iranian relations with Saudi Arabia and Israel, countries where Iran has no specific hard-core territorial conflicts, are represented by the most hostilely stereotypical views. And with Turkey, the UAE, and Qatar, countries with which Iran has a modicum of interest overlap, complex imagery tends to prevail. In other words, the existence of pragmatic interests, even if at times conflicting, tends to support more complex and less stereotypical imagery.

In terms of ordinal ranking, Iran's views of Israel represent the most stereotypical and simplified hostile views. Views of Turkey at the other extreme tend toward greater complexity. What makes this interesting is that Turkey like Israel is an American ally. And Turkey (unlike Israel) is a treaty ally of the United States through NATO. But Turkey under the current President Recep Tayyip Erdogan has shown a willingness to take an independent stand vis-à-vis the United States, rather than hide behind American coattails, like Saudi Arabia. Saudi Arabia is in the middle of the complexity-stereotypical scale, depending on how Tehran perceives the distance between American and Saudi policy preferences.

What this means is that the views Iran harbors of regional actors is highly dependent on their relationship with Washington, but that the portfolio of overlapping interests can be a mitigating factor, except of course for relations with Israel.

Iranian views of Israel

Iran's views about Israel are at the extreme end of the stereotypical scale. The current Supreme Leader of Iran, Ali Khamenei, said at the onset of the Iran nuclear deal in 2015:

> God willing, there will be no such thing as a Zionist regime in 25 years. Until then, struggling, heroic and jihadi morale will leave no moment of serenity for Zionists.[24]

In meetings with the late President Ibrahim Raisi in 2022 and 2023, he also denied legitimacy to the Israeli state, referring to it instead as the Zionist regime.[25] President Pezeshkian's animus toward Israel in meetings in 2024 wasn't directed at its intrinsic right to exist, but rather at Israel's assassination of Hamas leader, Ismail Haniyeh in Tehran on July 31, 2024, the day after his own inauguration as president. He argued that this brazen act by the Israelis robbed him of the potential to advance his agenda of more engagement with the west.

While Iranian leaders have off and on painted disparaging imagery of Saudi Arabia and the United States, the most consistent rhetorical venom is reserved for the state of Israel. There are several ways to understand what has become a hallmark of Iran's foreign policy, even though the issue fails to inspire most Iranians.[26] One straightforward explanation is that the strong ideological views about the injustice of Israel's treatment of the Palestinians held by the late Ayatollah Khomeini have become embedded in the ethos of the Islamic Republic. Whether these views represent something viscerally held by Iranian leaders or are a cynical, opportunistic attempt to use the issue of Israel to distract the Iranian public from the excesses of the Iranian regime is less important than the fact that it represents the official position of Iran.

There is also a more political explanation. The fact that the Shah of Iran, Mohammed Reza Pahlavi, had a functional relationship with Israel certainly prejudiced the relationship in the eyes of the revolutionary government in Iran starting in 1979. Also, keeping the Palestinian issue alive is a convenient way to shame Iran's Arab rivals who seem to disregard and look the other way when it comes to this issue. In other words, keeping the spotlight on the Israeli-Palestinian issue is what has connected Iran to Arab populations.[27]

The Abraham Accords, a 2020 US-brokered agreement normalizing relations between Israel and the UAE and Bahrain, gave Tehran fresh fodder for claiming that the Arab states have diverted their gaze from the plight of the Palestinians. Using the Palestinian issue by Iran is designed to undermine the legitimacy of these accords with Arab populations who might be more sensitive to the Palestinian plight than their leaders. Of course, Iranian opposition to the accords is also motivated by a concern that the agreements will be used to create a joint Arab-Israeli phalanx against Iran. Among Iranian officials there seems to be satisfaction that movement toward Israel and Saudi Arabia normalizing relations as a follow-on to the Abraham Accords has at least been set back temporarily by Israel's response in Gaza to the October 7, 2023 attacks by Hamas.

The other driver of Iran's opposition to Israel is Israel's hostility to it, and Israeli Prime Minister Benjamin Netanyahu's opposition to any normalization initiatives between Iran and the United States, particularly the JCPOA. Israel counselled the Trump administration to withdraw from the 2015 deal, which it did in 2018. Moreover, Israel's assassinations of Iranian nuclear scientists on Iranian soil, its participation in the Stuxnet attacks on Iranian nuclear centrifuges, and Israel's attacks on Iranian positions in Syria have contributed to the animus. Also, Iran's belief that Israel supports the Mujahedin e-Khalq (MEK), an enemy of the Islamic Republic, has solidified negative imagery.[28] And last, but certainly not least, was Israel's killing of Hamas leader Ismail Haniyeh in Tehran in 2024. While this act can be thought of as payback for the Hamas attacks on Israel in 2023, it can also be seen to safeguard against the new reformist Iranian President Pezeshkian fulfilling his campaign promise to reduce tensions with the west.

What is stunning is the mirror-like, diabolical, self-reinforcing imagery that has worked its way into the rhetoric of the two countries. Iran has at times challenged the Holocaust narrative of Israel, particularly the vehemently anti-Zionist former President Mahmoud Ahmadinejad, who painted Israel as an illegitimate state. Israeli leaders in turn have painted Iran as an irredeemable, evil actor and existential threat to Israel.[29]

Other states like Turkey and Saudi Arabia are also regional rivals of Iran. But for Iran, Israel is in a special category given its relationship with the United States and its possession of nuclear weapons. In many ways, Iranian decision-makers see Israel as part of a US-led phalanx against Iran. In fact, there is a tendency to conflate the two countries, often portraying Israel as controlling US policy toward Iran. This imagery was even evident in the rhetoric of the relatively moderate former Iranian President Mohammed Khatami:

> However, the impression of the people of the Middle East and Muslims in general is that certain foreign policy decisions of the United States are in fact made in Tel Aviv and not in Washington.[30]

That the United States and Israel are part of the same overall threat perception is evident in Iranian Supreme Leader Ali Khamenei's 2009 speech to the Assembly of Experts in Iran when he said:

They (U.S. and Israel) have come to oppose the Islamic regime. And in this war the main goal of the enemy is to transform the strengths of the regime into weaknesses and vulnerabilities.[31]

Iranian leaders also believe that the international community supports a double standard when it comes to Israel. Unlike Iran, Israel is not a signatory of the Non-Proliferation Treaty (NPT), yet its possession of nuclear weapons hasn't been a controversial issue in international forums. According to Iranians, Israel more broadly is exempt from compliance with international conventions and standards, while Iran is unfairly held to them.

A legitimate question to ask is the following: is Iran's imagery of Israel inextricably tied to the United States? Should the relationship with Washington improve, could we also see an attenuation of Iran's hostility to Israel? The quote from Khamenei suggests that the views of Israel are even more visceral and immutable than the imagery of the United States. While one could imagine relations improving with the United States under the current leadership in Iran, it seems more of a stretch to suggest that there could be rapprochement between Israel and Iran. I have been part of several Track II and Track 1.5 regional diplomatic initiatives. Even at the height of the spat between Iran and Saudi Arabia between 2016 and 2023, leaders and influencers met with one another informally in back-channel discussions. But never once have I witnessed the same between Iranian and Israeli officials.

That having been said, the situation between Israel and Hamas in Gaza, Israel and Hezbollah in Lebanon, and the strikes Iran and Israel waged on each other in April and October of 2024 could push Iran to manage risk by reigning in some of the anti-Israeli militias it supports. One indication that Iran's behavior could become more circumspect came shortly after the Hamas attacks on Israel on October 7, 2023. At the Islamic and Arab League conference held in Saudi Arabia in November 2023, even though the late President Raisi sported the Palestinian keffiyeh, he didn't grandstand and walk out of the talks when language supporting a two-state solution was included in the final communique of the conference.[32] This shows perhaps that there could be tension between Iran's extreme rhetoric toward Israel and more pragmatic policy considerations. Of course, given that Iran and Israel have already crossed the red line of attacking one another directly, another scenario could be that Iran becomes more aggressive.

It is important to be mindful of the fact that Israel wasn't always the Islamic Republic's primary nemesis. In the immediate aftermath of the 1979 Iranian revolution, Iraq with its 1980 invasion of Iran posed the primary threat. Iraq also posed a threat to Israel. While fundamentally the regime in Tehran was predisposed to hostility toward Israel, welcoming Palestine Liberation Organization (PLO) leader Yasir Arafat to Tehran only days after Ayatollah Khomeini returned to Iran in 1979, the crushing onslaught from Iraq in the early days of the Iran-Iraq war softened the rhetoric against Israel a bit.[33] In fact, Israel gave some support, albeit modest, to Iran during the war.[34] This was done largely to help prevent a strengthening of Iraq, an arch enemy of both Iran and Israel and a proponent of a virulent form of Arab nationalism that took aim at both countries. This bond of common threat perceptions about Arab nationalism preceded the revolution, extending back to the 1960s when Iraq and Egypt, both energized by Nasser's Arab nationalism, were seen as threatening non-Arab Israel and non-Arab Iran.

Right now, regional events militate against any improvement in relations between Israel and Iran. Iran's projection of power into Syria during its civil war brought Iran-led forces even closer to Israel than before. And of course, the activation of Iran-backed militias like Hezbollah after the Hamas attacks on Israel in 2023, as well as the back-and-forth military attacks between Iran and Israel in 2024, have poisoned the well even further. While we can't predict the future, it is likely that Iran's relationship with Israel will remain hostile.

Iranian views of Saudi Arabia

The late Supreme Leader Ayatollah Khomeini of Iran said this about Saudi Arabia in 1987:

> These vile and ungodly Wahhabis are like daggers which have always pierced the heart of the Muslims from the back. Mecca was in the hands of a band of heretics.[35]

This statement suggests that tensions between Iran and Saudi Arabia originated with the Iranian revolution and Khomeini's view of the Saudis as illegitimate apostates. But there were tensions between Iran and Saudi Arabia during the reign of Mohammed Shah Pahlavi, even though the depth of animosity never reached the level of Khomeini's post-revolutionary vitriol.

While the flashpoints between Iran and Saudi Arabia after the revolution were ideological in nature, Tehran claiming that the Saudis were illegitimate stewards of the holy cities of Mecca and Medina, the disputes between the two countries under the shah tended to be about more practical, earthly matters. Iran saw Saudi dominance over the Organization of Petroleum Exporting Countries (OPEC) oil cartel as troubling. And the two countries were rivals in the geopolitics of the Persian Gulf.[36] But there were some common interests as well. Both Mohamed Reza Shah and King Faisal bin Abdulaziz al Saud of Saudi Arabia worried in the 1960s about the spread of the virulent form of Arab nationalism propagated by President Gamal Abdel Nasser of Egypt. In fact, the shah proposed a defense arrangement with Riyadh as a hedge against this, but after the Saudis bridled at this proposal tensions between the two countries built up again.[37]

Like today, the relationship Iran and Saudi Arabia had with each other was affected by relations each had with the United States. While both countries were part of the Nixon administration's Twin Pillars policy to create a regional containment shield against the Soviet Union, it was clear that Washington saw Tehran as its senior partner. The Saudis sensed this inferior standing, believing they were the junior pillar in the eyes of Washington. Given that Iran was more militarily assertive than Saudi Arabia, more populous, and bordered the Soviet Union, there was something to this impression.

This sense of inferiority with respect to Iran during the Cold War helps us better understand Saudi consternation about the JCPOA nuclear deal. Among other concerns, the Saudis feared the deal would lead to a broader rehabilitation of relations between Iran and the United States. With the unraveling of US-Iranian relations following the Iranian revolution, Saudi Arabia was elevated to the key US ally in the Persian Gulf region, a status it has had for more than forty years. The Saudis fear this would change should relations between the United States and Iran become less frosty.

Revolutionary Iranian hostility to Saudi Arabia was always more complicated than ideological and religious sectarian differences. Ayatollah Khomeini also saw Saudi Arabia as the tip-of-the-spear of US efforts to undermine the Islamic Republic. This imagery became even more pronounced with Saudi Arabia's tilt toward Iraq after the invasion of Iran in 1980, a source of resentment that still today casts a pall on Iran-Saudi relations. The fact that the US also tilted toward Baghdad reinforced the imagery of a threatening US-Saudi phalanx against Iran.[38]

While there were multiple motivations for the Gulf Arab states, including Saudi Arabia, to form the Gulf Cooperation Council (GCC) in 1981, it was no coincidence that it was formed in the early years following the Iranian revolution. There were economic reasons for the organization, plus concerns about Soviet ambitions following its invasion of Afghanistan in 1979. But it was also seen as a collective security arrangement against Iran. Suspicions in Tehran were that the impetus for this pact was Washington, particularly since it came on the heels of the 1980 Carter Doctrine, which promised US defense of its interests in the Persian Gulf.

Relations between Iran and Saudi Arabia did improve somewhat during the Iranian presidency of Mohammed Khatami. In 1999, President Khatami became the first Iranian leader to visit Saudi Arabia since the revolution. It was no coincidence that improved Iran-Saudi relations correlated with a reduction in tensions between Iran and the United States. In the same year Khatami visited Riyadh, he made a proposal at the United Nations for a Dialogue of Civilizations which was aimed at reducing tensions both with Iran's neighbors as well as the United States.[39]

Another low-point in Iran-Saudi relations came during the civil wars in Syria, Yemen, and Iraq. As Iran projected power into these conflicts, Saudi Arabia and other Gulf Arab countries bridled at what they saw as Iranian expansionism into the Arab heartland, concerns they took to Washington. This in turn shaped Iranian attitudes toward the Saudis, reinforcing the view of a US-Saudi phalanx against Iran.

For Tehran its interventions in the Arab world were seen as both defense and offense. On the defense side these involvements were about Iran's ability to create strategic depth and protect the homeland. But at the regional level it was an offensive battle for regional influence with Riyadh. The civil wars became proxy battles by which Saudi Arabia and Iran competed for regional influence, a contest Iran was winning, at least up until October 7, 2023.[40]

This rivalry for regional influence with Saudi Arabia can be seen in how Iran is handling the issue of the Palestinians. Iranians for the most part don't have strong sentiments about the Israeli-Palestinian issue.[41] But for the Iranian leadership, support for the Palestinians was part of a regional influence game. The idea was to outshine the Arabs on Palestine, which had been a core Arab issue decades before. By doing this, the

Iranians believed they could create a rift between Saudi Arabia and Israel, preventing the expansion of the Abraham Accords. Iranian statements about the Abraham Accords betraying the Palestinians were designed to deter Saudi Arabia from joining the accords, which was a possibility before the October 7 attacks by Hamas against Israel. Comments from the Iranians about the accords focused more on the Palestinian betrayal than on any security threats Iran felt from the alliance.[42]

Iran and Saudi Arabia re-established diplomatic relations in 2023, after a seven-year hiatus. While China brokered the agreement ending hostilities, the Iranians give credit to their own strategy for bringing the Saudis to the negotiating table after President Trump withdrew from the JCPOA in 2018 and reimposed sanctions on Iran. In April of 2019, I sat with then Iranian Foreign Minister Javad Zarif when he articulated the strategy.[43] The logic was to demonstrate to the Saudis that the security umbrella they believed they had with Washington was a mirage. The belief was that the shock of this would give the Saudis an incentive to pursue diplomacy with Iran.[44] The view was that if the Saudis felt protected by the Americans, then they would take the path of least resistance and eschew negotiation. But if it was clear to the Saudis that their assumption of an American security umbrella was erroneous, the rational path would be to engage with Iran diplomatically.

The attacks on the Saudi Aramco facilities in Abqaiq in 2019 and attacks on shipping in the straits of Hormuz were part of this strategy. With these attacks came threats that the Saudis and Emiratis would be the target of Iran's reprisals should it be attacked by Washington or Jerusalem. In other words, the strategy was designed to impose a cost on Saudi Arabia for its support for and from Washington.[45]

The strategy worked but it consisted not just of threats, but also diplomacy. Concomitant with a ratcheting up of tensions in the Persian Gulf, Iran made several diplomatic entreaties. The initial talks took place in Baghdad, Iraq, then later in Muscat, Oman, and finally in Beijing. In March 2023, the Chinese government brokered an agreement between Iran and Saudi Arabia.

This shows that behind the simplified, stereotypical rhetoric used by Iranian leaders since Khomeini, Iran sees Saudi Arabia with greater nuance and more complexity than it does Israel, for whom Iran's imagery is virtually frozen. There is a duality in Iran's view of Saudi Arabia. On the one hand, Riyadh is seen as a lackey of the United States and therefore a threat to Iran. On the other hand, the view is that Saudi Arabia can be nudged back into a regional orbit, where it feels compelled to deal with Iran and acts more independently of the United States.

Iranian views of Turkey

The relationship between post-revolutionary Iran and Turkey has had its ups and downs. In the first decades following the revolution, relations were mostly turbulent. One symbol of frosty relations came when then Iranian Prime Minister Mir Hossein Mousavi arrived in Turkey for a state visit in the mid-1980s. When invited by his Turkish hosts to visit the tomb of Mustafa Kemal Ataturk, the father of modern Turkey, he declined what was standard protocol for visiting dignitaries, instead choosing to visit the tomb of Persian poet and Sufi mystic Rumi.[46]

Mousavi's refusal to visit Kemal's tomb was symbolic, but it also reflected Ayatollah Khomeini's extremely negative sentiments about Turkey's militant protection of secularism. Also, his perception was that Turkey was harboring the anti-Iran regime terrorist organization, the People's Mujahedin Organization of Iran (MEK), a view which was requited by Turkey's claim that Iran backed the Kurdish separatist Kurdistan Workers' Party (PKK).[47]

Relations improved after 2003, when Recep Tayyip Erdogan was elected to become Prime Minister of Turkey. Iranians looked favorably on Turkey's decision to deny the United States the right to use the Incirlik air base for bombing runs into Iraq in 2003, showing clear independence from Washington. Also, Turkey refused US attempts to use it to offshore balance against Iran, taking a more independent posture instead.[48] Turkey's self-image at the time was as a possible bridge between Iran and its Arab neighbors and perhaps even between Tehran and Washington.

It is instructive to compare Iran's views of Turkey with those of Israel. If Israel is seen in simplified, ideological, and stereotypical terms, Turkey is on the opposite end of the spectrum, seen through a lens of greater complexity. To provide context, it is important to point out that Saudi Arabia sits somewhere in the middle of this simplicity-complexity continuum.

Why would Turkey, a treaty ally of the United States through the North Atlantic Treaty Organization (NATO), be seen in a more complex light than Israel, a non-treaty US ally? One key reason is Erdogan's increasingly fierce independence from the United States, notwithstanding his transatlantic NATO affiliation. That distance has been evident most recently with Turkey's angry and vitriolic response to Israel's prosecution of the Gaza war that started in 2023, which contrasts with Washington's greater accommodation to the Israeli position.

Another explanation of close ties has to do with the practical interests that bind the two neighboring countries, including shared concerns about irredentist Kurdish independence movements. Also, trade interests have provided the glue between Turkey and Iran. Turkey's dependence on Iranian natural gas helped with cross-border trade, which ballooned from $1 billion in 2000 to $5.5 billion in 2023, making Turkey a key trading partner of Iran. Turkey (along with Brazil) also tried to help Iran out of its nuclear standoff with the United States in 2010, which hit a dead end in Washington due to the momentum of securing UN economic sanctions against Iran for its nuclear enrichment program. Iran and Turkey's joint support for Qatar after the Saudi and Emirati siege against that country in 2017 was also a common bond. And finally, Turkey and Iran worked together as part of the Russia-led Astana process to try to de-conflict the Syrian civil war.

Because of these factors, Iran's view of Turkey is more realpolitik than Iran's view of either Saudi Arabia or Israel. While there are conflict flashpoints in Syria, Iraq, and Nagorno-Karabakh between Iran and Turkey, relations have been reasonably stable. The flashpoints have been Turkey's support for Saudi Arabia's efforts to fight the Houthis in Yemen. Then came accusations from Tehran that Turkey supported ISIS.[49] In tit-for-tat fashion, Turkey counterattacked, accusing Iran of weaponizing sectarianism to weaken both Syria and Iraq.[50] And the Arab Spring and ensuing civil wars in Yemen and Syria added tensions to the relationship between Iran and Turkey. Iran sometimes portrays Turkish ambition as motivated by a neo-Ottoman impulse, and the charge is returned with Turkey seeing Iran's foreign policy in the Middle East as neo-Persian.

Iran's relations with Turkey show that Tehran can develop and sustain a realpolitik approach to countries where there are some shared regional interests. For Iran, Turkey is seen through an economic policy and interest lens in contrast to the more political and ideological prism used to consider relations with Israel and Saudi Arabia. This pragmatism is sustained and reinforced in the eyes of the Iranians due to Turkey's continued independence from Washington.

Iranian Views: Weak States in the Region

Each of the weak states of Lebanon, Iraq, Syria, and Yemen plays a particular role in Iran's foreign policy calculus. Overall, these states are seen as opportunities for offsetting the strategic disadvantages Iran has in competing with the stronger states in the region and with the United States. The militias Iran supports in these fragile Arab states are believed by Iran to provide deterrence against possible attacks by Israel or the United States. While these advantages are under challenge as the Iran-supported militias in the weak states are being pummeled by Israel in the aftermath of the October 7, 2023 attacks by Hamas, it is important to understand Iran's strategic calculus.

Iran's relations within these countries aren't limited to the security realm. Iran's projection of power into the weak states also provides economic benefits. But we shouldn't paint Iran's relationships in Iraq, Syria, Yemen, and Lebanon with a single brush. Iran sees each of these weak states very differently. From providing deterrence and a retaliatory capability to sanctions evasion and circumvention, each of these countries scratches a different strategic itch for Iran.

Iranian views of Iraq: Defense and sanctions evasion interests

When the United States invaded Iraq in 2003, Iran's strategic view was one of ambivalence. On the one hand, the US had brought down the regime of Saddam Hussein, an accomplishment Iran had been denied during its nearly eight years of war with Iraq. On the other hand, this feat, accomplished with a display of overwhelming American military power, instilled in the hallways of power in Tehran a fear that Iran might be next.[51]

Once the United States got mired in Iraq, as well as Afghanistan, the views of Tehran became less ambiguous as the threat of a possible military incursion into Iran ebbed somewhat. In fact, over time the threat gave way to cautious optimism and even opportunity.

There are two levels of strategic perceptions Iran holds of Iraq. The first is at the regional level and reflects how Iraq figures into Iran's threat mitigation calculus. Its priority is of course to keep Iraq from rising again into a powerful Arab nationalist state that can once again threaten Iran. While Iranian leaders don't want an Iraq that is prostrated or dismembered, as almost occurred in 2014 when ISIS captured large swaths of Iraqi territory, it does want to keep it militarily weak and dependent on Iran. In other words, it wants Iraq to have a modicum of internal security but remain militarily neutered.[52]

Iraq plays an integral role in what Iran views as its regional "axis of resistance" against Israel and the United States. Along with its own Quds Force, elements of the Hashd al-Sha'bi militia network in Iraq are part of Iran's portfolio of paramilitary assets strewn across the region that can provide deterrence against the US and Israel. Or as was witnessed after the start of the Gaza war in 2023, Iran's militia assets in Iraq can occasionally be used offensively against Israel as well against American troops stationed in the country.

While it is important not to overly exaggerate the importance of sectarianism when examining how Iraq is seen by Iran, Iranian leaders do see Iraq as part of its effort to strengthen Shi'i alliances against the predominantly Sunni Arab world. Iran sees the Shi'i holy cities of Najaf and Karbala as important to its overall influence and legitimacy in Iraq, and uses this to tap into the ambitions of Shi'i populations and institutions in Syria and Lebanon.

Iran's interest in and views of Shi'ism in Iraq also extend into the political realm. The Shi'i Marja in Iraq, Ayatollah Ali al-Sistani, subscribes to the quietist tradition, which sees a minimal political role for the clergy, intervening only under extraordinary circumstances. In contrast, the leadership in Iran comes from the tradition of Ayatollah Khomeini's *vilayat-e faqih* (rule of the jurist), which places a clerical leader atop the political system. Given Ayatollah Sistani's advanced age, his passing will likely lead to a power struggle for who will succeed him and which of the two traditions will prevail.[53] Iran will likely play a role in this.

The second level of views Iran holds of Iraq centers on how Iran influences the social, economic, and political systems of the country. The importance of this has increased since Iran was targeted with punishing sanctions by the Trump administration, essentially isolating it from the international community. The imperative of breaking out of economic isolation contributed to Iran doubling down on its regional activities in Iraq (and Syria and Lebanon). By curtailing Iran's horizontal outreach to the international community, US sanctions pushed Iran vertically down into its own immediate neighborhood of failed states. Iraq has provided Iran an economic conduit for circumventing American sanctions, primarily by giving it an outlet for selling its products. While the benefits of this did accrue to Tehran, this wasn't trouble free for Iraq. When Iran dumped tomatoes at low prices into the Iraqi market to raise much needed cash, it stoked the ire of southern Iraqi farmers who lost business and profits.[54]

Over the past few years, Iran has also started to see Iraq through a competitive lens. Since 2016, Saudi Arabia has tried making inroads into Iraq with a few high-profile economic development projects to attempt to pry the country away from the exclusive embrace of Iran. Turkey also has made some economic inroads into Iraq focusing on development.

But even with Saudi Arabia's overwhelmingly deep pockets, competing with Iran for influence in Iraq isn't easy. Iran has made its relations with Iraq intentionally complex and diffused, with multiple tentacles into Iraq's political, economic, and religious system. This system was erected in the aftermath of the American invasion of Iraq in 2003 in order that the Iranian presence in the country would be difficult to detect and counter by the US military. Since then, Iran's tentacles have only extended deeper into the fabric of Iraqi political, religious, and economic life. Today, this web of influence serves to create a shield against competition from would-be contenders like Saudi Arabia.[55] While Iran can't compete financially with Saudi Arabia, it can act as a spoiler against Saudi efforts to influence the Iraqi political system. Its web of government contacts and influence points throughout the political system act as a defensive web against contenders.

The Iranian leadership is aware that while Turkey and Saudi Arabia may have difficulty competing in Iraq, Iran's Achilles heel could be internal opposition against the Iranian presence. Iranians were psychologically prepared for protests in the Sunni heartland of Iraq. But they were more taken aback and rattled by protests in the Shi'i hubs of Najaf and even Basra in 2019, when the Iranian consulate in Najaf was sacked.[56] I was told by several Iraqis and Iranians that the resentment was really aimed at the Iraqi government, but that Iran was blamed because of its close association with the Iraqi political elites. They also said that since the protests in Iraq, and the killing of Major General Qassim Soleimani in 2020 by the United States in Baghdad, the Iranians have been a bit more nuanced in their dealings with the Iraqis.[57]

Going forward it will be important to keep a watchful eye for Tehran's reaction to the process of choosing a successor to Ayatollah Sistani. If

Tehran pushes for someone who embraces Iran's *vilayat-e faqih* tradition, then further resentment could build. But a sign of nuance might be accepting someone from the Sistani quietist tradition.[58]

Iran attaches a high degree of importance to its relationship with Iraq. This is attributable to a history of hostilities extending back to the Iran-Iraq war and the economic, cultural, and religious interests that Iran has developed over the decades. While Iran's view of Iraq is likely to adapt to changed political, security, and social realities, the salience of Iraq within the foreign policy establishment is likely to remain firm. Iraq represents both a buffer and a hedge: a buffer against potential Arab aggression and a hedge against a strengthened Iraq that could pose a renewed threat to the Iranian homeland.[59]

Iranian views of Syria: Defensive and offensive interests

Syria has been an unparalleled ally of Iran, reaching back to the early days of the Iranian revolution. Breaking ranks with the rest of the Arab world, Syria backed Iran during the Iran-Iraq war.[60] But Persian Iran and Arab Syria have been in many ways strange bedfellows. Syria once was a center of Arab nationalism, having been a seminal part of Egypt's Gamal Abdel Nasser's Arab unification plan in the 1950s. In fact, Syria from 1958 to 1961 conjoined with Egypt in the United Arab Republic (UAR). The more virulent forms of Nasser's Arab nationalism were seen as a threat to Iran during the reign of the last Shah of Iran, Mohammed Reza Pahlavi. And up until the 2024 toppling of the Assad regime, Syria had been the home of the Arab nationalist Ba'ath Party.

But by turning the looking glass a different way, we see that in many ways these bedfellows weren't so strange. The worldviews of Iran and Syria have been reasonably aligned since the early days of the revolution. Syria was part of the rejectionist front that became arrayed against Egypt after Sadat struck a US-brokered peace treaty with Israel in 1978. This was consistent with the views of the revolutionary government in Iran, which was almost genetically opposed to any US-sponsored peace deal involving Israel. And Arab-Persian differences aside, both Syria and Iran saw the reckless dictator of Iraq, Saddam Hussein, as a common menace who regularly threatened the regimes in Tehran and Damascus.

Once the Cold War ended with the collapse of Syria's Soviet benefactor, Damascus saw Iran as a strong regional ally against other enemies, namely Israel and the United States. This eventually led Syria along the path of becoming an integral part of the Iran-led "axis of resistance," which, until the 2024 toppling of Assad, tethered Iran, Syria, Lebanon/Hezbollah, Hamas, Palestine Islamic Jihad (PIJ), the Houthis, and militias in Iraq.

There are other threads that bound together Tehran and Damascus. Syria served as a conduit to Hezbollah of Lebanon, the jewel of the crown of Tehran's militia network. Since the 1980s, Syria was a training, logistics, and supply hub connecting Iran to Hezbollah in Lebanon. This allowed Iran to project power into the Mediterranean and Arab Levant, giving it leverage vis-à-vis Israel. This was true before the Syrian civil war but it became even more profound once Iran's Quds Force sat closer to Israel during the war as it helped stabilize and sustain the Assad regime.

Syria has been also part of Iran's overall Middle East worldview. As we saw earlier in this chapter, Iran has seen the failed and fragile states of the region as a borderless, malleable landscape within which it has established an integrated network of substate militias. Once Syria collapsed into civil war in 2011, it became an integral part of this strange, shadowy reality. In fact, the Syrian, Iraqi, Yemeni, and Lebanese strategic landscapes that had once been separate became merged into one battlefield for Iran. After the Iranians inserted themselves into the Syrian civil war with their own Quds Force and other militias, they brought Hezbollah into the Syrian theatre along with Iraqi and Afghan fighters.

This aggrandized role for Hezbollah and the expansion of the reach of the Quds Force gave Iran the strategic depth it believed it needed. For Iran supporting Assad was seen as a necessity, as the collapse of Syria would mean the loss of a critical strategic linchpin. In Tehran the view was that if the Assad regime collapses, Iran also loses its critical deterrence and retaliatory capabilities.[61] The importance of Syria for Iran was expressed in hyperbolic fashion by Mehdi Taeb, commander of Iran's Basiji force, in the early days of the Syrian civil war:

> Syria is the 35th province and a strategic province for Iran. If the enemy attacks and aims to attack both Syria and Khuzestan [in Iraq}, our priority would be Syria ... if Syria were lost, we would not be able to keep even Tehran.[62]

While Iraq gave Iran a buffer right on its border, Syria linked to Lebanon through Hezbollah gave it strategic depth into the broader region. This gave Iran both defensive and offensive capacity. On the defensive front, Syria gave Iran a hedge against a US or Israeli attack. But as was witnessed on April 13, 2024, Syria was also part of Iran's offensive capabilities. On that day, in response to an April 1 Israeli attack on Revolutionary Guard commanders in Damascus, Iran used its militias across the Middle East to wage an unprecedented direct attack on Israel. This offensive capability along with Iran's defensive capacity has been severely compromised with the toppling of the Assad regime in 2024 and possible eviction of Iranian personnel from Syria.

What is generally not expressed publicly but has been felt by Iranian strategic thinkers is that Syria and Iraq being under Iran's thumb represented a hedge against the re-emergence of a virulent form of Arab nationalism. The necessity for this became apparent to Iran during the Iran-Iraq war when all Arab states except Syria backed the Iraqi invasion of Iran. Pre-revolutionary Iran had a history of challenges from the Arab world when Gamal Abdel Nasser reigned over Egypt in the 1950s and 1960s.[63] In this vein, the utility of Iran's relations with Syria was to mitigate the threat coming from the Arab world, tying the Syrian, Lebanese, and Iraqi landscapes together. At the time of writing, Iran will need to reassess what the end of the Assad regime means for Iranian interests in hedging against Arab revivalism.

Prior to the toppling of the Assad regime, Iran had already planned for possible attempts by its Arab rivals to reintegrate Syria into the Arab world. In fact, Syria was reinstated as a member of the Arab League in 2023 after a decade long suspension due to the excesses of the Assad regime during the country's civil war. To sustain its influence in Syria, Iran suffused itself into the economic, political, cultural, and even religious landscape of the country, blocking any initiatives from Saudi Arabia or the UAE to fully reintegrate Syria into the Arab world. Iran has been trying to play down Syria's Arab heritage and play up its connection to the Shi'i world. It has invested in fortifying the Shi'i shrines in Syria and promoted tourism around them. This was designed to build support for the Alawite regime as well as the Ismailis and other Shi'i sects in the country.

Iran also benefited economically from Syria's isolation during its long civil war, by flooding it with Iranian exports.[64] This took on particular importance in 2018, when the Trump administration withdrew from the

JCPOA and reimposed punishing sanctions.⁶⁵ Also, Iran has built housing developments, such as the Marota City project in Damascus, right behind the Iranian embassy. The idea was that this would house 50,000 supporters of the Assad regime and Iran.⁶⁶ What happens to the economic, cultural, and political links between Syria and Iran is unknown at this time. But Iran needs to prepare for the worst. The investment Iran made in keeping Syria outside the Arab orbit will be challenged in the post-Assad era. Given the support Iran gave to the murderous Assad regime, this will be a difficult needle to thread.

In summary, Syria has been seen as essential to the security of Iran. There is plenty of cynicism about this from its rivals in the region, who suggest that this claim of defense has been merely a cover for Iranian hegemonic designs. Of course, this narrative became amplified after the attacks on Israel by Hamas in October of 2023, and the ratcheting up of conflict between Israel, Iran, and the United States.

But it is fair to say that Iran has also been motivated by the perceived need to create deterrence, something that perhaps now has been lost. Since Iran's conventional military assets aren't sufficient to deter the United States and Israel, Iran's presence in Syria, Lebanon, and Iraq has been thought to give Iran the retaliatory capability needed to establish deterrence. Moreover, the degree to which Iran had suffused itself into Syria made it difficult for Israel and the United States, as well as the Arab states, to counter its influence and presence.⁶⁷ This is likely to change as Syria goes through a leadership transition, with Iran likely losing its foothold in the country and the linchpin of its "axis of resistance."

Iranian views of Lebanon

Iran's view of Lebanon, like most of Iran's connections to the fragile states in the region, should not be considered in a vacuum, but rather in the context of a broader system of deterrence and power projection. Iran has linked Lebanon to Syria in a web of both offensive and defensive assets through its own Quds Force and Hezbollah, which, until Assad was toppled, operated in both countries.

If there is a hierarchy in Iran's portfolio of militias, Lebanon's Hezbollah is the apex. Given the war Israel waged in Lebanon against Hezbollah in 2024, it is unclear how effective the group will be in protecting Iran in the future. But Iran taking the risk of attacking Israel for a second time with a barrage of missiles a few days after the assassination by Israel of Hezbollah leader Hassan Nasrallah on September 27, 2024 is a good indication of how important the group is to Iran. Hezbollah was the first militia created outside Iran after the revolution, has the longest track record of fealty to Iran, and has followed Iran on its road to project power into the weak states of the region. It has sent men and material to Syria, Iraq, and Yemen, largely to do Iran's bidding.

The relationship with Hezbollah is also considered by Iranians to be its most strategically successful partnership. It certainly has been the most impactful in terms of consistently advancing Iran's foreign policy agenda. Until the October 7, 2023 Hamas attacks on Israel, it was thought to be the primary deterrent to an Israeli or US attack, keeping Israel's northern borders with Lebanon and Syria uncertain and precarious. Hezbollah fought Israel to a draw in 2006, after which the group with help from Iran acquired a significant arsenal of highly sophisticated missiles, aimed at Israel.[68]

Hezbollah's contribution to fortifying President Assad of Syria during the country's civil war may have cut it down to size reputationally in the Arab world, but it further strengthened its ties with Iran. For sure, Hezbollah has a revered spot in Iran's strategic calculus. While Iranian leaders rarely state this publicly, Hezbollah has greater strategic importance than Hamas and even Palestine Islamic Jihad (PIJ). During the war between Israel and Hamas that followed the October 7 attacks on Israel, Iran signaled to Hezbollah circumspection about engaging in an all-out war with Israel. Even though Iran itself launched attacks on Israel on April 13, 2024, it counseled Hezbollah not to spark an all-out war.[69]

But calibrating the red lines of an opponent is difficult during wartime. On October 8, 2023, one day after Hamas's deadly attack on Israel, Hezbollah started lobbing missiles into Israel in support of Hamas. For almost a year, this became a war of attrition between Israel and Hezbollah. In September of 2024, Israel raised the stakes and waged war on Hezbollah in Lebanon, culminating in the killing of Nasrallah and the bombing of key Hezbollah assets. We don't know the degree of coordination left between Iran and Hezbollah. But if Hezbollah is significantly weakened, Iran's entire deterrence strategy will be compromised. Aside from its own Quds Force, Hezbollah has been the centerpiece of Iran's forward defense approach of creating strategic depth in its surrounding environment. Whether Iran can reconstitute Hezbollah or will make a dash to a nuclear weapon to re-establish deterrence is unknown at this time. What is known is the central role Hezbollah has played in Iran's strategic doctrine and its sense of national security.

Iranian views of Yemen: Game of offense with Saudi Arabia

In talking to Saudi and Emirati political elites since 2015, it is clear they see Iran as having established a hegemonic stranglehold over the Arab world, with a presence in Syria, Iraq, Lebanon, and Yemen. But for them, Iran's presence in Yemen is the most menacing due to its strategic location on the Arabian Peninsula.[70]

But there are significant differences between how Yemen fits into Iran's strategic calculus and the role played by Iraq, Lebanon, or Syria. Iran's support for the Houthis goes back to 2011. But it increased significantly when the group took over the Yemeni capital Sana'a in 2014. Support for the Houthis in Yemen increased further in 2015 after Saudi Arabia entered the civil war there. Initially Iran's aim in Yemen was to mire Saudi Arabia, hoping to deprive it of victory over the Houthis and to degrade its capability. The evidence suggests that Iran responded to an opportunity provided by the Saudi onslaught into Yemen, rather than as part of any broader strategic plan.

But under the maximum pressure campaign during President Trump's first term, the Iranian calculus changed. The Houthis gave Iran at least an opportunity for implausible deniability when it came to aggressive actions in the Persian Gulf area, including attacks on the Saudi Aramco facilities in 2019 and on shipping in the Red Sea after the Hamas attacks on Israel in 2023. The Houthi attacks in 2019 and 2023 redounded to the strategic benefit of Iran, without the direct attribution that could drag it into an unwanted war. The ambiguity as to whether these attacks were attributable to Iranian command and control or simply the free will of the Houthis has played to Iran's strategic advantage.

In the aftermath of the attacks on Israel by Hamas in 2023, it is less clear whether Iran will be able to maintain this ambiguity and deniability with the Houthis. On April 13, 2024, Iran was able to coordinate missile and drone attacks on Israel with the Houthis, Hezbollah, and other militias. This public demonstration of a coordinated attack capability may give Iran pause in thinking that future attacks by the Houthis give Iran any real credible deniability.

To what degree the aftermath of October 7 makes the Houthis a more strategic part of Iran's network remains to be seen. What is clear is that since October 7, Iran now sees the Houthis as part of a more active component of the resistance front against the United States and Israel. The continued attacks by the Houthis on shipping in the Red Sea keeps pressure on the United States, with little risk so far to the Iranian homeland.

Conclusion

One lingering question is whether Iran has an interest in maintaining the region in its current state of disorder, dysfunction, and conflict, or does it believe it benefits from a more stable and less violent Middle East? As was said at the beginning of this chapter, Iran operates simultaneously in two Middle East realities, one being the reality of sovereign states and the other a more shadowy Hobbesian world without boundaries in the weak states of the region. In the first reality, Iran conducts diplomacy with the likes of Saudi Arabia, Turkey, Egypt, and Saudi Arabia. In the second world, Iran supports and operates militias. Which of these Iran shifts its weight to going forward cannot be foreseen today.

What we can say is that Iran has been more successful in parlaying the civil wars and dystopia in the region into strategic influence for itself than it has been in engaging diplomatically in the region. The question for the future is whether it can compete on a more conventional basis with other strong states in the region. Or does it need the fragile states and alliances with militias to maintain its influence?

In discussions with senior Iranian officials, they evinced an understanding that Iran cannot thrive politically or economically in a region fraught with civil wars and conflict. But the question is whether they have the political will and maneuverability to shift Iranian foreign policy in a more constructive direction. In a post-October 7 environment, Iran may be forced to make some key decisions about how much emphasis it places on its substate militias, since this strategy designed to create deterrence could create more risk with Israel and undermine deterrence. This is particularly the case given the likelihood that Iran's militia network could be compromised for some time to come after being pummeled by Israel in 2023 and 2024, and with the loss of Syria as Iran's only real state ally in the Middle East.

Iran does have realpolitik responses to regional dynamics. Today it sees the region for what it is: a degraded state system, within which regional rivalry has been shaped by what has unfolded in the civil war zones of Syria and Yemen and weak states of Iraq and Lebanon, and of course since 2023, Palestine. Prior to 2023, Iran could rely on its foothold in these weak states to give it regional influence. But with the possibility that Iran's militia network might be further compromised with the loss of Syria as an ally, it may be forced to rearticulate and recalibrate its regional foreign policy to lean more heavily on conventional diplomacy to assure itself continued influence in a region in flux.

4 IRAN'S VIEW OF ITSELF

Most countries are built on and sustained by national narratives. Sometimes these are myths that give meaning to the present in context of the past. Some of these narratives are stories of grievance and others are expressions of grandeur. The Palestinian story is built on grievance: the usurpation of land at the hands of Israel. The Egyptians see themselves in the context of their pharaonic past. The United States is built on a story about revolution, freedom, and American exceptionalism. And nascent countries and communities, such as the European Union, are built on visions of a better and more peaceful future than the past.

Iran's narrative is a hybrid of greatness and grievance. Its story takes us back over 2,500 years to Cyrus the Great and what many Iranians describe as a benevolent expansion of the Persian Empire. But the Iranian national psyche is also shaped by a sense of grievance: conquest and domination at the hands of more powerful opponents, starting with the Arab invasion in the seventh century, then the Ottomans, Russians, British, and finally the United States.

Iran's strategic outlook and priorities are shaped by this Janus-faced and dialectical view Iran has of itself. It is tricky to write about Iran's self-image, as there is no singular self-identification held by Iranians. Clearly, there are some who embrace the Shi'i Islamic narrative as core, while others hew to their more secular Persian past.

In this chapter, we are interested in how Iran sees itself within a strategic context, how it defines its foreign policy aspirations relative to the region and other countries, and how it defines and identifies its strategic priorities. We also look at how Iran sees its role in the region and how it articulates its interests.

Iran's Foreign Policy Interests

There are few purely objective foreign policy interests of any country. Of course, there are vital interests common to all states, such as national security, economic growth, and territorial sovereignty. But how these get interpreted can depend on the regime in power. For example, there have been different interpretations about the role nuclear enrichment plays in Iran's national security interests, some saying that its nuclear program undermines its interests, inviting international opprobrium and even possible attack, while others say it is essential to national security, grandeur, prestige, and deterrence.

Also, Iranian leaders seldom interpret their country's national security interests in a political vacuum. Some interests that are sold to the Iranian people as essential to national security are also about regime preservation, a front-of-mind concern of all Iranian leaders. One question is what is the scope or horizon of Iran's foreign policy interests? Iran is a regional power, like Turkey, Saudi Arabia, and Egypt. But because of the threats Iran perceives and the ideology it holds, Iran thinks about its interests more broadly and deeply than most. We have seen this evidenced in Iranian behavior over the past decade. Its forward defense doctrine is built on the premise that Iran has security interests that necessitate power projection far beyond its borders. The searing lessons of the Iraqi attack of 1980 and the subsequent eight-year war are the foundation for this kind of thinking.

Iran's zone of interests expanded in the aftermath of the Arab Spring, significantly beyond the minimal buffer zone required by forward defense. The civil wars that followed the Arab Spring created a vacuum through which Iran could project power and enlarge its range of regional influence. Iran expanded this zone in Syria, Yemen, and Iraq to satisfy its security and economic interests, but also to block Saudi and Turkish entry into these areas.

Also enlarging Iran's scope of interests has been its entanglement with global powers.[1] One motivation for Iran's power projections into the failed states of the region was a belief that support for militias such as Hezbollah, the Houthis, and Hamas is the best way to deal effectively with the threat from the United States.[2] Russia's war in Ukraine has further widened the aperture of Iran's foreign policy interests. Iranian leaders believe that its support for Russia has expanded its leverage with Moscow. Iran's supply of critical drones to Russia gives Iranian leaders confidence in this leverage, notwithstanding the disappointments Iranians felt at Russia's silence after Israel attacked the Russian-supplied S-300 anti-air systems in Iran on October 26, 2024.[3] Iran also believes this relationship with Russia as well as China gives it an alternative to better relations with the United States, with which it sees little hope of redemption. While Iranian President Pezeshkian ran on a platform of improved relations with the west, including the United States, in meetings he seemed almost resigned to this being out of reach given what he saw as military aggression from Israel.

Iran's enhanced scope of interests is also shaped by the fact that it sees the United States as both a global and regional power, with its own military assets in the region coupled with those of its allies. Iranian leaders often conflate the threat it sees from the United States with how it sees Israel and even Saudi Arabia. In the Iranian worldview, these US allies are part of a US phalanx arrayed against Iran.[4]

Iran's missile program and its nuclear enrichment capabilities are a response to how Iran defines its interests. While these programs are linked to Iran's regional security concerns, they also relate to how Iran sees its global standing. Iran sees itself as isolated, even though its adversaries would claim this is self-inflicted. In fact, there has been much written about Iran's "strategic loneliness," pointing to the country's dearth of natural allies and plethora of adversaries.[5]

This sense of aloneness plays into Iran's dialectical view of being both a victim and victor, as a country imbued with greatness and a country isolated and vulnerable. It sees itself simultaneously threatened by the United States and emboldened to thwart and frustrate Washington's regional ambitions. This duality in how Iran sees itself in the regional and global context helps us understand how important preservation of prestige is to its foreign policy interests.[6] Iran's nuclear enrichment program fits into this drive for prestige and grandeur, in addition to its obvious interest in creating a deterrence against Israel and the United States.

One question that needs to be addressed is whether the foreign policy interests of Iran have changed significantly since the Islamic revolution of 1979? For a country like the United States, where national security challenges tend to evolve rather than occur suddenly, interests remain reasonably stable over time. But Iran, as a middle power, is subject to the vicissitudes of rapidly changing international and regional environments and, lacking the natural strategic depth of the United States, interests and how they are defined can shift much more rapidly.

For example, how Iran conceived of the interest of creating strategic depth changed from the Iran-Iraq war of the 1980s to the US invasion of Iraq in 2003. While Iran identified strategic depth as an interest and enshrined it in its forward defense doctrine during its war with Iraq, how it operationalized this interest changed with the toppling of Saddam Hussein in 2003 and again with the onset of the civil wars in Syria in 2011 and Yemen in 2014. It opportunistically projected power into these zones and established a network of militias. The principal interest of strategic depth remained constant, but how Iran acted upon that interest changed with a shifting strategic regional landscape.

One question that needs to be addressed is how might Iran's interests govern its relationship to the broader region going forward? In other words, does it have an interest in preserving or disrupting the regional status quo? It is a strange twist of history that the regime in Iran which believes it is the heir to the mantle of the revolution is preserving the status quo in Lebanon, Iraq, and Yemen, and also tried to stabilize and preserve the Assad regime in power in Syria. It helped maintain President Assad in power in Syria until 2024 and supported Hezbollah's efforts in Lebanon. Iran also kept the Iraqi government beholden to it, and helped sustain the Houthis in power in Yemen.

Despite the regional bravado, when it comes to its own national security interests, Iran is careful with disruption. While from an Israeli perspective, Iran is a reckless and dangerous actor, Iran's actions since October 7, 2023 suggest it is calculating and even circumspect. Even its egregious and unprecedented attacks on Israel on April 13 and October 1, 2024, were done with some careful calculation and risk mitigation measures. While Iran demonstrated its ability and willingness to launch attacks from the Iranian homeland and from across the region using its militias, it seemed to have the aim of restoring deterrence and avoiding further escalation.[7]

One way of thinking about the tension between Iran's interests of preservation and disruption is that they exist at two different levels—Iran is participating in a two-level interest game.[8] Iran has an interest in preserving the status quos in Syria, Lebanon, Iraq, and Yemen, from which it derives significant benefits. And it is cautious when it comes to its own state security. But it also is using its involvement in these countries to disrupt the regional order and shape it into something that favors its competitive advantage. In this spirit, Iran gloated and reveled in the aftermath of one of the most regionally disruptive events in decades: Hamas's attack on Israel in 2023. Iran tolerates and even encourages regional disruption if it compromises the interests of Israel and the United States, but not to the extent that it also creates risk to its own security.

The question going forward is whether Iran has stakes in a more cooperative and competitive Middle East or whether its long-term interests can be served by the disruptive effect of its militias? Part of this depends on how dominant the United States remains in Iran's strategic thinking. With the United States at the center of Iran's strategic universe, the region is seen as a zero-sum game. In that game, anything that challenges Israel or the United States redounds to the benefit of Iran, even if it leads to risky regional disruption.

There are signs that even within this zero-sum game involving the United States, Iran might be moving toward diplomacy, potentially improving Iran's standing in the global community. Its rapprochement with Saudi Arabia in March 2023 and improvement in relations with Egypt are evidence of this. In the international arena, Iran joining the Shanghai Cooperation Organization (SCO) is also a sign of Iran wanting to integrate with the global order, albeit an eastern dominated one. Of course, this move is designed to situate Iran in an eastward alliance system and isn't a healthy sign for future US-Iran relations. But it might augur well for Iran focusing more on diplomacy and state-based integration into the global system than on a more destructive substate militia approach.

How Iran evaluates its interests in terms of future risk is still an open question at the time of writing. Prior to October 7, 2023, Iran was able to secure its national security interests using two parallel foreign policy tracks of a substate militia strategy and state-to-state diplomacy, arguing both were aimed at preservation of the status quo, the militia strategy aimed at maintaining a system of deterrence and the state-to-state diplomacy preserving stability. After October 7, it was hard for Iran to make the case that its militia strategy was preservationist. Whether Iran can continue advancing its national security interests without rebalancing its foreign policy toward a more conventional state-to-state diplomacy now that the preservationist veil of its militia approach has been exposed remains to be seen.

Iran's Identity

During the negotiations on the JCPOA Iran nuclear deal in July of 2015 in Vienna, there was a moment when the Iranian delegation felt besieged by demands from the United States and other members of the P5+1 (permanent members of the Security Council plus Germany). In response, Foreign Minister Javad Zarif yelled, "never threaten an Iranian."[9] To break the tension, apparently Russian Foreign Minister Lavrov quipped, "nor a Russian".

While a singular event, this outburst is emblematic of the duality of Iranian identity as it relates to the outside world. On the one hand, Iranians are steeped in the glory days of an ascendant and enlightened Persia, when the expanding empire burst with cultural, intellectual, and economic activity. On the other hand, Iranians reflect a sense of extreme vulnerability, and even at times insecurity at the hands of outside powers.

The meeting in Vienna played on both sides of this duality. Iran had some bargaining power given how advanced its nuclear enrichment program had become, and the outsized role Iran played in the Middle East. In fact, what brought Iran to the table, in addition to sanctions, was a concession on the part of the United States. Washington conceded that Iran had a right to enrich uranium under the Non-Proliferation Treaty to which it was a signatory but drew a red line on the quantity and potency of its fissile material.[10] This was a recognition on the part of the Americans that previous attempts to deny Iran any enrichment capability had been flawed non-starters. But despite the leverage and bravado from the Iranian delegation, it was apparent to Zarif that Iran was a middle, regional power negotiating with global powers. In fact, all the powers which had passed UN Security Council Resolution 1929 unanimously in 2010 to sanction Iran for its nuclear-related activities were in that room in Vienna, a fact that gave Iran an added incentive to negotiate in good faith but also accentuated its sense of strategic loneliness.

Iran has endured several identity crises over the course of its history, which weigh on decision-makers to this day. Iranians in general are aware of their long history, proud of what they see as the halcyon days of the Persian Empire when it encompassed broad swaths of the current Middle East and Central Asia more than 2,500 years ago. But they are also painfully aware of the Arab invasion nearly 1,300 years later and the effect this had on Persian society. But in the minds of Iranians, the Arab invasion reflected a duality. Iran was politically and geographically pummeled and subdued, but the country's culture, language, and sense of Persian identity remained intact. It was a kind of inversion of the previous Persian Empire, during which it became the target of cultural penetration efforts by what Iranians today see as an inferior Arab enemy.

In the 1500s, during which Persia experienced penetration from Russia and Ottoman Turkey, the Safavid shahs redefined Persia as a Shi'i jihadist power, having previously been Sunni. In a way, this was a reassertion of a distinct Persian identity, albeit within an Islamic context. We can interpret this as Iran redefining itself on its own terms, a symbol of its indomitability after the Arab invasion. This transformation, along with all other revolutionary spasms, including the 1979 revolution, fundamentally was about the generation of military, social, and political power after periods of foreign domination.

Iran has struggled as have many former empires, including modern-day Russia, with the tension between perceptions of a glorious past and the less glorious realities of the present. Iranians tend to be highly patriotic, but nationalism has had a mixed historical record of resolving this tension. The gains of the Constitutional Revolution in Iran of 1906 were quashed by Britain and Russia. And even the transformations imposed by Reza Shah Pahlavi in the early days of the twentieth century didn't generate enough power to years later spare Iran from the overthrow of its star nationalist, Prime Minister Mohammed Mossadegh, in 1953.[11]

Iran's Islamic identity is complicated, as at times it is indistinguishable from a nationalist identity. This was apparent in Zarif's comportment in Vienna, where he represented the Islamic Republic of Iran, but his nationalist sensibilities and pride were on full display. During the lead-up to the 1979 Iranian revolution, Islam for many was a symbolic receptacle for generating power at a time when the secular shah was being discredited as a stooge of the west. Many secularly minded women donned Islamic garb in support of the revolution, but underneath the embers of nationalist passion burned. For some, talk in 1979 of exporting the revolution tapped into a longing to spread Iran's reach into territory once part of ancient Persia, meaning that Islamic fervor became blended with Persian nationalism.

One question is whether Islam as an identity construct has been successful in terms of generating power for Iran, and whether this serves the interests of the Iranian people? As we know, the Iranian revolution at its core for many Iranians was a nationalist revolution, using the symbols of Islam to generate sufficient power to topple the shah. In other words, Islamic symbols for many were instrumentalized to generate political power and engender change. This isn't to cast doubt on the authenticity of the symbols of the Islamic revolution of 1979, but it is important to acknowledge that the attraction Islamic symbols held for many was due to the charismatic leadership of Ayatollah Ruhollah Khomeini, who promised a more independent and powerful future for Iran. For some Iranians, the revolution was at its core about Islamic ideology, but many secular nationalists were drawn to the symbols of Khomeini and the revolution because of the promise of political power to produce positive change.

For these folks, the Islamic revolution was built atop a history of power deprivation. Iranians were hungry for striking a path independent of outside powers and for ridding themselves of leaders who did their bidding. They were hungry to reverse the historical record set with the American and British assisted 1953 overthrow of Mossadegh and were still seething with grievances about foreign governments undermining their nationalistic and democratic aspirations. They were also rejecting what they saw as the excesses of the shah and the lack of democratic norms and institutions in their country.

Record low turnout numbers during recent presidential elections in Iran suggest that the Islamic fervor that ignited a revolution over four decades ago has been mostly extinguished. Also, the brutal suppression of protests by the Iranian regime and overall repressive policies related to Islamic dress have weakened the legitimacy of the regime. It is questionable whether the symbols of the Islamic revolution will animate Iranians going forward. It will be up to future Iranian leaders to decide how to handle the dialectic of Islamic and nationalist strands of Iranian identity that have been such a part of Iranian history.

Iran's Role

Another piece of the puzzle of self-perception is how Iran identifies its role within the regional and international systems.[12] Does Iran see itself playing a regional stewardship role, a hegemonic role, or spoiler role? Because Iran sees the United States as both a global and regional actor, there is a complexity to how it sees its own role within that context.

It is hard to get a clear delineation of how Iranian leaders see their country's role in the Middle East and beyond. Iran has seen itself as part of a "resistance front" to blunt US penetration in the region, consisting of Syria, Hamas, Hezbollah, the Houthis, and its militia network in Iraq. Also, it sees itself as the one truly independent actor in the region, unlike Saudi Arabia, the UAE, and Israel, which to a large degree it sees as proxies of the United States.[13]

Iranian leaders toggle back and forth between talk of Iran as a disrupter and Iran as a stabilizer. They have been vocal about what they see as the need for Iran to disrupt US allies in the region through its resistance front. But in addition to seeing itself as part of a resistance front, it also sees itself as a regional leader, willing to collaborate and cooperate with other regional powers toward stability when necessary to serve Iran's national interests. Iranian President Masoud Pezeshkian said the following to the United Nations General Assembly on September 24, 2024, which was reiterated the following day in greater detail in meetings I had with him:

... the new regional order must be inclusive and beneficial for all neighbors. An order that fails to safeguard the interests of each neighboring country cannot be sustained ... Our region suffers from war, sectarian tensions, terrorism and extremism, drug trafficking, water scarcity, refugee crises, environmental degradation and foreign interventions. We can collectively address these common challenges for a better future for coming generations.[14]

There is an additional paradox that appears when analyzing the mindset prevalent among Iranian leaders. They pride themselves in being the only power in the Middle East willing to defy the United States and its allies. But they also see Iran as a middle, regional power amid several intervening great powers, fully aware of the limitations of defying the interests of a greater power like the United States.

In some ways, Iran has convinced itself that it has found a way out of this paradox with the Ukraine war and what its leaders perceive to be a more symmetric relationship with Russia. Since the war and improved relations with China, Iran increasingly sees itself as part of an emerging eastern order that can defy the United States on a global scale. Iranian leaders tend to increasingly see their regional defiance of the United States as linking up with a broader trend of an emerging eastern-dominated international order. In headier moments, these leaders see Iran as part of an eastern phalanx, which with the heavyweights of Russia and China, can act as a counterbalance to US power.[15] The belief is that Iran could tether its regional resistance strategy to Russia and China's global resistance against American attempts to impose on the Middle East a new Pax Americana.

In some ways, migration from the 1979 revolutionary worldview of opposing all global powers to today sidling up to Russia and China is quite remarkable. In the immediate aftermath of the revolution, there was the view that Iran needed to resist the efforts of both Cold War era superpowers, for fear they could collaborate with each other against Iran. This fear was borne out during the Iran-Iraq war when both the United States and Soviet Union tilted toward Iraq. But after the Cold War, the focus of perceived threat was singularly on the United States, which then ran unopposed in the Middle East. The end of the Cold War was a strategic mixed bag for Iran, with the US unbridled yet also feckless. While this unipolar moment was initially daunting to the Iranians, they started to observe that without the Soviet threat, the United States had become purposeless and rudderless. This observation of a lumbering United States coupled with Iran's relationship with a rising China, created a belief that Iran could play a strong regional and even global role.

If Iran's perceived role is dependent on tethering itself to the efforts by Russia and China to resist the United States, there are some perils in that strategy. This is particularly the case since Iran's militias have wreaked havoc on regional stability, and direct back-and-forth military attacks between Israel and Iran in 2024 risk a broader regional war. If Iran is seen by Russia and China as a regional wildcard that stokes instability and threatens their commercial interests, then Iran may be disappointed by the tentativeness of their support. This has already started to happen. Russia and China remained mum after the October 26, 2024 attack on Iran by Israel, something that greatly distressed the Iranians.[16]

What does the risk with respect to Russia and China mean in terms of how Iran will see its role going forward? Will it see its role to be more of a disrupter or preserver of stability in the region? Clearly, Iran wants to disrupt a US-dominated status quo in the region without completely destabilizing the region in the process. This seems to have injected Iran with some caution when it comes to actions that might drag it into a major regional war. We clearly see the disrupter/spoiler role in how Iran has supported Hamas and Hezbollah against what it sees as a US and Israeli system. But we also need to understand that there are limits to how far Iran wants to go in completely disrupting the Middle East. Iranian leaders point to evidence of having played a regulatory, stabilizing role in the Middle East in recent years. They point to successful campaigns to prevent ISIS from overtaking Baghdad, and prior to the collapse of the Syrian government of President Bashar al-Assad in 2024 the Iranians ballyhooed their stabilization efforts in that country. They also describe Iran's rapprochement with Saudi Arabia in regional stability terms. And it appears that in the early days after the 2023 Hamas attacks on Israel, Iran counseled Hezbollah to limit its attacks on Israel to those that wouldn't spark a wider war. Going forward, the risks of supporting disruptive actors like Hezbollah and Hamas might increase due to changing American and Israeli red lines, and to constraints imposed on Iran by Russia and China. Whether Iran tacks hard in the direction of stabilizing diplomacy with Saudi Arabia, and possibly even with the United States and Europe, or hunkers down further in its role as spoiler depends on events in the region, and the makeup of Iranian leadership going forward.

How Iran Sees Its Strategy

There is an understandable skepticism in the west and the region about Iran's characterization of its strategic doctrine of forward defense. Speaking with Saudis and Emirati elites on many occasions revealed a view of Iran's strategic pronouncements as window dressing for its true hegemonic and aggressive ambitions.[17] Moreover, the October 7, 2023 attacks on Israel by Hamas rendered the claim that Iran's network of militias is defensive in nature disingenuous and laughable. Even though there is no evidence linking Iran directly to the attacks, Tehran's rhetorical support for Hamas, Hezbollah, and the Houthis in the aftermath of the attacks strips the façade off the Iranian claim of defense.

But whether we trust or distrust the sincerity of Iran's pronouncements about its strategies, it is important to look at how its leaders justify and explain their foreign policy decisions. Even if others see these claims as disingenuous and a veil for naked aggression, discussions with Iranian officials over the past several years, both during the Rouhani era and later with the late President Raisi and current President Pezeshkian, indicate that they have internalized their own rhetoric and are committed to the soundness of their justifications.

Iranian officials don't deny they have ambitions for greater regional influence. But at the same time, they see their country's current foreign policy as necessary to cope with what they see as intentions by the United States and Israel to subjugate Iran and even topple the regime. They see and justify their strategies as necessary to attaining strategic depth in their neighborhood, against what they see as the aggressive intentions of the United States and its allies.

This puts the regime in a quandary when faced with the prospects for engagement between the US and Iran. For many hardliners in Tehran, the political and strategic risks of rapprochement are greater than the rewards. For hardliners in the Iranian government, maintaining a hostile stance toward Washington made it easier to defend their regional activities in Lebanon, Syria, Iraq, and Yemen as defensive in nature and necessary for deterrence. For them, an open and outstretched hand from Washington translates into greater difficulty in justifying on purely defensive and existential grounds Iran's involvement with militias. In other words, a hostile America lends a geopolitical context and logical consistency to Iran's regional policies that otherwise might ring hollow. Without the external threat, Iran would have a more difficult time justifying its foreign policy priorities to itself, its population, and to the world.

In discussions with Iranians close to the regime in 2022, I learned of efforts by the United States to attenuate Iran's ties to the countries that are part of its "axis of resistance" network and where it has militias. They described the United States blocking attempts by Iran to create constructive ties with its Arab neighbors.[18] For example, they blame the United States for delays in the still unfinished strategic rail links between the Iranian city of Shalamcheh and the Iraqi city of Basra.[19] The effort is being paid for by the Iranians to improve trade ties between Iran and Iraq.

There have been debates within the Iranian government about the efficacy and wisdom of engaging with the United States. Since the Trump administration's unilateral withdrawal from the nuclear deal in 2018, the debates have narrowed, with the closing of ranks between those who previously favored engagement and those who took a hard-line approach. Even some reform-minded leaders painted engagement with the west as a dead-end after the United States walked out of the JCPOA nuclear deal.[20] I saw this firsthand with former Foreign Minister Javad Zarif, who had been the lead Iranian negotiator of the JCPOA. By 2019, one year following the US withdrawal from the deal, his position had hardened and very much resembled that of the hardliners, led at the time by Major General Qassim Soleimani, head of the Quds Force.

What we saw in the wake of Trump's peremptory withdrawal from the nuclear deal was a shift in strategic thinking. The emergent thinking was as follows: if the strategic calculus of the United States can't be changed through negotiation, then Iran will focus instead on changing the strategic calculus of its Middle East allies. In other words, if diplomacy with the United States isn't a reliable path, then the emphasis will shift to disrupting Washington's bonds with its regional allies. The knock-on effect of this would be to compromise the gravitational pull of the United States in the region.

This strategic approach started gaining legs the year after the US withdrawal from the nuclear deal. Iranian leaders were emboldened by the success they believe they had in demonstrating to Saudi Arabia and the UAE that the United States was an unreliable ally, thereby giving these US allies an incentive to pursue engagement rather than conflict with Iran. The goal was to convince these Gulf Arab states to rely less for security on the United States and more on diplomacy with Iran.

The first shot across the bow came with drone attacks on Saudi Aramco facilities at Abqaiq in 2019. Then came attacks on shipping in the Persian Gulf in 2020–21, with the objective of demonstrating to the Gulf Arab states that the US wouldn't act to defend them, and that the only reasonable path forward was to pursue diplomacy with Iran. It was in the aftermath of these and other attacks in the straits of Hormuz that Riyadh became more serious about seeking better relations with Iran. This strategy culminated with the rapprochement between Iran and Saudi Arabia in March of 2023, brokered by China. While Iran saw the impossibility of prompting a US withdrawal from the region, its leaders believed that their strategy of attenuating the ties between Washington and Riyadh worked.

The other piece of the Iranian strategy was to link these Gulf activities to a broader global strategy of pivoting to the east. Iranians understand that they alone can't attenuate the ties between the Gulf Arab states and the United States. It is no coincidence, then, that after several years of the Iranians negotiating with the Saudis in Iraq and Oman, it was China that helped broker the final agreement in March 2023. In other words, Iran leveraged China's diplomatic heft to provide further octane to its own efforts.

This accomplished several things for the Iranians. The first was a demonstration to the United States that its efforts to use the Gulf Arab states as a cudgel against Iran would backfire, bringing the Saudis closer to rather than farther from Iran. The second accomplishment was to show the United States that Iran had diplomatic options, despite the maximum pressure campaign of the United States to isolate it. The late President Ibrahim Raisi told me directly in 2022 that the maximum pressure campaign had left Iran few options other than pursuing diplomacy with China to normalize relations with Saudi Arabia.[21] And third it was to give Beijing a win against Washington, demonstrating that it too could play a significant diplomatic role in the Middle East.

The piece of the puzzle we can't see is how Iran will weigh its relations with Saudi Arabia in the wake of the events of October 7, 2023. Will it follow the logic of trying to use diplomacy with Riyadh to pull it further away from the United States orbit? Or, instead, will it double down on its tried-and-true strategy of leaning on its militias? If it follows the diplomatic logic, then its relationship with Saudi Arabia could become an important hedge against an increasingly hostile Israel or Washington. The thinking would be that if Saudi-Iranian relations are constructive, Riyadh will be less likely than before to push Washington toward a more aggressive posture toward Iran. Given that Iran's strategic objective was to divide Riyadh from Washington, it seems that Iran, particularly with the re-election of Donald Trump as president in 2024, won't want to lose the advantage it believes it gained by now jettisoning or jeopardizing this relationship.[22]

But how this plays out depends also on how Iran's battle with Israel unfolds. It is hard to imagine Iran yielding on its anti-Israeli stance for practical and ideological reasons. But its entire charm offensive with Saudi Arabia, and even its relationship with China, could be jeopardized by all-out war with Israel. A war could devastate all diplomatic initiatives and make it difficult for Iran to balance its diplomatic initiatives with its continued support for its militias. The attacks on Beirut that killed Hezbollah commander Fuad Shukr and Hezbollah head Hassan Nasrallah, the killing in Tehran of Hamas head Ismail Haniyeh in July 2024 and then Yahya al-Sinwar in Gaza in October 2024 don't augur well for avoiding further battles between Iran and Israel.

In the coming years, we will see what transpires with the recently elected President Masoud Pezeshkian, and whether the debate within the Iranian government about engagement with the United States widens or narrows further.

Conclusion

How Iran sees itself is as important as how it views the regional and global environments. As much as Iran has shown flexibility in how it has adapted to its global and regional milieus, in some ways it seems stuck in a view of itself from the past. Whether Iran can adjust its self-view to future exigencies will determine whether Iran and its people can thrive.

The way Iran sees its interests today in many ways is consistent with the geopolitical realities it has faced. Iran has been invaded, controlled, and influenced by outside powers for centuries. While the way in which the current regime defines its interests is a product of the revolution, it is also a product of the stubborn geopolitical realities of the past.

Intertwined with how Iran sees its interests is how it self-identifies. On the one hand, Iran has the confidence of a power with an ancient and powerful past, but also the fragility of a country which has been under the thumb of countries more powerful than itself. This duality is the prism through which Iran also sees its role and its strategy. Iranian leaders try to punch above their weight by taking advantage of regional vacuums and international opportunities. It views its strategy as more about playing on the weaknesses and missteps of others than about leveraging its resources. While it currently is disadvantaged when it comes to competing in a conventional manner with regional and global actors, it has figured out a way to protect its security interests using non-conventional means.

Whether these views will adapt to changes in the environment in a post-October 7, 2023 set of realities that include diminution in the power of Hamas and Hezbollah, and the toppling of Assad in Syria, will be a test of Iran's strategic maneuverability and its ability to accurately assess its capability and strategy.

5 ASSESSING IRAN'S CAPABILITY

Strategy is about improving the probability of success, nothing more. There is no guarantee that even a well-conceived strategy will work. There are too many variables at play for any strategy to be a sure thing success. One definite path to failure, however, is to launch a strategy underpowered, with scant regard for the requisite capabilities.

According to the venerable military historian Richard Betts:

> Strategy is most important when it provides value-added to resources, functions as a force multiplier, and offers a way to beat an adversary ...[1]

What Betts is essentially referring to by "value-added" and "force multiplier" is capability. He is implying a lesson that is oft forgotten: not to conflate and forget the distinction between inert resources and more muscular capability. Resources are generally tangible, like military or economic assets, while capability is more intangible, like a deterrent or retaliatory capability. Assets are the more inert raw material that go to make up a more muscular capability.[2] Developing capabilities involves marshalling resources toward generating the muscle a country needs to power its foreign policy strategy.[3]

According to the late French Army officer and strategist Andre Beaufre:

> Strategy is not like chess; its pieces have no permanent, defined value. It must therefore produce its solutions by a sort of cookery, fusing constantly changing ingredients.[4]

What Beaufre means by "cookery" is the process by which assets are combined and put into the service of more muscular capabilities. The complexity of strategy at the country level is that it entails stringing multiple capabilities together to serve a coherent strategy.

Historically there has been a mismatch between Iran's ambitions and its capabilities. Outside powers have for centuries put a crimp on Iran's capacity to realize its aspirations. In 1911, Morgan Shuster, an American lawyer, became the Treasury-General of Iran, with the idea of building up Iran's financial capability to give it the muscle and coherence for dealing with its external challengers, which at the time were Great Britain and Russia. These two dominant powers sometimes competed, but they also often collaborated to subjugate Iran to their purposes. The most egregious example came when they conspired to overturn the gains of Iranian nationalists made during the 1906 Constitutional Revolution.[5] Shuster, incensed by what he saw as these abuses, tried to frustrate the efforts of these two great powers by verbally opposing them, but more importantly by trying to modernize and turn around Iran's flagging public finance system and by extension its overall economy. What Shuster was attempting to do was give Iran a muscular economic capability that could be used to create greater independence from Britain and Russia. Unfortunately, the efforts of these two powers were more successful than Shuster's, ultimately denying Iran this critical capability.

Ayatollah Khomeini didn't see economic vitality as the key capability needed for Iran to become truly independent of great powers. In fact, in his mindset economic development had only made Iran more, not less, dependent on the United States. Rather, he believed that fervent adherence to Islam provided the key for unlocking the capability and power of the Iranian people. For Khomeini, Islam maximized the extractive capabilities of the state to demand from and marshal the strength of the Iranian people.[6] His belief also was that it was western ideals and values during the shah's era, plus the active interference by the United States, which detracted from Iran's capacity to be truly independent.

In the present day, creating a system of mutually reinforcing and interlocking capabilities is a critically important element of Iran's foreign policy, arguably the most important. Given Iran's history of interventions by outside powers, creating a network of interlocking capabilities that can protect the homeland, and the regime, is a stated priority. Over time, Iran has become less reliant on the extractive capabilities of Islam that Khomeini had tapped into and more on the geopolitical leverage it garners through its network of militias, like Hezbollah, Hamas, and the Houthis.

If strategy is about tailoring a country's capabilities to its challenges, does Iran's capacity to activate its militia network across the region match Iran's geopolitical challenges? While Iran's network of Hamas, Palestine Islamic Jihad (PIJ), the Houthis, Hezbollah, and militias in Iraq and Syria seems to serve it well today, is this a capability that can carry the aspirations and interests of the Iranian people or even the state forward in the future?

There are a couple of considerations here. One is the state of the region going forward. With the events that took place in 2023 and 2024 between Israel and Hamas in Gaza, Israel and Hezbollah, and Israel and Iran directly, it is unlikely that the region will stabilize in the foreseeable future. This means that Iran will likely be able to leverage its capability of operating with its militias in the failed states of the region for some time to come. Of course, with both Hamas and Hezbollah weakened by Israeli attacks, and Assad having fallen in Syria, Iran will have to do an assessment of how Israel's actions and events in Syria have compromised Iran's capability vis-à-vis the militias. And it will have to decide whether to double down on its militia strategy or recalibrate its foreign policy toward more conventional diplomatic means. This gets at a broader question of whether Iran's system of capabilities positions it well toward the future in a changing region? This latter question is particularly important to answering whether Iran has an interest in perpetuating the status quo, or whether its capabilities can be transformed to adapt to a modernizing region?[7]

But should the region stabilize at some point in the future, Iran may be less able to rely on its militia capability and need to lean on the economic, military, and diplomatic capabilities of a more conventional state. Moreover, there are signs that Iran's foreign policy adventures aren't supported by many Iranians, who through protests have asked why their government is supporting adventurist activities outside the country at a time when the economy is in freefall and the domestic needs are so pressing.[8]

Assessing whether Iran's capabilities match its strategic requirements requires that we go a bit deeper by scrutinizing its current array of capabilities, looking for signs of gaps. John Lewis Gaddis said that strategy involves marrying theoretically unlimited goals with more stubbornly finite means:

> Because ends exist only in the imagination, they can be infinite: a throne on the moon, perhaps, with a great view. Means though are

stubbornly finite: they're boots on the ground, ships in the sea, and the bodies required to fill them. Ends and means have to connect if anything is to happen.[9]

In terms of connecting Iran's ends and means, by which Gaddis means goals and capabilities, respectively, there are two significant considerations. One is identifying Iran's current capabilities, and the other is ascertaining how these key capabilities interact strategically with one another. For example, Iran's hybrid and more conventional military capabilities work together to give Iran competitive advantages within weak states like Syria, Yemen, Lebanon, and Iraq. While they don't translate into broader competitive advantages against strong states, such as Saudi Arabia, they do give Iran the ability to block these states from establishing beachheads in the weak states, giving Iran a perception of regional dominance.

Part of the story of Iran's strategic capabilities is that their creation has evolved over time. Iran made investments in capabilities in the early days of the revolution, which only bore fruit much later. The Quds Force, formed in the wake of the Iran-Iraq war in 1988, really became a core part of Iran's regional capability after the US invasion of Iraq in 2003. Another asset was Hezbollah, which was established in Lebanon in 1982, but really was deployed on a large scale when civil war broke out in Syria, Yemen, and Iraq.[10]

Another question is which of Iran's capabilities serves as a linchpin or keystone, that if absent, neutralizes the power of all the other capabilities. The traditional way of thinking about Iran's capability is that the linchpin is its hybrid, asymmetric capability. While Iran may currently differentiate itself from its rivals with this hybrid capability, we should be cautious about assuming this will hold in the future. Iran's system of capabilities is complementary today, but as conditions change this could too. Which of these capabilities could become a linchpin later is unclear and dependent on how the regional environment evolves.

The argument made in this chapter is that while Iran's capabilities are used to project power in the region, strategically they are built to give it a defensive crouch. While these capabilities, particularly Iran's militia network, have allowed it to use offensive tactics, strategically they have mostly given Iran the capacity to defend, adapt, and maintain the status quo. And, more critically, they have given Iran the capacity to block other contenders from creating sustainable inroads into Syria, Lebanon, and Iraq. But it is questionable as to whether these capabilities can be adapted to forge a more competitive position for Iran in the region, particularly on the economic front. Iran's current repertoire of capabilities isn't increasing Iran's competitiveness in an increasingly interconnected world or meeting the growing needs of the Iranian people. We will examine the different capabilities in some depth, asking questions about how they interact and whether they give Iran a sustainable competitive advantage going forward.

Iran's Soft Power

Most analyses of Iran's power projection into the region focus on Iran's hard power, that is its military and paramilitary capabilities. These analyses provide comparative estimates of how Iran's hard power capabilities compare to its Gulf Arab rivals. Included are missile arsenals, including their throw-weights, size of both Iran's army (Artesh) and its Revolutionary Guards forces, and budget allocations to Iran's conventional and unconventional military capabilities.[11]

But it is also important to understand Iran's non-security capabilities, such as soft power. Soft power encompasses the brand, values, and communication approaches the country uses to complement its hard power. It also includes measures taken to create cultural and social bonds within another country.[12] For Iran, this means the capacity to embed itself into the social, political, and cultural fabrics of Syria, Lebanon, and Iraq.

There have been serious questions raised about the efficacy of Iran's soft power campaigns in Syria, Lebanon, and Iraq. Protests in 2019 in Lebanon and Iraq point to an attenuation of Iran's soft power appeal in these countries.[13] The striking thing about the protests in Iraq was that they were predominantly located in the Shi'i strongholds of the southern part of the country. In Lebanon, the protests of 2019 and 2021 were against Hezbollah and Iran as its benefactor, expressing disgruntlement about the lack of governance and Hezbollah's role in the Syrian civil war.[14]

There was a time when Iran's star shone brighter in Lebanon. After its 2006 war with Israel, Hezbollah took on the task of rebuilding hard-hit areas of Lebanon. The belief was that Iran helped with the funding of these reconstruction efforts.[15] But there are also limitations to the receptivity of Lebanese citizens to Iranian influence in the country. The specific grievances of the Lebanese were related to the ineffectuality of the Lebanese government, something that many blamed on Hezbollah and by extension on Iran, even on bread-and-butter issues.[16] While Hezbollah had never directly run the government, the fact that it was the principal powerbroker in the country meant it was saddled to some degree with the ineptitude of the government.[17] This, plus the view that Hezbollah and Iran backed the Assad government in Syria until it fell in 2024 also tarnished the reputation of both in Lebanon.

Iraq, too, should be fertile ground for Iranian soft power. The Shi'i sectarian connections, particularly in the southern part of Iraq, are strong in the holy cities of Karbala and Najaf. Also, the political connections at the highest levels of government are strong, not to mention the role Iran and its related militias played in liberating the country from ISIS between 2014 and 2017.

But there has been resentment over Iran's heavy-handedness on issues such as economics and water. Diversion of waters away from Iraq created resentment. There was also resentment over Iran's undercutting the price of local Iraqi agriculture in the southern Shi'i areas of the country, particularly in Basra. Iranians purportedly dumped agricultural staples such as tomatoes into Iraq at a fraction of local market pricing, to raise cash for circumventing American sanctions.[18] Perceptions that Iran gouged Iraqis on gas prices, when they could have bought cheaper gas from the Qataris, also contributed to the erosion of support.

In other words, Iran's use of Iraq as an economic escape hatch for circumventing sanctions hurt Iran's brand and soft power in the Shi'i areas where support would expectedly be strongest. While perhaps Tehran believed that much cheaper agriculture would be welcomed by the Shi'i populace in southern Iraq, it led to resentment among farmers and became a symbol of both Iraqi government ineffectiveness and Iranian heavy-handedness.[19] This culminated in protests and the sacking of the Iranian Consulate in Najaf in 2019.[20]

There has also been pushback against Iran casting a long shadow on Iraq, with perceived overreach by Iran striking at the Arab and Iraqi nationalist sensibilities in the country.[21] The perception that Iran has backed a corrupt state apparatus since the Americans invaded in 2003 has contributed to the erosion of Iran's soft power. The fact that Iran advised the Iraqi government on how to suppress the protesters in 2020 hasn't been forgotten by Iraqis. This, plus the securitization of Iran's presence in Iraq, relying on the militias at the expense of the political system, started to tarnish the image of Iran among Iraqis.

In interviewing both Iranian and Iraqi officials, there seems to be a couple of insights into Iranian thinking about this. It seems that Iranians calculated that cross-border Shi'i unity with Iran would be stronger than Iraqi or even Arab nationalism. Given this presumption, the protests in Shi'i areas shook the Iranians. But they were confident that this could be overcome, with a strategy of receding more into the shadowy background in Iraqi intragovernmental decision-making. They said that this new approach contrasted with the more conspicuous and heavy-handed methods used earlier by the late Major General Qassim Soleimani. But there seems to be no shift in the overall strategy. While Iran may be working more behind the scenes than before, its leaders are confident that their capability to assert influence in Iraq is unshaken. Even the Iraqis concede that it would be very difficult to dislodge the Iranians, given how many tentacles they have in the political, social, security, and economic systems of the country.[22]

Competition from Saudi Arabia could add to the image problems of Iran in Iraq. The Saudis, who had written off Iraq as an Iranian satrapy under King Abdullah, started to recognize under King Salman bin Abdulaziz Al Saud in 2016 that this approach may have pushed Iraq into Iran's corner. Over the past several years, Riyadh has tried to rehabilitate Iraq into the Arab state system. Should Saudi investment plans materialize, this could create a contrast between the soft power image of the Saudis and the more heavy-handed image of Iran.

The re-establishment of diplomatic relations between Iran and Saudi Arabia in 2023 could make the Arab reintegration of Iraq even more viable. But there is very little evidence that Saudi efforts have developed significant traction, and complete reintegration is unlikely.[23] But there are signs of Gulf Arab investment in Iraq, particularly in the real estate markets.[24] And in the long term, if there is already a residual and growing resentment against Iran, then these Saudi efforts could play to Arab or Iraqi sentiment, which in turn could disadvantage Iran.

Given that Syria has been in some stage of civil war for more than a decade, we have little access to polling data as to public sentiments about Iran. We do know that Iran has been instrumental in renovating revered Shi'i shrines, such as Sayyida Zaynab and Sayyida Ruqayya, but it isn't clear that this has really increased support for Iran among the Syrian populace.[25] Iran has supported schools and hospitals, which has generated some conversions to Shi'i Islam by grateful recipients and supplicants. There have also been significant investments in the billions of dollars from Iran in the energy, agricultural, and communication sectors, which creates commercial ties between the countries.[26] But beyond anecdotal evidence, the soft power progress in terms of shaping the hearts and minds of Syrians is doubtful.[27] Some of this is because a Syrian Arab identity militates against a strong identification with Iran. But also, the support base in Syria for Iran would be necessarily narrow given Tehran's support for a widely unpopular leader, President Bashar al-Assad, and his regime, up until the time it collapsed in 2024 and he fled to Moscow.

One question is whether Iran's carrying of the flag for the Palestinians will redound to its soft power? Adoption of the Palestinian cause extends back to the early days of the Iranian revolution, beginning with Yasir Arafat's trip to Iran and support received from Ayatollah Khomeini.[28] Part of Khomeini's thinking was that support for the Palestinians would delegitimize the more conservative Arab states and position Iran as a revolutionary force in the region.[29]

The Palestinian issue for Iran is not driven by sectarian preferences, given that Hamas and Palestine Islamic Jihad (PIJ) are predominantly Sunni. Rather it is driven by Iran's imperative of positioning itself at the head of a resistance front against a US-Israeli phalanx. One way this has been described is "talking over the heads" of Sunni leaders in the Arab world.[30] It was aimed at Arab populations, demonstrating to them that Iran is the only real standard-bearer for the Palestinian cause. We saw this in the aftermath of the attacks by Hamas on Israel on October 7, 2023, when many Iran-backed groups activated in support of the Palestinian cause. This contrasted with several of the Arab countries which were willing to normalize relations with Israel prior to October 7 without consideration for the Palestinians. Several studies show that the impressions of Iran became more positive in the Arab world in the immediate aftermath of October 7 and those of the UAE, a country that normalized relations with Israel, declined.[31]

The problem is that this image of Iran as a revolutionary state that champions just causes could attenuate over time. The tricky part will be whether Iran will act as a spoiler in possible progress toward a two-state solution. Or will it play a more positive and constructive role? If serious movement toward two states emerges, Iran will have to carefully navigate this issue. In other words, if there is a serious diplomatic track between Israel and the Palestinians, Iran could risk its soft power image should it be an impediment toward progress and an end to Palestinian suffering. But in the absence of diplomatic progress between Israel and the

Palestinians, Iran could remain opposed in theory to any conciliation with Israel while burnishing its image in the Arab world.

Iran uses a wide range of institutions and programs that push Iranian soft power across the region and beyond. Some of these focus on specific audiences in Lebanon, Iraq, and Syria, while others are aimed at the Arab world writ large. The Islamic Republic of Iran Broadcasting (IRIB) disseminates throughout the region messages tailored for each target country and community. Programs like "Al Alam" purport to compete with Al-Jazeera. And there are also TV programs tailored to western audiences.[32] Together, these represent attempts to use revolutionary ideology to connect different audiences to causes in the region.

Moreover, the Islamic Culture and Relations Organization (ICRO) has programs that are organized by the cultural attachés in each of the Iranian diplomatic missions abroad to promote understanding and goodwill in the host countries.[33] As part of this, Al-Mustafa International University has programs globally that propagate Islamic values. Based in the Iranian holy city of Qom, it has affiliates across the globe pushing an Islamic agenda.[34]

One of the issues for Iran on all these efforts will be the loss of support at home for its government. In the absence of support at home, the sustainability of Iran's soft power outside the country is suspect.[35] Soft power involves attraction rather than coercion. With protests at home and heavy-handedness abroad, the effectiveness and legitimacy of Iran's communication message can suffer over time.[36] In other words, a loss of legitimacy at home can lead to a soft power erosion in the region. How Iran manages this in the future will determine the sustainability of the efforts outlined in this chapter.

Iran's National Will

In the lead-up to the Iranian revolution of 1979, secular women who otherwise would have shunned wearing the chador worn traditionally by pious Muslim women donned it in support of what they thought would be a nationalist revolution. This same piety in the service of the nation materialized during the Iran-Iraq war, when young boys holding "keys to paradise" ran over the minefields laid by the Iraqis in an almost guaranteed suicide mission. The war commenced with a land attack by Iraq on Iran. When the Iranians gained the offensive in 1982, most of the world tilted toward Iraq, but the nation was nonetheless galvanized and at least momentarily unified. This is not to suggest there was complete unanimity about the war. The Mujahedin-e Khalq (MEK), which supported the revolution, sided with Iraqi President Saddam Hussein during the war.[37] But the war did tap into both Islamist and nationalist passions across a wide swath of Iranian society.

Tensions between Islamists and nationalists appeared early in the revolution with the purging of the nationalists and the imposition of strict requirements of Islamic dress. But the inflection point, where the regime's legitimacy became challenged and popular support waned, was the 2009 presidential election. At the end of the first term of President Mahmoud Ahmadinejad, elections were widely believed to have secured a victory for Mir Hussein Moussavi, a reformist politician. But the regime, nonetheless, asserted that Ahmadinejad had won, a claim supported by Supreme Leader Ali Khamenei. Demonstrations erupted throughout Iran, with the charge that the regime had stolen the election from the people. These mass protests were brutally suppressed.

Since then, we have seen protests taking aim at the legitimacy of the regime, the Supreme Leader himself, and the foreign policy agenda, particularly its involvement in Syria.[38] What was surprising was that these revolts were not just among the privileged elite in Tehran but among the base of core supporters of the regime. Also, the gasoline protests of 2019 are telling about the sensitivity of Iranians to economic privations, such as price increases and the removal of government subsidies.[39] Aside from the charge of stolen elections, economic issues also tore at the legitimacy of the regime.

The culmination of this breach in popular support were the protests after the brutalized death of Mahsa Amini in September of 2022 over her hijab being askew. While the protests have died down after months of ruthless suppression, popular support for the regime seems at an all-time low. Another indication even before the death of Mahsa Amini was the historically low turnout for the presidential elections of 2021, which delivered the late President Raisi, a hardliner, to the country. The parliamentary elections in 2024 also showed very low voter turnouts, a further indication of apathy or even antipathy toward the regime. The snap presidential election after President Raisi's death also revealed voter apathy, though the second round of voting that brought Masoud Pezeshkian to the presidency showed slightly higher numbers.

From a foreign policy capability perspective, it is unclear whether the regime has a strong reservoir of support among the people to draw upon for foreign adventures. Of course, if the country comes under sustained attack by Israel or the United States, the regime will likely be able to tap into the patriotism of the country to marshal a defense. But short of that it appears that the support Iran can garner from the population has waned somewhat. Unless the government can figure a way out of the current economic malaise, which has its roots in sanctions imposed by the United States and internal corruption, it is unlikely that Iran's foreign policy adventures will generate much popular support.

Iran's Militia Capability

Iran has a competitive disadvantage compared to its primary adversaries in the Middle East. Washington has allies such as Saudi Arabia, Qatar, the UAE, Egypt, and Israel, all of which have well-developed and modern military capabilities. Iran's only state ally in the region was Syria, a shell of a country embattled by war and heavily dependent on Tehran up until the time the Assad regime fell in 2024. Moreover, Iran spends about $24 billion on military defense while US-aligned Gulf Cooperation Council (GCC) states spend close to $80 billion.[40] This doesn't consider the fact that the equipment supplied to US allies is superior technologically and in terms of interoperability to anything Iran has access to.

Iran's signature capabilities have been in the unconventional sphere with its network of militias. We saw in the aftermath of October 7, 2023 the ability for Iran to coordinate operations across its entire militia network. The vivid demonstration on April 13, 2024, of Iran's ability to choreograph missile and drone attacks on Israel from multiple geographic locations was a surprise to many western analysts.[41] The surprise wasn't the attack itself, as Iran had uncharacteristically telegraphed its intentions far in advance; rather, it was the capability to coordinate the attacks among its various militias.

But Iran's much-vaunted militia capability is heavily a product of the regional dysfunction plaguing the Middle East today. The region today is a weak state system, with several countries burdened by unresolved civil wars, namely Syria, Yemen, and Libya, and other states which are fragile, such as Lebanon and Iraq. In each of these countries, Iran has alliances with substate actors, such as Hezbollah in Lebanon and Syria, Hashd al-Sha'bi in

Iraq, and the Houthis in Yemen. These alliances enable Iran to project power into the civil war zones, something that countries allied with the United States don't have to the same degree and effect.

The question is what is the durability of this capability? Even though the alliances may endure, if the region should ever return to a stronger state system, will Iran have the same competitive advantage it now enjoys? Or, will the basis of competition change in a way that renders this core part of Iran's capability ineffective?

Unless Iran has the capacity to balance these asymmetric means with other strategic advantages, it may have a competitive problem in generating power. There are several risk factors that could water down the efficacy of Iran's militia capability. One is if existing regional security arrangements become arrayed against Iran. For instance, if the Abraham Accords, which formalized relations between Israel, the United Arab Emirates (UAE), and Bahrain, and later Morocco and Sudan, expands to include Saudi Arabia, this could provide a counterpunch to Iran's militia network. It wouldn't challenge the network itself, but it could render the deterrence it provides to Iran less effective by challenging it with a more unified US-backed phalanx of Arab countries and Israel. This could become even a higher risk factor during a second Trump administration, should it have an appetite to further challenge Iran directly and weaponize the Abraham Accords.

It appears that Riyadh will only seriously consider joining the accords if the Israelis commit to, and show evidence of movement toward, a two-state solution for the Palestinians. While the war between Israel and Hamas in Gaza and the recalcitrance of Israel's right-wing government militates against this, if conditions on the ground change, expansion of the Abraham Accords could become a reality. The threat of this becomes amplified should there be further deterioration of Hamas, Hezbollah, or the Houthis at the hands of the Israelis.

A more aggressive Israel believing it has a mandate and capability to once and for all seriously damage or even eliminate the threat from Hamas and Hezbollah would also pose a serious threat to Iran's capability. Because Israel's deterrence failed on October 7, 2023 with Hamas's attacks, there will be a race to re-establish deterrence by setting new red lines.[42] We saw this in the 2024 audacious Israeli attack in Beirut targeting senior Hezbollah commander Fuad Shukr and the assassination of Hamas chiefs Ismail Haniyeh in Tehran and Yahya al-Sinwar in Gaza, as well as the killing of Hezbollah head Hassan Nasrallah in Beirut in 2024. Also, Israel is likely to be emboldened to act against Iranian interests given the collapse of President Assad of Syria. Israel will remain committed to limiting Syria's military capacity and will be vigilant against Iran trying to re-establish its position with a new regime in Damascus.

Another risk factor for Tehran is in the arena of world opinion. Iran had claimed to anyone who would listen that its network of militias was required for deterrence against attacks by Israel or the United States. Iranian leaders were able to make the case that diplomacy with the Arab Gulf states, the United States, and Europe was what they desired, but their strategy of working with militias was one of necessity, as an offensive capability to shore up deterrence. The attacks by Hamas on Israel on October 7, 2023 destroyed the claim that Iran's support for its militias was merely defensive. The attacks tore off the veil of Iran's narrative and made it clear for anyone to see that Iran had aggressive and hostile intentions against Israel. While there is no evidence suggesting that Iran had any foreknowledge of Hamas's plans, its pronouncements supporting Hamas in the aftermath made clear its true intentions.

Given this context, a more aggressive Israel against Iran's militias will continue creating security risks that will need to be managed by Iran. Tehran will have to weigh the risk of an overreliance on its "axis of resistance" going forward. And it will have to figure out how to deal with the blow to the deterrence system it has had with its militias for decades. Will it work hard to resurrect Hezbollah? If it does, the Israelis will most probably try to interdict those efforts. Will Iran make a mad dash to finally assemble a nuclear weapon? Or will it double down on diplomacy?

At the time of writing, it appears that Iran is relying more on its conventional capability to challenge Israel, something that potentially plays to its competitive disadvantage. We have seen the unprecedented direct military attacks both Israel and Iran waged against each other in 2024. This poses a dilemma for Iran. Iran's strategic advantage came from its capacity to fight a shadow war with Israel and the United States using its militias, while at the same time preserving deterrence. But if it chooses or is forced to fight Israel or the United States directly using conventional military means, it will be playing with a much weaker or perhaps even losing hand, given its inferior military capability. And without Hezbollah and Hamas to back it up, Iran will be exposed.

How this plays out will also affect the prospects for Iran pursuing and maintaining regional diplomacy with Saudi Arabia, Turkey, and Egypt, as well as broader diplomacy with the United State and Europe. If there is an escalation in direct fighting between Israel and Iran, it will be hard to sustain any kind of lasting or significant diplomacy at any level. Given the relative silence from Russia and China since Iran's military salvos with Israel, it is likely it will have to navigate the treacherous shoals of these dilemmas alone.

Iran's Conventional Military Capability

Despite the bravado of statements by Iranian leaders, there is general acknowledgement that Iran cannot effectively defend itself against a military attack by the United States and its regional allies. Iran's annual military expenditures of just over $24 billion pale in comparison to the budgets of Saudi Arabia and Israel, which together total over $100 billion. And when compared to the United States, Iran is a regional, middle power. Moreover, Iran's existing military equipment and material isn't as technologically advanced as those of its adversaries due to decades of economic sanctions.

Despite these deficits in being able to repel an attack by the United States and Israel, Iran's military capability is designed to deter such aggression by giving it a retaliatory capability through Iran's proxies and an advanced ballistic missile program. As has been mentioned already, both of these assets have been challenged in 2024 by Israeli missile strikes on sites related to Iran's vaunted missile program as well as by deadly and destructive attacks on Hamas and Hezbollah.

There are several pillars to Iran's overall military capability. The core of Iran's military strategy is the two-headed hydra of Iran's conventional military apparatus, the Artesh, which includes the Army, Navy, and Airforce, and the Islamic Revolutionary Guard Corps (IRGC). While the Artesh is focused mostly on defending Iran's borders, the IRGC's mandate is to create strategic depth by projecting power and influence into neighboring countries, such as Lebanon, Iraq, Syria, and Yemen. The Quds arm of the IRGC is the expeditionary force that interfaces with Iran's militias, such as Hezbollah, Hamas, the Houthis, and Iraqi Hashd al-Sha'bi (Popular Mobilization Forces). Iran has been able to integrate the Artesh and IRGC into a single strategic capability, giving the country the capacity to defend the homeland while also projecting power into the broader region.

Another pillar of Iran's military capability is its personnel. Iran has over 500,000 active-duty troops and about 350,000 reserve troops, one of the largest in the region. The 125,000 troops of the IRGC brings Iran's potential fighting force up to nearly one million. While hobbled by archaic equipment, Iran makes up for this deficit with overwhelming numbers.

Central to Iran's deterrence strategy is its missile program, the most advanced in the Middle East. It includes mostly short- and medium-range ballistic missiles, such as the Shahab-3, Ghadr, and Sejjil missiles, giving Iran the capacity to reach Israel and US bases in the region. Iran's missile program compensates for weaker airpower. The world witnessed in 2024 Iran's capacity to launch missiles with some degree of accuracy at Israel. While Iran's missile program is formidable, the anti-missile defense shields of Israel and the United States reduce the deterrent effect of this.

One of the key elements of Iran's military strategy is its Anti-Access/Area Denial (A2/AD) capacity. Involving mostly Iran's naval forces, the idea is to deny adversaries access to areas of critical strategic concern. Iran's naval swarming capacity is central to this. This gets operationalized mostly in Iran's defense of the Persian Gulf and Strait of Hormuz.

Other critical components of Iran's conventional military capability are its production and use of unmanned aerial vehicles (UAVs) commonly known as drones. These drones have been supplied to Russia for its war in Ukraine and have been used by Iran-backed militias in the Middle East. This gives Tehran some added leverage in its critical relationship with Moscow. Iranian drones were on full display during the Iranian attack on Israel in April of 2024.[43]

There are other capabilities that augment Iran's more conventional capabilities. Its cyber warfare program isn't much publicized by Iranians but is part of an integrated approach to its offensive and defensive missions. The program is known for its skills in espionage, disruption, and propaganda, targeting US and Israeli infrastructure. While Iran's program doesn't yet match US or Israeli capabilities in this area, it is a significant part of Iran's military portfolio. In many ways, this program is a response to earlier cyber efforts by Israel and the United States to target and disrupt Iran's nuclear enrichment program.

In aggregate, Iran's military capabilities have given it an adequate defensive posture, both in terms of protecting the homeland and in terms of being able to project power into the broader region, consistent with Iran's forward defense doctrine. Since Iran can't project sufficient power into the region using conventional means, it has had to rely on its unconventional capabilities of IRGC-supported militias.

What is uncertain is whether with Iran's militias degraded by Israel in 2023 and 2024, it can beef up its conventional capacity sufficiently to compensate. Given that the country is still burdened by sanctions and facing the possibility of a more aggressive US posture under a second term of Donald Trump, it is unlikely that Iran will be able to resurrect its deterrent capacity using conventional means anytime soon, particularly with its likely loss of influence in a post-Assad Syria.

One possibility is that Iran makes a dash to finalize production of a nuclear weapon. It already has sufficient fissile material to do this, though there seems to be still work required to integrate this with Iran's missile program. Debates were taking place in Iran late in 2024 as to whether Iran should develop the weapon and extend its missile range beyond the self-imposed limit of 2000 kilometers.[44] If this happens, Iran's entire defense doctrine and array of capabilities will need to adjust. Of course, these intentions could be undermined by preemptive actions by Israel or the United States.

Iran's Economic Capability

Iran has tremendous economic potential given the education levels and demographic profile of its population. Data for 2023 for average years education of the population shows Iran's at 10.7 years, compared to Turkey's 8.8 years and Egypt's 9.8 years.[45] Iran has a well-trained youth. In 2023, 98% of Iranian youth were literate; in 2020, nearly 58% of Iranian youth were enrolled in tertiary education, and the college enrollment rate for Iranian women is 60.7%, and higher in urban areas. It has a large workforce potential of 69 million people aged 15–64 years.[46] In terms of energy resources in 2023, Iran ranked third in the world in known crude oil reserves and second in the world in known natural gas reserves.[47]

But Iran also faces significant constraints on its growth and development. It has been suffering from poor economic management which has magnified the adverse impact of the trade and financial sanctions imposed by the United States on its economy. Although Iran's economy and exports are more diversified than in some of its Arab counterparts on the southern tiers of the Persian Gulf, it continues to be highly dependent on oil export revenues.[48] And there is endemic chronic corruption. One of the most significant economic constraints comes from the sanctions it has endured since the revolution, but most profoundly since US President Donald Trump withdrew from the JCPOA nuclear deal in 2018 and reimposed old sanctions and levied new ones.

This has put a damper on the economy in several ways. One is in terms of overall performance: high levels of inflation, high unemployment among the youth, low levels of foreign direct investment, and a significant deterioration in standard of living, with nearly 30% of the population being in extreme poverty compared to 20% before the Trump administration imposed the so-called "maximum pressure" sanctions starting in 2018.[49] But also sanctions have distorted the Iranian economy with a high percentage of critical industries having been captured by the Islamic Revolutionary Guards Corps (IRGC). This has led to crony capitalism that benefits a small portion of the elite, with little trickle-down benefits to ordinary citizens. While there are plenty of small companies and industries outside the clutch of the IRGC, several major industries are controlled by the security apparatus of the government.[50]

One of the greatest indications of poor economic performance is the low labor participation rate in the formal economy. In 2023, less than 40% of the working-age population had employment. Men participate at a higher level of 70.6% while women lag at a much lower rate of 14.4%.[51] This is due to inadequate job creation, particularly for more educated men and women, and religiously inspired restrictions on the employment of women. A large percentage of working-age Iranian women remain outside the workforce due to home care responsibilities.[52] As a point of comparison, the overall labor participation rate in the world is 61% and in the United States is over 62.5%.

There are some bright spots in the Iranian economy. Growth in gross domestic product (GDP) was 5% year-over-year in 2023 and is on a positive trajectory, primarily due to increases in oil production and exports from the low levels in 2019–21 due to the US-imposed sanctions. Its growth is also due to the recovery of the services sector from the lows experienced during the Covid-19 pandemic during 2020–22. Oil export sales have increased to nearly 3.9 million barrels per day, a significant increase since the early days of the Trump-era maximum pressure campaign. Actual financial revenues from oil exports have grown more slowly due to volatility in oil prices and heavily discounted prices of petroleum exports to China.[53] As a point of comparison, oil production was at 6 million barrels per day before the Iranian revolution and represented 50% of the Iranian economy versus 22% in 2024.

Iran's non-oil growth has been more anemic, with non-petroleum energy and agriculture showing contraction. Iran's historical dependence on the oil sector and the poor investment climate, which has discouraged domestic and foreign private investment, as well as the capture of key elements of the economy by the Revolutionary Guards, have suppressed growth and limited the degree of economic diversification.

In terms of diversification, while Iran is less reliant on oil production as an overall contributor to the economy, it is more reliant on oil exports because of currency devaluations and the persistence of sanctions. One measure of the problem of diversification is the correlation between the volatility in oil pricing and swings in vibrancy of the Iranian economy. The busts and booms in the oil sector are strongly associated with similar cyclical adjustments in the overall Iranian economy.[54]

Iran has put an emphasis on certain industries that have potential to lead a growth economy if Iran is ever able to operate free of sanctions. Its advances in satellite, drones, rocketry, and nuclear technology show that the country has the talent pool and institutional knowledge to advance under a more competitive economic model.

Another factor affecting Iran's economic potential is regional rivals. Turkey pursued an export-led strategy that contributed to its growth in contrast to Iran's import substitution model, which led to more self-reliance but less growth. But this alone didn't drive Iran's lackluster results. Iran's import substitution approach was forced upon it due to sanctions, rather than representing some principled lurch toward substitution. That having been said, there was a socialist bent to the revolution, which led to the nationalization of key industries and banks and made foreign direct investment something to prevent rather than encourage. While Turkey's exports are mostly industrial goods, Iran's are mostly hydrocarbon related, though Iran is the largest exporter of cheap cars in the Middle East and has started to export military equipment.[55] In sharp contrast to Iran, Saudi Arabia and other Gulf Arab states have growth plans that look to the next decade, with strategies to better diversify their economies and balance trade ties with both eastern and western economies.

Iran has put large stakes in its tilt to Asia. It had high hopes for stronger economic growth due to membership in the Shanghai Cooperation Organization (SCO) and BRICS, but sanctions from the United States have limited the upside growth potential of these memberships for Iran. Iran has stated a desire to grow its economy through relationships with Asia. And in fact, it finds the China model of growth quite attractive. But endemic corruption and the effect of sanctions make full realization of this unlikely, at least in the short to medium term.

The key to Iran's long-term economic prospects is linked to its political decisions relating to foreign policy. Iran has been able to survive economically for the past four decades despite having been sanctioned and engaged in regional conflicts for most of this period. But for Iran to move beyond the current situation economically, it will face the tough question of whether it is willing to make the necessary concessions to wriggle out from under the weight of sanctions. This would require rebalancing its foreign policy away from its "axis of resistance" militias and more toward diplomacy at both the regional and global levels. And it would require dialing back its illogical and self-defeating obsession with Israel. The factor militating against this happening is the distortive effects of sanctions in creating vested interests for the Revolutionary Guards. While the Iranian people have languished under sanctions, the Revolutionary Guards have benefited due to ownership of key industries. If Iran is ever open to foreign markets and investments, these protected industries could face competition for the first time. In other words, under sanctions Iran has out of necessity followed an import substitution approach, with many benefits accruing to the interests of the Revolutionary Guards.[56]

The wild card in the Iranian economy, other than sanctions, is the risk of geopolitical tensions in the region. Should war break out between Israel and Iran, or the United States and Iran, much of Iran's economic and military infrastructure is likely to be destroyed. Moreover, Iran's oil exports will mostly likely suffer. Also, investments in the Iranian economy by China will likely be negatively affected. At a time when countries like Saudi Arabia, the UAE, and Qatar all have growth plans by picking different spots in the global economy, Iran remains reasonably isolated. While its tilt to the east may pay off in the long term, there is little substitution for integration into the global economy in the short to medium term.

An Integrated Capability Model?

Iran has some impressive capabilities that have become integrated into its national security apparatus. Iran's conventional military capabilities have become integrated with its asymmetric militia capabilities. Its much-vaunted missile technology has been used to augment the efforts of the militias that are part of its "axis of resistance" approach. The swarming capability of its Navy vessels has been used to harass the US military in the Strait of Hormuz. But all of this has been compromised by the conflicts that have arisen between Iran and Israel in 2024. Iran's keystone capability has been its network of militias that has allowed it to avoid direct conflict with Israel and the United States, while providing deterrence against these adversaries. This entire system has collapsed with the degradation of Hezbollah and Hamas by Israel, the potential loss of influence in Syria, and Iran's direct conflict with Israel, all of which play to Iran's competitive disadvantage.

Iran will need to recalibrate its foreign policy around new capabilities. That could take Iran further in the direction of diplomacy or in a worst-case scenario for global security, a nuclear weapon. With the collapse of its keystone capability of its militia network, Iran in the months and years ahead will be struggling with what its signature capability for dealing with the challenges it faces will be.

As it struggles with this, there will be other weaknesses and vulnerabilities Iran will need to consider. One is its overall economic capability as well as a flagging soft power capacity. Iran's soft power challenges could become more profound in the future. One question is to what degree Iran's flagging soft power, both at home and abroad, will affect its ability to project power and influence in the current environment. Even if the region doesn't transition to greater stability, how will loss of popularity affect Iran's ability to play the outsized role its rivals ascribe to it? One variable is whether in the Arab world, Iran's consistent support for Hamas continues to play well. There are two layers to Iran's soft power. One is at the country level in Iraq, Syria, and Lebanon, and the other is more broadly regional and involves Iran's support for the Palestinian cause. Will the uptick in popularity of Iran for its support for the Palestinians be sustainable at the regional level?[57] This could hinge on whether Iran continues to act as a spoiler for a diplomatic solution on this issue or becomes at least a passive contributor to a solution. And it depends on the outcome of the direct conflict between Iran and Israel, and how this plays out as the region and the world contemplate the second administration of Donald Trump.

At the country level, the decline in popularity of Iran in Iraq and Lebanon seems decoupled from its support for the Palestinians. Rather, the downturn is more about Iran's heavy-handedness in those countries and the impact Iranian influence is perceived to have on the lives of ordinary people. The degradation of Hezbollah could lead to a further deterioration in the support for Iran.

Another factor is whether the region shifts to a more stable footing. The degradation of Hezbollah could lead to a more independent and stable Lebanon. And with Syria reeling from Iranian heavy-handedness, its reintegration to the Arab League, and a new regime in Damascus, Iran's reliance on the failed states to project power and influence into the region could become compromised.

Iran's set of capabilities works for it within the current environment. With lagging soft power and an anemic economy, the question will be how Iran's capabilities prepare it for a more normalized competition with other states in the region. The current set of capabilities satisfies its security itch, but it isn't clear whether Iran has the capability set to compete in a more normalized region, or whether even Iran has an interest in helping move the region in that direction. We see Iran moving to improve its relationships with Saudi Arabia, the UAE, Egypt, and even Turkey.[58] This is suggestive of perhaps an interest in burnishing Iran's diplomatic capability. But the question is whether there will be a recalibration of Iran's foreign policy in this direction, or whether we can expect more of the same. Another way of thinking of this is whether Iran will try to perpetuate the status quo, which enhances its tactical short- and medium-term interests, or whether it moves to a longer-term approach for its overall strategic benefit?

6 UNPACKING IRAN'S FOREIGN POLICY STRATEGY

In this chapter, we will look at Iran's foreign policy using a strategic lens. In many ways, that is what we have been doing all along. Since foreign policy doesn't take place in a vacuum, we have looked at the context within which Iran's foreign policy has evolved. We started with Iran's long history, peering deeply into Iran's past and foraging for clues as to the antecedents of the patterns we have seen since the Iranian revolution. From there we looked at how Iranian decision-makers analyzed the global and regional environments. To broaden the story, we then looked at how Iran interprets itself within its regional and global contexts and the capabilities that it has leveraged to deal with the challenges it faces. The broad story told was of Iran's foreign policy reflecting the country's unique interpretation of the threats and opportunities it has faced.

When commencing this book project, several colleagues warned me of the perils of embarking on such an endeavor. When told I was writing a book on Iran's foreign policy strategy, one of them said, "good luck with that." That individual questioned the premise that Iran has a clear and definable strategy. My response was that the book doesn't presuppose that Iran has a single grand strategy. I also said I was more interested in teasing out the patterns of Iran's response to its unique geopolitical environment than I was in trying to uncover some hidden plan.

But at every step, I have struggled with the question of whether the patterns I was seeing qualify as a strategy, or rather were just tactical maneuvers and responses to changes in Iran's environment. What I discovered was that both can be true. Iran, like most countries, reacts tactically to the threats, opportunities, and crises it faces. But if we look hard, we can see the outlines of how these tactical responses add up to a pattern. While perhaps not qualifying as a grand strategy, the patterns do nevertheless push Iran in an identifiable direction.

The other struggle I wrestled with is does a continuation of Iran's current path position it for the challenges it is likely to face in the future, or will the crossroads it confronts be profound enough to necessitate a significant course correction? The conclusion I have come to is that Iran in 2024 is at that crossroads, and that it needs to figure out how to re-establish deterrence against Israel and the United States, given the pummeling of its allies, Hamas and Hezbollah, by Israel and attacks on the homeland by the Israelis for the very first time.

Strategy can be an elusive concept. At the most general level, it entails how a country either adapts to or shapes its external environment to protect or advance its interests. The criterion for a good strategy isn't elegance or even the objective correctness of its underlying assumptions. But rather a good strategy needs to be assessed empirically: did it achieve the stated goals and advance a country's interests? Where does this definition leave Iran? Iran has become a master of adapting to its external environment. Adapting to changes in the Middle East also altered it in the process. We witnessed this on and after the October 7, 2023 attacks on Israel by Hamas, when all the militias allied with Iran became arrayed in one way or another against the United States and Israel.

But rather than being part of some predesigned grand plan for the region, the influence Iran wields through this network of militias has largely been built on the failures of other actors, and on the failures of the region itself. Iran has skillfully taken advantage of these failures and used them to help reorder the region, but it didn't create these failures. What this means for Iran's future given possible changes in the region will be the focus of Chapter 7.

In assessing Iran's foreign policy strategy, we need to avoid looking at it through a one-dimensional lens that could distort reality and lead to improper and incorrect conclusions. Instead, this chapter will look at Iran's strategic responses through a multidimensional lens. It will attempt to tell multiple stories that together will illuminate how Iran approaches its international environment. The stories will ideally generate insights into Iran's strategic response to the challenges and opportunities the country faces.

We are not presupposing that these stories reflect exactly how Iran's leaders conceptualize strategy in their minds. Most leaders think more about specific policies and decisions than strategy per se. It will be our job to ascertain if there is a policy pattern that adds up to something approaching a strategy, or whether what we are witnessing is just a string of disconnected tactical maneuvers. In meeting with some of Iran's senior leaders I was expecting to and did find some clues about this. But I wasn't looking for a eureka moment where a grand strategy would somehow appear to me. Trying to tease out a grand strategy from Iran's foreign policy can be a quixotic quest. A more reasonable expectation is to identify patterns of how Iran responds to the challenges it faces that are worth paying attention to.

Some words about the notion of strategy itself are in order. It is a misconception that strategy needs to be like a blueprint for a house. In some cases, countries will arrive at an overarching grand strategy that lays out the priorities, goals, and capabilities of the country a priori. In the 1950s, the US strategy of containment was a deliberately constructed grand strategy for confronting what was seen as a Soviet threat. But the Cold War was a singular moment in world history when leaders were confronted with one principal adversary. The realities of today are very different and therefore our sense of what strategy entails will likely be different too.

Grand strategies of Cold War vintage, or what we might call deliberate strategies, are only one type. Other types of strategy can be more emergent than deliberate, evolving over time more organically.[1] I would argue that while there are deliberate aspects to Iran's foreign policy, much of it is what could be characterized as an emergent strategy, which are adaptive responses to challenges and opportunities in the external environment. While deliberate strategies are clear bets on the future, adaptive strategies are more iterative calculations in response to a changing environment. Emergent strategies are different from mere tactical responses in that they represent a sustained pattern and direction over time, even though they are not preplanned.

Sometimes emergent or adaptive strategies start out as a series of tactical maneuvers but eventually take the shape of a coherent pattern over time, becoming institutionalized as an official strategy. In other words, over a sustained period adaptive strategy can become more deliberate. In the Iranian case, we see that what started out as adaptation has morphed into a more consistent, deliberate type of strategy over time. We see that while many instances of Iran's support for its affiliated militias started out as opportunistic responses to the civil wars in the region, they became part of a more integrated whole over time. In other words, the militias which emerged from threats and opportunities in the environment became later connected to a broader, more encompassing deliberate strategy.

Because strategy can be such an elusive concept, looking at it from different angles is the way I have chosen to go. Each of the following stories represents a turn of the kaleidoscope, hopefully generating different insights into how Iran has responded to the challenges it sees in its environment. Iran's foreign policy represents a dialectic between a grand past and a more prosaic present. It also represents the challenge of dealing with great powers with large capabilities, while Iran itself is a middle power with significant resource constraints. The different stories that follow about Iran's response to its struggles will hopefully get us closer to decoding Iran's foreign policy.

Story #1: A Strategy of Denial

If we look closely at Iran's foreign policy today, we see that it is built on top of a collapsed regional order. Much of Iran's foreign policy strength has come from projecting power into the states that have collapsed at some point into civil war, namely Lebanon, Syria, Iraq, and Yemen. The question is, has insinuating itself into failed states led to foreign policy success for Iran? Whether this positions Iran for success long term will be covered in the next chapter. But for the short term, Iran's priorities are to use its presence in these failed states to extract resources in the face of economic sanctions and create deterrence against the United States and Israel. And its presence is also designed to win in the regional influence game by ensuring that the failed states never reintegrate into the Arab world. In other words, Iran's definition of winning is to deny Saudi Arabia and other Gulf Arab states re-entry into Syria, Yemen, Lebanon, and Iraq. In other words, they win by keeping the Arab world dislocated and on the defensive.

In denying the Arab world a return to coherence, Iran is playing a multileveled game. It operates both in the subterranean world of failed states and in the more terrestrial world of strong states. While many aspects of Iran's foreign policy today are sui generis, operating a foreign policy at various levels isn't new. Even before the revolution of 1979, Iran had a multilevel approach to its foreign policy. During the reign of Shah

Mohammed Reza Pahlavi, Iran used conventional state-to-state diplomacy with both friends and rivals. But Iran also operated in the shadowy substate realities of the region. While we typically ascribe substate meddling to post-revolutionary Iran, under the shah Iran meddled in the 1970s in the internal workings of Iraq by supporting the Kurds. While the shah (and Washington) ultimately betrayed the Kurds when it settled its dispute with Iraq, nonetheless this occurred after an active intervention had taken place.[2] Similarly, in 1972 the Shah of Iran entered a civil conflict in Dhofar, Oman on the side of the imperialists against the rebels.[3]

The difference is that the shah led with and emphasized its state-to-state relations, delving into the substate world on the margins, while the Islamic Republic has it reversed. In terms of regional politics, Iran today leads with its substate strategy, with its diplomacy toward its Arab neighbors more volatile and nascent. This goes back to the early days of the revolution when Iran promised to export its revolution to neighboring states. The most provocative statements aimed at states were aimed at Saudi Arabia, which the Iranian regime saw as illegitimate Wahhabi heretics. Menacing statements were also leveled at the state of Iraq prior to that country's invasion of Iran in 1980.[4]

Ayatollah Khomeini said in 1980:

> I hope that [Iran] will become a model for all the meek and Muslim nations in the world, and that this century will become the smashing of great idols . . .[5]

President Bani-Sadr took it a step further:

> Our Revolution will not win unless it is exported. We are going to create a new order in which deprived people will not always be deprived. As long as our brothers in Palestine, Afghanistan, the Philippines, and all over the world, have not been liberated, we will not put down our arms.[6]

As incendiary as the revolutionary statements made by Iranian revolutionary leaders sounded to the leaderships in Riyadh and Baghdad in 1979, they turned out to be more aspirational than operational. Beyond the rhetorical flourishes on radio broadcasts, there was no clear capacity for operationalizing the desire to push the revolution to the broader region, particularly during the Iran-Iraq war. But an opportunity appeared in 1982 to establish what became the foundational piece of a shadow foreign policy in helping establish Hezbollah in Lebanon. This came about because of the chaos in Lebanon from the civil war, and the invasion of southern Lebanon by Israel in June of 1982. Since then, on the backs of the US invasion of Iraq in 2003 and the civil wars a decade later in Syria and Yemen, Iran expanded on what had been built in Lebanon with Hezbollah decades earlier. Iran's Quds Force, the expeditionary arm of the Islamic Revolutionary Guard Corps (IRGC), spread its tentacles into these countries at war and formed an alliance with Hamas and Palestine Islamic Jihad (PIJ) in Gaza, as well as the Hashd al-Sha'bi militias in Iraq and the Houthis in Yemen. The thread that connects what had started as an emergent strategy with Hezbollah in 1982 into a broader strategic thrust was the Quds Force which, in close coordination with Hezbollah, sent forces to Syria, Iraq, and Yemen as these countries collapsed into disorder and civil war.

The question is, how does this subterranean, shadowy strategy tie into Iran's more conventional state-to-state approach to the region? While seldom will Iranians describe their foreign policy in these terms, Iran's two-leveled foreign policy represents a strategy of preclusion or denial.[7] It is designed to deny Saudi Arabia, the UAE, Egypt, and other Arab countries a strategic opening for reintegrating Iraq, Lebanon, Yemen, or Syria back into the Arab fold, despite modest success by the Arab League with Syria and the Saudis with Iraq to do just that.[8] The Iranians have spent the last decades insinuating themselves into these countries, establishing military, political, economic, cultural, and religious roots that are hard to dislodge, giving them a competitive advantage with other states in the region. In the Iranian strategic mindset, this protects Iran against re-formation of an Arab phalanx that can surround it, as happened during the Iran-Iraq war of the 1980s. And it is core to the doctrine of forward defense, which is that Iran must project power into the region to protect the homeland.

Lebanon and Iraq provide pertinent examples of how effective this has been. The Lebanese Army had been supported by Saudi Arabia principally as a counter to the influence of Iran-supported Hezbollah. But the Saudis suspended its $3 billion aid package in 2016, presumably because of Lebanon's refusal to condemn attacks on Saudi Arabia's diplomatic mission in Tehran.[9] It was also the reality that Iran's and Hezbollah's influence in the country extended into Lebanon's political realm, in effect blocking any possible Saudi inroads, that motivated Riyadh's withdrawal of support.

Whether the Saudi decision was wise or shortsighted can be up for debate. But what is incontrovertible is that the Iranians with Hezbollah had erected a virtual firewall, creating significant obstacles for any external actor who might tread into the treacherous political and security landscape of Lebanon.

What transpired in Iraq also shows the degree to which Iran penetrated weak states in the region, making reintegration back to the Arab fold difficult. The US invasion of Iraq in 2003 brought the regime of Saddam Hussein down. While the Americans were threateningly in striking range of Iran, they quickly became mired in the murky security and sectarian structure of Iraqi society. This weak spot for the United States was turned into a strategic advantage for Iran, which fortified old ties with Shi'i politicians and clerics. Saudi Arabia seeing this creeping Iranian influence shortsightedly shunned Baghdad, rebuffing any attempts by Iraqi politicians to engage.

Finally, starting in 2016, Saudi Arabia under the new reign of King Salman, re-engaged with Iraq, tacitly acknowledging that shunning Baghdad had been a blunder. There have been some successes with specific economic development projects. But in speaking to Iraqi and Iranian officials it became clear that slow progress has been attributable to Iranian blocking tactics. One Iraqi official said that while the Saudis excel at using their immense sovereign wealth funds, they can't compete with the Iranians in the chaotic and treacherous "badlands" of Iraq.[10]

This strategy of preclusion or denial in the failed states of the region gave Iran an effective way to compete for regional influence against its heavyweight rivals Saudi Arabia, Turkey, and Israel.[11] It enabled Iran to compensate for the fact that on conventional military and economic grounds, it is significantly behind its regional rivals.[12] It also gives Iran a way to withstand the counterstrategies of the United States, Israel, and Saudi Arabia, by denying them a base from which to compete in Iraq, Syria, Lebanon, and Yemen.[13]

It is important that we do not aggrandize this strategy of preclusion into a grand strategy. It emerged over time due to Iran's capacity to navigate and operate within a region that had collapsed. It was the US invasion of Iraq in 2003 and the epidemic of civil wars that started in 2011 that gave Iran the opportunity to expand on what it had built with Hezbollah in the 1980s and to project power to the broader region. While the Iran-Iraq war seared into Iran's consciousness the need to create a buffer zone to prevent another Arab assault, it was the fallout from the US invasion of Iraq in 2003 and the civil wars in the next decade that allowed Iran to act upon this.

But by denying the Gulf Arabs re-entry into Iraq, Lebanon, Syria, and Yemen, Iran has spooked their leaders who fear Iranian hegemony over the Arab heartland. While Iran's presence in these countries gives it export outlets for goods that show up in the souks of Iraq and Syria, circumventing American sanctions, it is a strange kind of regional influence that doesn't translate into broad economic and political benefits for Iran or Iranian citizens.[14] It gives Iran regional security benefits, but this is a narrow, overly securitized conception of competitiveness when compared to more regionally and globally powerful states such as Saudi Arabia and the UAE who are competing using a broader spectrum of foreign policy tools, including diplomatic and economic initiatives. Going forward, Iran will likely need to compete more broadly, not relying merely on denying its rivals access to the failed states, but by creating a value proposition for itself that enables it to compete more directly and effectively in a way that benefits the Iranian people. It could be forced into this position with the inability to deny Arab access to a new post-Assad reality in Syria.

Story #2: Strategies of Diffusion

Strategy traditionally relies on the principle of concentration—that is, arraying a set of resources in a laser-focused way toward a clearly articulated direction. Carl von Clausewitz, the seminal Prussian military strategist of the eighteenth and nineteenth centuries, opined about the importance of the concentration principle, calling it "center of gravity," which is the source of strength but also vulnerability of an opponent. It is the fulcrum upon which everything else depends.[15] For the United States, an emphasis on concentration was a legacy of the Cold War, during which it was critical to focus resources on the historic challenge of containing the Soviet Union.

Concentration for all states, but particularly smaller states, also has attendant risks. Concentrations of forces and resources create exposure to attack by larger and more powerful states. Iraq learned this the hard way in 2003, after the United States collapsed the regime of President

Saddam Hussein quickly by attacking its overly concentrated central command structure.

Having witnessed how quickly the Iraqi regime collapsed under American attack, Iran mitigated its risk of this by relying on a more organic strategy of diffusion.[16] There are two dimensions to an Iranian rendition of a diffusion strategy. The first is horizontal, where Iran has strewn its assets and forces widely across the region, rather than concentrating them at home. Having militias distributed in multiple states across the region gave Iran a retaliatory capability that it believed acted as a deterrent, something Iraq had lacked. And it assured the Iranians that one knockout blow couldn't completely cripple them.

We saw this horizontal diffusion operationalized in 2024 with attacks on Israel by Hezbollah, Houthis attacks on shipping in the Red Sea, and attacks on American forces in Iraq and Syria. We don't know the degree to which there was any Iranian direction of these attacks, but we do know that Tehran cheered them on. Together they were designed to sow chaos and create sufficient complexity across a wide geographic area to confuse and overwhelm the ability of Israel or the United States to cope.[17] And they were designed to re-establish deterrence Iran believed it had lost after several Israeli assaults on its militias and direct attacks on Iran itself by Israel in April and October 2024. Both attacks followed Iranian direct missile and drone attacks on Israel.

The other dimension of a diffusion strategy is vertical and involves Iran suffusing itself deeply into the political, cultural, and religious structures in Syria, Lebanon, and Iraq, making countermeasures by rivals very challenging. It involves combining security ties, economic dependence, and cultural affinities into a web of influence. By extending its tentacles across these various domains, it makes it very difficult to dislodge Iran from these countries. A major chink in Iran's armor that might benefit its rivals could be a potential loss of influence over events in Syria with the collapse of the Assad government.

This strategy has worked because of its asymmetry, meaning that Iran has become somewhat impervious to the more conventional approaches taken by the United States and its allies. But it also works by playing to the weaknesses inherent in a more powerful adversary like the United States, which lacks the ability to counter Iran's presence in the subterranean crevices of failed states. The asymmetry between Iran's subterranean strategy of diffusion and the United States' more conventional strategy of concentration has favored Iran.

The question is, how does a strategy of diffusion relate to the issue of Iran's nuclear enrichment program? In a perverse way, the nuclear issue has helped shield Iran's strategy of diffusion. Iran's willingness to negotiate only on the nuclear issue separate from other concerns created a tacit acceptance of Iran's regional militia activities and missile arsenal. The JCPOA nuclear talks compartmentalized the nuclear file from these other issues, giving Iran a strategic advantage. The willingness of the international community to negotiate nuclear matters without addressing these other issues was in a way a tacit concession.

But the strategy of diffusion becomes more parlous for Iran in the context of the Gaza war. The risk is that Israel and even the United States will have a lower risk threshold relative to threats to their national security than before. If Israel continues to retaliate against Iran for attacks by its affiliated militias, which happened in 2024, then the strategy of diffusion will no longer have protected Iran but would instead have created liability. Given how central deterrence was to the diffusion strategy, there will likely need to be a strategic reconsideration by Tehran.

Story #3: Strategies of Sun Tzu

We have no indication that Iranian leaders have read *The Art of War* by Sun Tzu, the consummate Chinese strategist from the fifth century BC. Nevertheless, the pattern of Iran's actions embodies several of his strategic principles. Sun Tzu argues that direct confrontation with the enemy should be avoided in favor of indirect engagement, if possible. Given Iran's resource and capability constraints and how it sees its strategic environment, it makes sense that it would lean on indirect means for dealing with the threats it perceives. There are obvious exceptions to the rule, such as the direct attacks on Israel in 2024. But overall, Iran has eschewed direct confrontation and has worked more comfortably in the shadows.

Sun Tzu: Indirect approaches

For Sun Tzu, direct kinetic fighting isn't the consummate skill of the strategist. For him, victory should be secured before the battle begins, or ideally without fighting at all:

To win one hundred victories in one hundred battles is not the acme of skill. To subdue the enemy without fighting is the acme of skill.[18]

It would be wrong to suggest that Iran always avoids direct confrontation in favor of indirect measures. The 2024 missile and drone attacks on Israel suggest otherwise. And, of course, during the Iran-Iraq war of 1980–88 when conflict was thrust on Iran by an Iraqi invasion, it fought an intense direct war for eight years.[19]

But from the Iran-Iraq war came the imperative of Iran reducing the risk of another direct military assault in the future by building a protective shield to deal with threats before they come to the homeland. Since that time, there is strong evidence of an emphasis on Sun Tzu's indirect approach to war, which tries to eschew a direct fight with the enemy.[20]

One of Sun Tzu's principles was to manipulate the environment in a way that disadvantages the enemy, obviating the necessity of fighting directly. Iran's foreign policy has largely embodied this principle by taking advantage of vacuums in its regional environment to create competitive advantages in its longstanding conflict with the United States and its allies. Those vacuums are the weak or failed states of Lebanon, Iraq, Syria, and Yemen.

Avoiding a direct confrontation has meant building a system of affiliated militias in these weak states that would give Iran a deterrent capability against attacks by the United States and Israel. While Iran lacks the military capacity to win a direct fight with the United States or Israel, creating a regional system of militias was intended to establish deterrence by raising the costs and risks of a military move against Iran. And in the Iranian mindset, it gave them a multi-headed retaliatory capability, should deterrence fail.

The key part of the strategy was to surround Israel with allied militias, creating a specter of fear of Iran activating all its militias in a way that would overwhelm Israel's defensive missile shields. A test of this occurred on April 13, 2024, when Iran launched a coordinated attack on Israel using its own assets and those of its allies. It was designed to be a signal of its capability, not necessarily a provocation of all-out war.

Another advantage of this indirect approach is that Iran can hide in plain sight. It can create enough ambiguity within its strategic environment that it gives Iran some plausible deniability of the actions of its proxy militias. We saw this when there were drone and missile attacks on Saudi Aramco facilities in 2019. Iran denied responsibility and the Houthis from Yemen claimed it. While the United States claims to have evidence that the attack came from Iran, there was enough ambiguity to give Iran some protection.[21]

Sun Tzu wrote that the warrior should act like water, becoming formless and adaptive, rather than fixed and inflexible:

> A military force has no constant formation, water has no constant shape. The ability to gain victory by changing and adapting according to the opponent is called genius.[22]

Iran has embodied this principle by diffusing its assets across the region and suffusing itself into the weak countries in the region, making it difficult for Saudi Arabia, Israel, and other rivals to target it. It makes identifying Iran's strategic center of gravity challenging.[23] One example of this was how Iran disbanded its military units and bases in Syria, and instead embedded its Quds Force fighters within the Syrian Army, rendering it difficult for Israel to identify and target them.[24] This strategy of avoiding detection was in response to Israel's targeting of Iran's Islamic Revolutionary Guard bases and units in Syria.

There is a belief among Iranian decision-makers that an indirect approach is necessary but that there are attendant risks. The risk is that a purely indirect approach will be construed by Washington and Jerusalem as a sign of weakness. This is related to the view that Iran cannot placate Washington. Its mindset in this regard was forged in the aftermath of 9/11 when Iran assisted the United States in confronting the Taliban in Afghanistan.[25] A few months later, this effort was rebuffed when Iran was grouped with Iraq and North Korea in President George W. Bush's "axis of evil" reference in his State of the Union Address in 2002.[26] Ayatollah Khamenei lays this out explicitly in response to these comments:

> Another reality is that whenever we showed flexibility towards the enemy and used certain justifications to retreat, the enemy adopted bolder positions against us. For example, at one point we said that we should not give the enemy an excuse and at another point we said that we should dispel the enemy's suspicions against ourselves. The day the statements of our government officials were contaminated with flattery for the west and western culture, they labeled us "axis of evil."[27]

So, for the Iranians an indirect approach is necessary, yet insufficient. The belief is that it needs to be augmented with direct approaches. The thinking is that to deter and discourage adventurism, Iran needs to strike a balance between confrontation avoidance and demonstrations of strength. In other words, it needs to show strength without provoking an attack. How Iran balances its indirect and direct approaches to resurrect deterrence against Israel and the United States in the fraught region of 2025 will test the strategic acuity of Iranian leaders. Failure to properly balance its foreign policy raises the risk of an all-out regional war.[28]

This will be a difficult task, given how conflict escalation affects Iran and Israel differently. For the Israelis, the attacks by Hamas in 2023 and the follow-on attacks by Hezbollah proved that their deterrence and detection systems were flawed. They have been and will continue being aggressive in trying to re-establish deterrence. For Iran, the notion that its support for its militia network was justified on defensive grounds is no longer a credible claim given the unprovoked aggression by Hamas and Hezbollah. This in turn creates a risk of more attacks on Iran by Israel.

Given the Iranian belief that inaction can be perceived as weakness, there will be tremendous pressure to respond to all Israeli attacks in kind. What this means is that the efficacy and risks of Iran's indirect approach to conflict will be tested in the months and years to come. The idea that the indirect approach of supporting militias reduces the risk of direct attack on Iran has been proven wrong in 2024. Whether Iran can balance its direct and indirect approaches in the future will determine whether deterrence and stability can be recreated.

Sun Tzu: Disrupt the enemy's plans

In a similar vein of fighting the enemy indirectly, Sun Tzu advocated attacking the enemy's strategy, rather than the enemy's army. In other words, disrupting the mechanism of the enemy's strategy has higher value and lower risk than attacking the enemy's forces.

Sun Tzu said:

> The highest realization of warfare is to attack the enemy's plans; next is to attack their alliances; next to attack their army; and the lowest is to attack their fortified cities.[29]

Ayatollah Ali Khamenei said something similar:

A nation should know its enemies; it should uncover the enemies' plots, and it should fully prepare itself for them.[30]

After a year of enduring maximum pressure sanctions from the United States under President Donald Trump, Iran in 2019 was determined to demonstrate to the Arab states that had supported Trump's hostility to Iran that the security umbrella they believed they had from the US was a mere mirage. This was designed to disrupt the strategies of both the United States and Saudi Arabia.

The United States under Donald Trump had actively dissuaded Saudi Arabia from responding positively to any diplomatic advances from Iran, in support of Washington's maximum pressure campaign. Reciprocally, Saudi Arabia encouraged the Trump administration to withdraw from the JCPOA and to wage a campaign of hostility toward Tehran. The United States assumed it could cower Iran into submission using these methods. And Saudi Arabia believed that US sanctions boxed Tehran in. For the Saudis, the actions of the United States obviated the need to engage diplomatically with Iran. The belief was that they could afford to eschew diplomacy with Iran due to a reliance on Washington for security.

The Iranians operationalized its disruption of the strategy of the United States and Saudi Arabia by waging aggression in the Persian Gulf and Strait of Hormuz, detaining several ships. The intent was to show Washington that waging economic warfare against Iran using sanctions wouldn't cower it but instead would incite it to disruptive behavior that could cause a rise in oil prices. There were also drone attacks on the Saudi Aramco facilities in Abqaiq and Khurais in 2019, claimed by the Houthis but believed to come from Iran. These actions were designed to demonstrate to the Saudis that Washington wouldn't come to their assistance.[31] The Iranian gambit paid off, as Washington didn't respond in a forceful way against Iran. And after vigorous diplomacy, Iran and Saudi Arabia resumed diplomatic relations in 2023.

The goal of the strategy was to break the mechanism of dependence that tied the Gulf Arabs to the United States by demonstrating that Washington wouldn't come to their aid if attacked. The Iranians knew that if they frontally and directly attacked Saudi Arabia in a major way that created casualties, Washington would likely respond. But they calculated that a damaging, but not lethal, attack on oil facilities would likely not elicit any real reprisals. What it did do is disrupt the US strategy of keeping the Saudis squarely in the US fold and outside the diplomatic forcefield of Iran. The Iranian strategy was designed to signal to the Gulf states that the United States wasn't a reliable ally, thereby pushing them off their position of recalcitrant unwillingness to negotiate and toward a more pliable and negotiation-ready posture.

This Iranian approach drew from several other Sun Tzu principles.[32] By having the Houthis launch their limited attacks on the Aramco facilities in 2019, Iran followed another of Sun Tzu's principles by using concealment and deception in hiding its direct role in the attacks.[33] The mechanism for the overall strategy of peeling Saudi Arabia from the clutches of Washington draws from the Sun Tzu principle of altering the psychology of the enemy. In this case, the alteration came from raising the intensity of perceived threat of the Gulf Arabs by showing them that Washington didn't have their back, *and* that the US maximum pressure campaign created risk for them. The message the Iranians tried to convey through heightened Saudi threat perceptions was that diplomacy with Iran was the only way to mitigate risk and reduce the threat. By betting that the United States wouldn't respond robustly, the Iranians raised Saudi threat perceptions, causing Riyadh to see diplomacy with Iran as the only reasonable way forward.

Sun Tzu would approve of how the Iranians handled this, as he favored a disruption of the system of alliances of the enemy over a direct attack. Iran's actions in the Persian Gulf of mining and interdicting ships and then the attacks on the Saudi Aramco facilities were designed to attenuate the bonds between the United States and Saudi Arabia by dispelling the perception of a security commitment from Washington.[34] The idea was that shorn of security commitments from the United States, Saudi Arabia would be more receptive to negotiation.

In sum, the costly and searing effects of the Iran-Iraq war of the 1980s helped solidify Iran's approach to war and strategy, embodying many of the principles of Sun Tzu.[35] Iran's approach was also a response to its relative weakness vis-à-vis the United States and Israel. It operated in the shadows, following more of an indirect strategy, at least until October 7, 2023. And it worked on the psychology of Saudi Arabia to bring it to the bargaining table. Whether Iran will be able to follow the principles of Sun Tzu going forward or will need to transition to more direct engagement with its enemies remains to be seen.

Story #4: Iran's Strategic Doctrines

The United States has a history of national security doctrines which generally are eponymously linked to individual presidents. Among others there is the Monroe Doctrine, which laid out a marker against European involvement in the western hemisphere, and the Carter Doctrine, which committed the United States to the security of the Persian Gulf. Each of these presidential doctrines came about because of threats or opportunities that prevailed on policy-makers at the time.

Iran, too, has doctrines, though they are seldom articulated and formalized in the American style. But similarly, Iran's doctrines are associated with threats (or in some cases opportunities) from the international environment. Most of those treated below were developed in the aftermath of the Iranian revolution of 1979. But others have their roots in pre-revolutionary Iran. All of those presented here are relevant to Iran's strategic thinking today and reverberate in Iran's foreign policy-making process.

One of the overarching themes in Iran's strategic history has been the struggle for generating political power. For this reason, all of Iran's doctrines deal with questions around the use of power. They signal Iran's intentions to use power to defend the homeland or project power into the region to advance what it deems its vital interests. And they address issues of dealing with more powerful, global powers.

Forward defense doctrine: Deterrent power

As presented in Chapter 1, Iran has been exposed to foreign threats for centuries. The revolution of 1979 to a large degree took place because of a perception that the Iranian political system, its economy, and even its social structure had been penetrated by the United States during the reign of Shah Mohammed Reza Pahlavi.

But it was the Iran-Iraq war, starting in 1980 with an Iraqi invasion, that became the crucible for Iran's strategic thinking that weighs on Iran's foreign policy to this day. Out of this seminal event came the forward defense doctrine. After having its economy ravaged by war and after close to a million Iranians killed or wounded, Iranian leaders decided that it needed to build a buffer zone to protect the homeland.

Critics and skeptics will understandably see Iran's claims of defensive motives as a clever concealment of naked expansionist ambitions. But gleaning foreign policy motivations can be inherently complex and laden with ambiguity. Iran's leaders and their critics can both be right. Defensive and offensive impulses can and do coexist in Iran's foreign policy. The evidence that the pummeling and isolation Iran experienced during the Iran-Iraq war was the raison d'être for the forward defense doctrine is incontrovertible. But it is also true that Iran has taken every opportunity to project power into the region to confront the interests of the United States, Israel, and Gulf Arab states.

One of the core principles behind Iran's forward defense doctrine is strategic depth. How this gets operationalized can vary depending on circumstances. In wartime, control of physical territory on the battlefield is what yields strategic depth. The concept encompasses both space and time. It puts high value on control of territory as a buffer against the enemy, maximizing the time it would take for the enemy to get to you.[36] In circumstances of peace, alliances can be the currency of strategic depth. Strong alliances can add a virtual buffer between you and a strategic adversary, assuming the ally can be relied upon for steadfast support in the eventuality of an attack.

The notion of creating strategic depth isn't unique to Iran's forward defense doctrine. The well-known American diplomat, Charles W. "Chas" Freeman Jr. defined strategy as "the effort to gain and retain the initiative, and to minimize the effects of chance."[37] This is apropos of Iran's forward defense doctrine, which doesn't leave to chance the intention of adversaries. It means confronting threats closer to the source and as far away from Iran as is possible. This has become operationalized in Iran's relationship with Hezbollah of Lebanon, which takes Iran's conflict with Israel to its backyard and away from Iran.

Iran's forward defense doctrine is broader than just encompassing military strategic depth, but also includes political strategic depth. Iran's political influence in Iraq is designed to create a buffer that prevents a previously aggressive neighbor from ever threatening the Iranian homeland again.[38] Iran's presence in Iraq, Lebanon, and Syria has acted as a bulwark against Saudi attempts to reintegrate these countries into the Arab fold, creating a virtual political buffer zone around Iran. Iran has tried to create this buffer zone by playing on its cultural and religious heritage to embed itself in these countries. In a speech in 2008, Ayatollah Khamenei argued that political strategic depth was the cornerstone of Iran's security policies and that Iran's interventions and relationships within the Muslim world are core to this. What this means is that

Khamenei sees Iran's religious affinities as key to its notion of strategic depth.[39]

Iran has some dilemmas when it comes to creating strategic depth. Given the intensity of threat perceived from the United States, Iranian leaders see themselves under constant siege, neither in a state of peace nor war. For this reason, the purpose of strategic depth and forward defense is about creating deterrence.[40] As much as Iran believes ultimate strategic depth will only come from a US pullback from the Middle East, its leaders understand they need to rely on deterrence to protect the homeland. The dilemma for Iran is whether, considering the events of October 7, it can rely on its presence in Iraq, Yemen, and Lebanon to create strategic depth and deterrence as it has before, and how it will adjust to the likely loss of Syria as a loyal and reliable ally. It is harder for Iran to claim its support for militias in the region is motivated by a need for defense, given the offensive nature of the brutal attacks by Hamas on Israel. With Israel now surrounded by Iran's militias, the chief one being Hezbollah, there is risk that Iran will be held more accountable than before for any actions by these groups. Iran will have to weigh how to navigate in a world where the mere existence of Iran-supported militias could become a red line for the Israelis. In such a situation, Iran's militias would work against strategic depth, not for it.

There are other risks to Iran's forward defense doctrine. Iran's current forward defense formula is well-suited to the moment when there is a plethora of failed or fragile states in the Middle East for Iran to project power into with its militias. If the region transitions to a more stable platform, and governance and sovereignty improve in Syria with a new post-Assad regime at the helm, and conditions become more stable in Iraq, then what options does Iran have? It is likely that Iran will need to rely more on conventional diplomacy to give it political strategic depth.

In this scenario, diplomatic relations with Saudi Arabia and other Arab states could be leaned on to a greater degree than before. If Iran's support for militias detracts from rather than yields deterrence, and the region transitions to greater stability, then a greater reliance on regional diplomacy may become an imperative. This could help reduce the risk of an American administration or even Israel taking aggressive actions against Iran. Whether Iran rebalances its foreign policy in the direction of diplomacy given the risks is something that will need to play out in the future. Of course, in the absence of strategic depth and a compromised forward defense, Iran's missile program and possible advancement in its nuclear program would still likely remain core to Iran's security portfolio as an augmentation to a possible tilt toward diplomacy.

Indigenization doctrine: Internal power

While Iran's forward defense doctrine is based on security threats, the indigenization doctrine is based on economic threats, mostly due to western-imposed sanctions since the Iranian revolution.

Iran's indigenization doctrine, which is really an economic resistance doctrine, has its roots in pre-revolutionary days. Prime Minister Mossadegh's nationalization of the Anglo-Iranian Oil Company in 1951 was clearly a provocative act of defiance against British control of Iran's lucrative oil industry, but also part of a strategy of limiting Iran's dependence on outside powers, something that had crippled Iran for much of its modern history.[41]

Today, the conditions are somewhat different. The thinking is that irrespective of sanctions, Iran needs to remain economically independent of the west, lest it become over-reliant on and unable to challenge the United States and its allies. But sanctions have forced Iran's hand as well. Absent foreign investment and lacking access to western goods, Iran has had to indigenize many industries.

Over the decades since the revolution, there have been debates within the ruling elite on this question of Iran's relationship with the global economy. The late President Rafsanjani as well as former President Rouhani believed that the best way to buttress Iran against sanctions is through some form of integration with the global economy. If Iran is integrated into the global economy, then there will be some systemic safeguards against future sanctions. The logic was that the costs of sanctions wouldn't be just borne by Iran, but also by those imposing sanctions in the form of lost export markets. The logic was that economic relations with the west would create a kind of mutually assured destruction safeguard against sanctions.

Another aspect of this is drawn from the Chinese model of economic development, which is to integrate with the global economy to engender political and military power.[42] Officials like the late Rafsanjani used China as an example of a country that had deep ideological separation from the west yet made compromises with the United States to serve the interests of economic vitality and growth. The corollary to this is that growing economic power of China would translate into political and military power that can help defend against the west.

The hardliners in Iran, including Ayatollah Ali Khamenei, take a different tack. They argue that it is impossible for Iran to maintain its independence while integrating with the global economy.[43] Moreover, they argue that a long-term relationship with the United States is unrealistic. This argument was buttressed by Trump's renunciation of the JCPOA in 2018 and the reimposition of sanctions that had been removed by the administration of Barack Obama.

One strategic question is with the collapse of the JCPOA and Iran's subsequent tilt toward China: how can it sustain its economic resistance approach? The dilemma will be that China, while it shares Iran's antipathy to the west yet itself is integrated into the global economy, may be only willing to go so far in support of Iran. We saw this during Trump's maximum pressure campaign, when China and Chinese firms were cautious not to stoke the full ire of the United States, lest they be slapped with secondary sanctions.[44] Also, the Chinese took advantage of the maximum pressure campaign imposed on Iran by the United States by buying Iranian oil at discounted prices.

Can Iran even thrive economically without some rapprochement with the west? Despite mixed support from Beijing on US-imposed sanctions, the Iranians are still bullish on their relationship with China. They are also relying to some degree on heightened animosities between Washington and Beijing over Taiwan to give the Chinese reason to hold Iran close.[45] Moreover, there is a belief that the international system is undergoing a shift, with the power of the United States waning and the power of China increasing on a relative basis.[46] If this is an accurate read of global economic and political power trends, then the strategy of aligning with China, and joining organizations such as the Shanghai Cooperation Council (SCO), might be a sound long-term bet. But in the short term Iran will likely not be able to satisfy the demands of the Iranian people solely by remaining a pariah in the west and tilting toward the east.[47]

Third power doctrine: Geopolitical power

Iran over the course of its history has toyed with several different theories for dealing with global powers. During the Qajar dynastic period, there was the theory of positive equilibrium, which suggested that given the inevitability of foreign intervention by two or more outside powers, Iran should engage with both, ideally playing one off the other.[48] The challenge to this theory came with the harsh reality that the dominant powers at the time, Britain and Russia, while competitive rivals were also conspiring to weaken Iran by dividing it up into spheres of influence among themselves.

In 1951, during the Cold War, Iranian Prime Minister Mohammed Mossadegh nationalized the British-controlled Anglo Iranian Oil Company, an act that led to his overthrow in 1953. His fateful and courageous action, though, was a repudiation of the whole notion of positive equilibrium. Mossadegh's thinking had transitioned from the prevailing notion of positive equilibrium to something he dubbed negative equilibrium, which was to deny all outside powers the ability to subjugate Iran in any way.[49] This obviously fell by the wayside through much of the Cold War, after Mossadegh was overthrown and Iran tilted toward the United States.

But the concept was resurrected during and after the revolution of 1979 with the mantra "neither east, nor west,"[50] which reflected the view that Iran needed to eschew aligning with either the United States or the Soviet Union. This notion of non-alignment sprung from the belief that the superpowers, while global rivals, had common interests in subjugating the countries of the region. Distinctions were made between the United States and Soviet Union, however, with the former being the Great Satan and the Soviets being a Lesser Satan.[51]

Another theory that has a long history in Iran's strategic thinking about global powers is the "third power" theory. It emerged in response to the stranglehold Britain and Russia had on Iran during much of the nineteenth and early twentieth centuries. The third power doctrine was that Iran should align itself with a third power that could counterbalance the effect of the other two. Reza Shah Pahlavi tried this during the Second World War by aligning with Hitler's Germany against the two dominant powers of the time, Britain and the Soviet Union. This ended disastrously for Reza Shah when the two powers he was trying to resist invaded Iran in 1941, ousted him, and occupied it for the remainder of the war.

Ironically, in the early part of the twentieth century Iran saw the United States as a third power candidate, particularly given the comments by then President Wilson of the principle of self-determination. The hope was that Washington, which had minimal commercial interests in Iran, as a remote power could act as a counterweight to Britain and the Soviet

Union. This wasn't just blind hope. The history of Morgan Shuster, the American financier who became Iran's Treasurer General and railed against both Britain and the Soviets, added some credibility to this belief.[52] And the United States supported Iran in 1946 when the Soviet Union on its way out of Iran after the Second World War stopped short of the border in Iranian Azerbaijan. It was the US intervention that solved the crisis.

But there are several problems with the theory. One is that if the third power lacks significant interests in Iran, then why would it spend political and perhaps even financial and military capital on behalf of a midsize state like Iran? The other is that once the third power develops interests in Iran, they are likely to act to protect those interests. This happened with the United States, which previously had been supportive of Iranian self-determination. Once the Cold War was underway, the US quickly developed significant interests in Iran that would militate against giving primacy to the principle of self-determination. The United States prioritized containment of the Soviet Union (and oil) over Iranian independence and democracy. This ultimately led Washington to help overthrow Mossadegh in 1953 in Operation Ajax.

The parting question is whether there is a doctrine today that effectively guides Iran's relations with great powers. Forward defense deals with Iran's relations with Israel, Saudi Arabia, and the United States, but it has little bearing on how Iran handles the expansion of great power involvement in the Middle East more broadly. Saudi Arabia and other Gulf states are using the opportunity of great power involvement in the region to their advantage by maintaining proper relations with Washington, while also courting Russia and China. Iran doesn't have the luxury of balancing relations with the United States against Russia and China, given toxic relations between Washington and Tehran. The bet on the future Iran is making is that power in the international system will shift to the east to the detriment of the United States. Even if this bet proves to be prescient, Iran will have to navigate the competing pressures of short-term economic demands from its people against the long-term possibility that an eastern tilt will eventually pay off in terms of economic and political benefits.

Story #5: Strategic Events

In the lead up to the signing of the Joint Comprehensive Plan of Action (JCPOA), otherwise known as the Iran nuclear deal, Israeli and Arab voices decried the deal on the grounds that it would help fuel Iran's hegemonic designs on the Middle East.[53] There is little to dispute that Iran has successfully projected power into Syria, Yemen, Lebanon, and Iraq. But it is also important to understand that much of Iran's "success" has come from its adaptation to events that have occurred, rather than from any grand design. In other words, Iran has been exceedingly successful in parlaying regional and global circumstances to its benefit.

Of course, the revolution of 1979 was the big bang moment for setting the course of Iran's foreign policy. But there has been a strategic evolution for Iran based largely on circumstances not of its making. Let's examine Iran's foreign policy evolution through the lens of seminal events.

The Iran-Iraq war

Strategy typically doesn't spring from some theoretical concern, but rather is forged out of necessity. In the case of post-revolutionary Iran, it was the Iran-Iraq war that commenced with an attack by Iraq in 1980 which served as the crucible for Iran's strategic thinking.

The war did several things to affect the course of Iran's strategic thought process. The first is it reinforced a worldview that has been outlined in previous chapters. It reinforced that both the United States and the Soviet Union, despite Cold War rivalries, would ultimately conspire to suppress the wishes and ambitions of the Iranian people. The view was that the superpowers would work in tandem to preserve the Cold War structure. While this was a theoretical and ideological view before the revolution, the Iran-Iraq war added credence to that view.

Solidifying this view was that the United States and Soviet Union both backed Iraq, particularly once Iran gained the initiative in the war in 1982. Both superpowers were involved with reflagging Kuwaiti tankers in the Persian Gulf in 1987 to deter Iran from continuing its attacks on ships.[54] Both the rivalry and cooperation that was embedded in Iran's worldview about great powers were evident in this incident. After the United States learned that Kuwait was close to a deal with Moscow on reflagging Kuwaiti oil tankers, Washington swooped in and preempted Moscow. But notwithstanding the rivalry around reflagging, the lesson the Iranians took from this was that both superpower rivals were on the same side against Iran. The rivalry between the superpowers was on full display, as was their mutual commitment to preventing an Iranian victory.

The second is that it laid the foundation for the forward defense doctrine. The fact that Iran was invaded by its neighbor exposed Iran's vulnerability at the height of its revolutionary fervor. Iran has had a history of interventions, invasions at the hands of both regional and global powers, from the Ottomans to the Russians and British. But the invasion from Iraq at such a formative moment in the revolution became seared into Iran's strategic consciousness. It contributed to Iran's sense of isolation, as no country other than Syria took the side of Iran against Iraq's aggression.[55] And it fortified Iran's commitment to building strategic depth so as not to be as vulnerable to attack as it had been.

Third, the Iran-Iraq war tested Iran's capacity to extract sacrifice from the Iranian people. Khomeini always felt that the secret sauce of the revolution was Iran's ability to tap into the Islamic fervor of the people. Iran did survive the initial onslaught of the war due to the passionate wave of young people it threw at the war. This is one of the legacies of the war that may have passed its expiration date. The protests in the past few years, culminating in the wave of unrest following the killing of Mahsa Amini in 2022, suggest that Iran's extractive capacity at home may have waned. The question will be how the Iranian people will weather the post-October 7 environment, when they may be asked to sacrifice even more than in past years. The Palestinian cause has limited appeal to many Iranians. So, sacrifices on behalf of Hamas and the Palestinian people may be tough to swallow for many ordinary Iranians.[56]

In sum, the Iran-Iraq war affirmed several of the biases of the Islamic Republic and helped inform Iran's strategic priorities going forward. It affirmed that great powers, particularly the United States, couldn't be trusted. It also reinforced skepticism toward the international community writ large, leaving Iran convinced that it is truly alone in the international system and committing it to establishing a strategic buffer zone to deter and repel any foreign attack on Iraq. The opportunities for creating this buffer zone came with the collapse of Saddam Hussein under withering US attacks on Iraq in 2003 and the civil wars that arose in Syria and Yemen a decade later. The Iran-Iraq war set the imperative for how Iran would respond to later events, such as the Arab Spring, the civil wars in Syria and Yemen, post-2003 Iraq, and even the aftermath of the attacks on Israel by Hamas in 2023.

The Lebanese civil war and establishment of Hezbollah

In the early, headiest days of the Iranian revolution, Khomeini and his minions made the commitment to export the revolution to other areas of the Middle East.[57] But any plans they may have had for this were precluded by the eight-year Iran-Iraq war that started in 1980. But even amid this war, an opportunity presented itself in Lebanon in 1982. The Israeli invasion of Lebanon had ultimately sparked outrage from the Lebanese Shi'i in the south, creating an opportunity for a new, more activist Shi'i force that could be supported by Iran.[58] That force was Hezbollah.

The importance of Hezbollah to Iran increased over time. Supreme Leader Ali Khamenei in 2006 said the following after the month-long Israel-Hezbollah war that was fought to a standoff:

> Heroic Lebanon and Hezbollah showed that one can stand up against and defeat Israel with resistance and firm determination. This is something that some politicians in Islamic countries could not at all imagine, but it happened. Israel was defeated because Hezbollah and the people of Lebanon showed steadfastness and resistance, because they relied on Allah the Exalted and because they utilized all their capabilities.[59]

In the aftermath of the Israel-Hezbollah war, Iran's popularity rose in Lebanon and even in the broader region due to Tehran providing aid for social services and reconstruction money to the Shi'i communities in Lebanon that had been devastated by Israeli bombers. For many in the Arab world, Hezbollah (and by extension Iran) became the darlings of resistance groups, having evinced the capacity and will to tangle with the Israelis and the Americans.

As Khomeini indicated, Hezbollah gave Iran both offensive and defensive capabilities. On the offensive side, Hezbollah had acted as a terror arm of the Islamic Republic with the attack on the US marine barracks in Beirut in 1983, and the kidnapping of President of the American University of Beirut, David Dodge.[60] And in the months following the attack by Hamas on Israel in 2023, and the subsequent counterattacks by Israel in Gaza, Hezbollah lobbed missiles against Israel. Defensively, Hezbollah gave Iran a deterrence capability via its large arsenal of short-, medium-, and long-range missiles that could rain terror on Israel should Iran be attacked.

In retrospect, Lebanon in the 1980s with Hezbollah became a blueprint for how Iran could take advantage of state failure thirty years later in the broader region. Iran learned in Lebanon how to operate effectively within failed states and leveraged those lessons decades later in dealing with other state failures. Starting in 2003 with the American invasion of Iraq, and then in 2011 as the Arab Spring morphed into multiple civil wars, Iran scaled up its presence in the region using Hezbollah as its expansionist vehicle for interventions in Syria, Yemen, and Iraq. In other words, Lebanon of the 1980s with Hezbollah was a proof of a concept that became scaled up decades later in response to the epidemic of state failure that hit the region during the Arab Spring. It used the foundation it had built in Lebanon in the eighties and refined in Iraq after 2003, to scale up operations in Syria and Yemen a decade later.

It may appear that Iran's relationships with Hezbollah and other militias in its portfolio are permanent fixtures of the Middle East. But it is important to keep in mind that Iran's substate shadow strategy using groups like Hezbollah exists against a backdrop of a collapsed regional order. Should the region start to stabilize, and should Iraq, Lebanon, and Syria start to assert their sovereignty, the strategy may be a less robust basis for competitive influence in the region.

Also, the question of what role Hezbollah will play in a post-October 7 world is still open. Much of this depends on how degraded Hezbollah becomes under Israeli attack. But whether Hezbollah is permanently damaged or is rebuilt with the help of Iran, we shouldn't overlook the centrality this group has played in Iran's national security strategy. The creation of Hezbollah in the 1980s became an early foundation of what decades later became Iran's shadow strategy of tying together the various militias in Syria, Iraq, and Yemen into an integrated whole. While the collapse of these countries into civil war could not have been foreseen in 1982, the decision to support Hezbollah during the civil war in Lebanon became part of a much broader strategy once Iran had the opportunity to extend its operational reach into the broader region. While support for Hezbollah may have been a tactical move in 1982, it later became part of a broader and more deliberate strategy.

9/11 and the US invasions of Afghanistan and Iraq

The events of September 11, 2001 sent shockwaves across the globe. In Iran, vigils were held in support of the families whose loved ones perished in New York and Washington, and on the flight that crashed in Pennsylvania. And most Iranians disapproved of the attacks.[61] Even Iran's President Mohammed Khatami said the following:

> I would like to again express my deepest condolences to the nation of America and express my sorrow for the tragic event of September 11. What occurred was a disaster.[62]

Notwithstanding this early paroxysm of sympathy, the official policy from the Iranian government to the events that followed September 11 was one that could be described as complex. While the US invasion of Afghanistan that followed the attacks rattled the Iranians, the silver lining was that it toppled the Taliban regime that was reviled in Tehran. Understanding the tightrope of opposing US interventions in principle yet also acknowledging the risks of not cooperating with the wounded superpower, the Iranians offered logistical support to US operations in Afghanistan.[63]

But the honeymoon ended, and the dynamic shifted quickly with the hostile rhetoric coming out of the Bush administration. President Bush in his State of the Union Address in January 2002 labeled Iran as part of an "axis of evil," along with Iraq and North Korea. In addition to being interpreted as an insult, the signal this sent to the Iranians was that goodwill gestures on the part of Iran are misconstrued by Washington as weakness, and that further cooperation would be futile and unproductive.

In 2003, Iran's fortunes changed again with the US invasion of Iraq. Initially, it solidified the view that the United States was an irremediably aggressive actor and brought home the reality that Iran was flanked by US forces on two of its borders. The Iranians believed that they could be the next target of US aggression, particularly with the "axis of evil" moniker. And in fact, the Bush administration did toy with the idea of invading Iran.[64]

But the US invasion of Iraq was a double-edged sword for Iran. Notwithstanding the potential for aggression from the United States, the toppling of the regime of Iraqi President Saddam Hussein provided a boon to Tehran given Iraq's previous aggression. Moreover, once the Americans became mired in both Afghanistan and Iraq, the fear of an invasion from the United States was felt less intensely by the Iranians.

Supreme Leader Ayatollah Khamenei said that the removal of Saddam Hussein was a gift from God.[65] Whether granted by the heavens or the missteps of the United States, the invasion of Iraq after 9/11 presented Iran some opportunities to operationalize some of the strategic priorities that had emerged out of the Iran-Iraq war, decades earlier. The toppling of Saddam allowed Iran to build on the model it had established with Hezbollah in Lebanon to extend its capability into the region using its Quds Force of the Revolutionary Guards. This laid the foundation of a strategy of working with and establishing militias that could later penetrate weak countries like Yemen and Syria.

It is important to understand that the toppling of Saddam had some inherent perils for Iran, aside from the obvious threat of the United States sitting just across the border. It would be a stretch to say it was a gift that fell into Iran's lap. A significant risk Iran had to contemplate was that a complete collapse of the Iraqi state could lead to instability in Iran, particularly in the Arab province of Khuzestan and in perennially restive Kurdistan. And the threat of Sunni groups rising as a backlash against a Shi'i majority-led Iraqi state, as happened in 2014 with the Islamic State (ISIS), was omnipresent.[66]

Iran had to manage through these risks of further American aggression and of instability in Iraq. In the emerging landscape of post-Saddam Iraq, Iran was able to successfully penetrate its new Shi'i-dominated political structure, leveraging ties it had with groups before the fall of Saddam in 2003. Tehran had connections to the Supreme Council for the Islamic Revolution in Iraq (SCIRI), which later was called the Islamic Supreme Council of Iraq (ISCI). These ties extended back to the period in the 1990s when the United States invaded Iraq during the first Gulf War. It also had close connections to the Badr Brigade, which had sheltered in Iran since the Iran-Iraq war, but then set up offices in Baghdad with Iranian support after the US invasion in 2003.[67]

These relationships in Iraq had to be finessed by Tehran, as improperly executed things could have worked out poorly for the Iranians.[68] In fact, the political alliances weren't trouble free for the Iranians. Tehran initially saw Muqtada al-Sadr, who led the Mahdi Army, a Shi'i militia, as an ally. Relations were tentative at times, but there was the common bond of opposition to the American presence. Initially, Sadr was seen by the Iranians as an Iraqi rendition of Hassan Nasrallah, the charismatic head of Hezbollah in Lebanon. While eventually Sadr fell out of favor with the Iranians, the initial dalliance speaks to a broader intention to "Lebanonize Iraq," meaning to use the Hezbollah model developed decades before in Lebanon of aligning with a local group to cement Iran's influence in the country. Iran had buy-in for this from the newly minted Iraqi political elite. Iraqi Prime Minister Ibrahim al-Jaafari, elected in 2005, approved the Iranian Quds Force plan to train and equip Sadr's Mahdi Army.[69] Iran's Quds Force, the expeditionary arm of the Islamic Revolutionary Guard Corps (IRGC), became the connective tissue between Iran and Iraqi militias and political groups. Right under the nose of the Americans, Iran's Major General Qassim Soleimani, head of the Quds Force, became the virtual Viceroy of Iraq, particularly after his relationship with Sadr soured.[70] This cemented Soleimani's position as the impresario of Iran's foreign policy, which would later be used in Syria and Yemen.

While Iran didn't favor complete chaos in Iraq, it did want a top-to-bottom clearing of the decks of the previous regime. Unbeknownst to the United States, Iran had ties to Ahmed Chalabi, an Iraqi exile who was America's "darling" pushing for a US invasion.[71] The plan of de-Baathification, which Chalabi had recommended to the Americans, apparently was devised or at least cleared by the Iranians.[72] If true, this shows the degree to which the Iranians had a stake in the complete dismemberment of the Iraqi regime, making it ripe for Iranian influence and penetration.

Even after it became clear that Iran accounted for a percentage of US casualties in Iraq due to its improvised explosive devices (IEDs), the Iranians believed that the United States was too mired in the civil war that eventually erupted in Iraq to do much about it. The audacity of the Iranians was stunning considering they publicly offered an $800 bounty for every American killed in Iraq.[73] *The Times* of London reported that Iran also offered a $1,000 compensation for soldiers killed in Afghanistan.[74]

Later in 2014, when the Islamic State (ISIS) posed an existential threat to Iraqi sovereignty, Iran turned the situation to its advantage. Before the Americans could assemble a broad international coalition for defeating ISIS, Iran helped prevent it from capturing Baghdad after Mosul had already fallen to the group. Iran's role in helping defeat ISIS in Iraq benefited Tehran on two fronts. First, it allowed it to dominate the Popular Mobilization Forces (PMF) or Hashd al-Sha'bi, which had been formed in response to Ayatollah Sistani's fatwa to arm to liberate Iraq from ISIS.[75] The majority of the sixty-six different groups, which comprised the PMF, took orders from Iran.[76] Most of these groups remained in place in Iraq after almost all Iraqi territories had been liberated from ISIS. Second, helping clear out ISIS created an opportunity for Iran to end its isolation. It was now doing the Arab world's bidding by fighting a regional insurgency that threatened many Arab states, including Saudi Arabia and Egypt. Third, like in Syria,

Iran's help in clearing out ISIS cemented it as the indisputable powerbroker in Iraq. Iran's presence was seen as instrumental to Iraq not falling back into civil war. It was also clear that even after Mosul and other areas of Iraq were liberated from ISIS, the Iraqi state remained dependent on Tehran.[77]

In my discussions with Iraqis, including then Ambassador to the United States, Fareed Yasseen, it was clear that Iran's role was seen as central to Iraq's independence from the likes of the Islamic State. He was clear that for the first three months after the fall of Mosul to the Islamic State it was Iran, and not the US-led international coalition, that saved Baghdad from falling. While he was clear that the sentiment of Iraqi officials was the desire for Iraq to be free of any foreign intrusions, the security exigencies of the Iraqi state militated against this.[78]

The question is whether these actions by Iran are part of a strategy. They might not individually be strategic, but they seem to be tied to a broader strategic thrust. Iran was able to maneuver around or even outmaneuver the United States by using its role as partner to the Iraqi government in the bid to defeat ISIS to strengthen itself inside the country. And it made the Iraqi government beholden to it, even in the face of pressure from Washington during the first Trump administration.

What strategic benefit did this have for Iran beyond Iraq? It certainly gave Tehran an advantage in the Saudi-Iran rivalry. Fears were heightened in Riyadh that Iraq had been wrested away from the Arab camp and would become a mere vassal state to Iran. This fear most assuredly was one driver of efforts by Saudi Arabia starting in 2016 to re-engage with Iraq. The other benefit was it played to Iran's self-image as a consequential power, as the Americans, which had only a shadow force in Iraq left, had to accept and work alongside Iran.

In sum, Iran's involvement in Iraq accomplished several things. First, it worked toward neutralizing the threat from Iraq, something that had been a priority since the Iran-Iraq war. By establishing itself militarily, politically, and even religiously in the country, it bought itself an insurance policy against a threat ever materializing on Iran's western border. Second, it weakened the US position in Iraq or at least it ensured that the Iraqi government, even if militarily dependent on the United States, would need to consider the concerns of Tehran. Also, starting in 2014, it was clear that the biggest threat to Iraq wasn't from Iran, but from internal insurgency groups like ISIS, or other like-minded Sunni groups.

The question is, are these advantages to Iran sustainable? Iran has been able to take advantage of circumstances over time, but in line with the theme of this book, coming up with a broad, sustainable grand strategy is very different than adapting to changing regional or international systems. The evidence as we sit on the cusp of 2025 isn't necessarily all positive.[79] The heavy-handedness of the militias of the Popular Mobilization Forces (PMF), the diversion of rivers in Iraq in response to the drought in Iran, as well as fuel shortages caused by Iran, could limit Iran's staying power in Iraq. Also, the demonstrations in Iraq that protested Iranian influence in 2019 could be repeated.

Moreover, as Iraq starts to try to normalize its international relations portfolio, Iran will have competition from Saudi Arabia and other wealthy Gulf Arab countries. While Iran so far has successfully countered these efforts, it is possible that Saudi Arabia and other Gulf states will see their influence grow in the future, due to the potential power of Gulf Arab investments.[80]

The Arab Spring and civil wars

For some Iranians, the onset of the Arab Spring in 2010–11 looked like redemption, as revolutionary spirits swept away old, stodgy Arab regimes in Tunisia, Egypt, and Yemen. Tehran tried to put claim to what was clearly an Arab revolution, suggesting that the Arab Spring was a consequence of its own 1979 Iranian revolution.[81] For a country whose revolutionary fervor had isolated it in the region and globally, it was a heady moment. But it was a double-edged sword for the Islamic Republic. The bloody putdown of protests in Yemen and Bahrain, and the later brutality in Syria seemed reminiscent of Iran's crackdown against protesters in 2009.

But the real threat came when, with help from the United States and Gulf Arab countries, the opposition movement in Syria had threatened to topple President Bashar al-Assad, the one Arab leader aligned with Iran. Shortly after Syria fell into civil war in 2011, Iran entered the fray with its own Quds Force, Hezbollah, as well as tens of thousands of Iraqi and Afghan volunteers. Russia entered the war in 2015 using its airpower to augment Iran's ground campaign.

The Syrian civil war

Like with Iraq, instability in Syria represented both a threat to and opportunity for Iran. The threat was that a longstanding ally and link to Hezbollah could fall during the Syrian civil war. Syria had been instrumental to Iran's strategy since the early days of the revolution, being the only Arab state to align with Tehran after the revolution and throughout the Iran-Iraq war. The Syrian civil war confronted Iran with the possibility of losing this critical ally should the protesters and insurgents prevail over the regime of Syrian President Bashar al-Assad.

The potential threat posed by the Syrian civil war to Iran's perception of security shouldn't be underestimated. In fact, Mehdi Taeb, head of the Revolutionary Guards intelligence wing and close advisor to Supreme Leader Ali Khamenei, reflected this thinking when he said:

> ... if we lose Syria, we won't be able to preserve Tehran. Syria is Iran's 35th Province.[82]

What the quote reflects is the view that the loss of Assad would have jeopardized Iran's deterrence against Israel, as it could have removed a Syrian threat from Israel's northern border. And because of Syria's role in Lebanon, it could have also compromised the Iranian position there. The Iranians believed that US support for the Free Syrian Army in the early days of the Syrian civil war was intended to cut Iran's link to Hezbollah.[83] Fortifying the Assad regime, therefore, was seen as critical to Iran's own security. In the coming months and years, we will learn whether the loss of Syria as a loyal and reliable ally has dire security implications for Iran, as Tehran tries to adjust to a post-Assad regime takeover in Damascus.

The opportunities provided by the relationship with Syria were apparent almost from the beginning of the Iranian revolution, with Syria acting as a strategic land bridge to Hezbollah after the group was established in 1982. It was also important to Iran as an escape portal from the isolation it experienced amid the sea of hostility from the Arab world. The hostility was understandable given the threats Iran made to export its revolution to surrounding Arab countries. But even if largely self-inflicted, the isolation felt by Iran was real. Also, relations with Syria were instrumental against a growing US-dominated political order in the Middle East following the Cold War. Syria moved even closer to Iran once Damascus had lost its Soviet benefactor.

There were significant benefits to Iran in coming to the rescue of the Syrian regime mired in civil war. Helping Assad remain in power would provide Tehran with both military *and* political strategic depth. Entering Syria amid war afforded Iran the opportunity to bring Damascus closer into the Iranian orbit and further away from the Arab fold. It brought

Iran's vaunted Quds Force closer to Israel and, along with Iraq and Yemen, created a crack in the already fragile Arab political order. Even before the civil war, Syria was a key part of Iran's attempt to build strategic depth. It became even more instrumental during the war.[84] It became part of an operationalization of Iran's forward defense doctrine, which entailed projecting influence and power beyond Iran's borders to protect the homeland. And it provided an insurance policy against the Arab world ever unifying against Iran again.

The Iranians understood that even with the help of their own Quds Force shock troops, Syria could be lost. In 2015, both the Syrian government and Iran desperately sought Russian help with much-needed air power. A key Russian advisor I met in Abu Dhabi in 2016 told me that when he arrived in Damascus in 2015, the Assad regime was more rickety and closer to collapse than Moscow had previously thought. Russian help ultimately did tilt the balance toward Assad, but this was lost when the group Hay'at Tahrir al-Sham (HTS) toppled the Assad regime late in 2024, threatening both Iranian and Russian influence in Syria, and potentially in the broader region.

It is tempting to see Iran's actions in Syria purely as a Machiavellian plan to build on its ambition to establish regional hegemony. One would have to have blinders not to see some naked opportunism in Iran's actions during the Syrian civil war, as well as the conflict in Iraq and Yemen.

But it is important to point out that Iran neither caused the Syrian civil war nor the collapse of the Arab political order. The civil wars in Syria and Yemen erupted out of the Arab Spring protests and local grievances against authoritarian governments. But the collapse of these two countries gave Iran the capacity to build on the capabilities established with Hezbollah in the 1980s and Iraq after the US invasion of 2003. It scaled up Hezbollah's capacity, taking it outside its Lebanese base. But it also created a venue for putting Iranian ground troops within striking distance of Israel. This scratched the itch of creating a broader phalanx against the United States and its allies, solidifying the resistance front, and enabling Iran to deal effectively with its regional rivals. And it played to the strengths and leadership of the now late Qassim Soleimani of the vaunted (and by many vilified) Quds Force division of the Revolutionary Guards. Soleimani was a master of marshalling non-state actors in service of Iran's interests in the collapsed states of Syria, Iraq, Afghanistan, and Yemen.

Additional value was the strategic depth provided by a land bridge between Iran, Syria, Iraq, and Lebanon. The land bridge concept involved seeing these fragile countries as part of one battlefield with which to fight the likes of ISIS but also an integrated force arrayed against Israel and the United States.[85] Beyond Syria, Iran had the ability to establish a one-battlefield approach, connecting its assets in Lebanon, Syria, Yemen, and Iraq. Iraq was in shambles and in Iran's orbit, and Syria was dependent on Tehran for regime survival. Yemen had also collapsed into civil war with Iran's Houthi ally at the helm. This wide swath of Iranian power gave Tehran the strategic depth it long coveted. Iran's view of the single battlefield concept was drawn from the Chinese Silk Road concept, only writ small. Both Ayatollah Khomeini and his successor Ali Khamenei were impressed with the Ancient Royal Road linking Khorasan in ancient Persia to China.[86]

This whole enterprise hinged on the survival of Assad, a bet that Iran potentially lost with the collapse of the Assad regime in December of 2024. Iran was backing and fortifying a minority Alawite government in a predominantly Sunni country, a dynamic unlikely to survive the demise of Assad. In other words, now that the Assad government has fallen to a predominantly Sunni group, the glue that held Syria to Iran could become attenuated.[87] With the fall of Assad, Iran's deterrence capability against Israel and the United States across both Syria and Lebanon could disappear.[88]

During the civil war in Syria, several operational capabilities of Iran were sharpened and then exported later to its operations in Iraq and Yemen. The operation to save Assad entailed stitching together several militia groups under the command of Iran's Quds Force and coordinating overall efforts with military units loyal to the Syrian government, and with the Russians. This established an organizational and coordination muscle that Iran drew upon for operations elsewhere. One of the fighting units which came to Syria in 2013 was drawn from the Hazara Shi'i refugees who had come to Iran from Afghanistan and fell under the command of Major General Qassim Soleimani of Iran's Quds Force.[89] The Shi'i refugees from the war in Afghanistan, organized into the Fatemiyoun Brigade, were motivated by gratitude to Iran and as well some pressure, and were ideologically predisposed to protect Shi'i shrines, such as the Sayyida Zaynab Shrine near Damascus.[90] As part of the Iranian network, Hezbollah's operations were enlarged to Syria. The Iranians leveraged the vaunted brand of Hezbollah to train and organize some of the other militias. The model had been successful in Lebanon and was an attractive model for recruits being sent to the Syrian theatre.[91]

The question going forward is whether Iran's investment in Syria has been completely lost with the collapse of Assad. This depends partially on any residual Iranian soft power that may remain in a post-Assad Syria. From where we sit today, it seems unlikely that any significant good will remains in Syria for Iran, given Tehran's longstanding support for the hated Assad regime.[92] Also, it is doubtful that what once was a proud Arab nationalist country could ever again fall into the orbit of non-Arab Iran. Given the historical peculiarities of the relationship that kept Iran and Syria aligned since the Iranian revolution, it seems that Iran will not be able to recreate the conditions in Syria that allowed it to operate as it once did during the Assad era. This will become even more critical as the civil war winds down and pressure grows for Iran to pivot to something less militaristic and more focused on governance. This will also be important as the Arab League, which readmitted Syria in 2023 after a long hiatus, tries to rehabilitate it in the Arab world in the post-Assad era.[93] Also, Iranian interests in Syria might be compromised by the fact that Turkey could become a new powerbroker given its relationship with the new post-Assad ruling elite.

The Yemeni civil war

Iran's motivation for its support for the Houthis in Yemen started out differently than for Syria, Iraq, and Lebanon. For the latter countries, the intent was to preserve and expand the country's strategic depth in the region, and to deter the United States and Israel. But Iran's motivation for its involvement in Yemen rested on a different and more opportunistic premise, which was to frustrate Saudi Arabia's ambition of imposing its will on its southern neighbor. Moreover, it was to protect Iran's ships in the Red Sea. Thus, Iran's initial motivation was more about competitive strategy vis-à-vis Saudi Arabia than part of a grand strategy. And it was in response more to opportunity to block Saudi ambitions than about threats from Israel or the United States.

We have seen, however, that the motivation and calculation have morphed over time, as Iran has more closely integrated the Houthis into its "axis of resistance." We saw this most profoundly in the aftermath of October 7, 2023, when the Houthis targeted ships in the Red Sea and became part of a network of Iran-supported militias that raised regional tensions in support of Hamas.

But in the decade before October 7, there were important sparks that fueled Iran's intervention in Yemen. First was the Arab Spring, which added tensions to an already brewing civil war in Yemen, weakening and then toppling the government of President Ali Abdullah Saleh. Second was Saudi Arabia's entry into the Yemen civil war in 2015, which both galvanized the Houthis and gave Iran an opportunity to further support them. While the relationship between Iran and the Houthis predated this, the priority Iran assigned to the Houthis spiked after the Saudi military incursion. This helped bog down Saudi Arabia in an unwinnable battle that would be enervating to its efforts to compete with Iran in the region. Being bogged down in Yemen would almost guarantee that Riyadh couldn't marshal an effective resistance against Iranian efforts in Syria, Lebanon, and Iraq.

Support for the Houthis gave Iran the ability to counter Saudi Arabia without the need to invest in or expose its own ground troops, which were being spread thin in interventions in Syria and Iraq. Iran seemed to understand as well that the weakness of the Saudi position was that they were mostly engaging from the air with no effective partners on the ground. It was perfect for the Iranians in that its involvement was low-cost, low-risk for them while high-cost, high-risk for the Saudis.[94]

In many ways, the Houthis were seen by the Iranians as the Hezbollah of Yemen. In fact, Iran tasked Hezbollah with helping to train the Houthis.[95] While Tehran never exercised the same degree of operational control over the Houthis as over Hezbollah, Iran saw both as regional insurgency movements that fit into Iran's overall design for its "axis of resistance" in the region.

Iran focused on augmenting the intrinsic capabilities of the Houthi leadership. It helped outfit the Houthis with Iran's 4GW (fourth-generation warfare), combining a war of attrition, urban fighting, and use of both conventional and unconventional means. And it also deployed Anti-Access, Area Denial (A2/AD) methods to ensure that the critical Bab el-Mandeb Strait remained open. The head of the Islamic Republic of Iran Navy (IRIN), Admiral Habibollah Sayyari, looking to 2025 said that Iran intends to influence the strategic maritime triangle that extends from the Bab el-Mandeb Strait at the southern end of the Red Sea to the Strait of Hormuz and even across the Indian Ocean to the Strait of Malacca.[96]

There is another strategic benefit to Iran of its involvement in Yemen that shouldn't be overlooked. Iran took advantage of its loose command and control relationship with the Houthis to give itself the cover of plausible deniability. While it was clear that Iran was supplying and training the Houthis, the ground battles themselves were perpetrated by the Houthi fighters. We saw the benefits of this ambiguity with the attacks on the Saudi Abqaiq facilities in September 2019 and the 2022 drone attacks on the UAE. The Houthis claimed responsibility, giving Iran the ability to distance itself from the attacks, even if they were conducted on Tehran's behalf.

Now that Saudi Arabia and Iran have re-established relations, and Saudi Arabia has lessened its involvement in Yemen, the original raison d'être of the relationship is less compelling. But with the Gaza war, the Houthis in many ways have greater strategic significance than before for Iran. They have become more strategic as part of Iran's "axis of resistance," having taken part in Iran's pro-Hamas efforts. The Houthis since October 7, 2023 have harassed ships from Israel, the United States, and other countries in the Red Sea. Time will tell whether this is an enduring foundation for the relationship or whether relations return to their more transactional roots. And time will tell whether the benefits of ambiguity provided by Houthi actions against Israel and the United States continue to protect Iran from Israeli and American reprisals.

The Ukraine war

The principles undergirding Iran's foreign policy have been remarkably consistent, with hostility toward the United States and Israel being hallmarks.

Concerns about the United States and Israel intensified when the Cold War ended. The United States had little great power competition in the Middle East for the first twenty years of the post-Cold War era. And then there was rapprochement between the United States and Russia in the 1990s, including Moscow joining NATO's Partners for Peace program in 1994. This made it more difficult for middle powers like Iran to play one global power off the other.

Iran's relations with Moscow in the post-Cold War era were partially derivative of the relations each had with the United States. Iran's relationship with Russia improved after the Trump administration unilaterally withdrew from the JCPOA nuclear deal and imposed punishing sanctions. Once the Europeans failed to provide Iran relief from sanctions, Tehran had few options other than moving closer to Russia and China. But there were perils in leaning hard to the east. In the Iranian mindset there was a concern that either Russia or China might trade its close relationship with Iran to get some concessions of greater value from either the United States or Europe. Sensitivities about Russian betrayals of Iran go back to the nineteenth and twentieth centuries.

With the Ukraine war, there has been a not-so-subtle shift in this thinking. This time it was a deterioration in relations between Washington and Moscow that led to the shift. Russia's invasion of Ukraine in February 2022 changed Iranian perceptions in some significant ways. There has been much less of a concern about Iran being sold out or betrayed by Russia since the war started. Iranian leaders believe that there has been a rebalancing of bargaining leverage between Russia and Iran. Since the Russians have become ostracized by much of the west, and like Iran is under severe sanctions, Iranians believe both countries need one another. Also, Iranians believe that Russia is likely to remain a pariah in the west and isolated for some time to come, calculating that this ensures some sustainability in the improved leverage Iran enjoys.[97]

Also, Iran has helped Russia with the know-how of circumventing sanctions, which has led to a perception of increased bargaining leverage. Iranians also see that the leverage dynamics have evened out due to a more balanced military trade relationship, with Russia now buying from Iran critical drones and other military material needed to prosecute its war in Ukraine.[98]

Iran's claims to a more level playing field with Russia don't seem to be mere rhetorical bravado; Iran has also become more forceful with Russia. In July 2023, Russia made comments supporting the UAE position that the three islands—Abu Musa, Greater Tunb, and Lesser Tunb—occupied by Iran since 1971, belong to the UAE. In response Tehran summoned the Russian Ambassador to express outrage and lodge a formal grievance.[99] Also, evidence of increased leverage I heard from Iranians has been their greater flexing of muscles in Syria, independent of Russia, an obvious concern to the Israelis.

The strategic question for Iran is whether the current leverage dynamics it sees can be sustained and turned into a long-term gamechanger. This hinges on several things. One is the length and outcome of the Ukraine war. It is possible that Russia will be rehabilitated if Putin falls or if Russia makes significant concessions, both unlikely scenarios at the time of writing. Also, the relationships between China and Russia and between China and Iran could also be wildcards in the equation. If Russia can use China to offset some of the lost leverage with the west, Iran could be demoted in the eyes of the Kremlin. And, of course, this all depends on whether there is eventually a lessening of tensions between Iran and the United States.

Israel's war with Hamas in Gaza

The war in Gaza creates both strategic risks and opportunities for Iran. The opportunities are that it potentially creates fissures between the major Arab players and Israel. The UAE and Bahrain were the first Gulf Arab countries to normalize relations with Israel under the Abraham Accords. Prior to October 7, 2023, Saudi Arabia was a candidate for joining the normalization with Israel as part of a three-way deal that included the United States.

The war in Gaza sows doubts about the future of a possible deal between Saudi Arabia and Israel, even though Washington would potentially offer Riyadh security guarantees. The likelihood is low of an Israeli government agreeing to a process toward a two-state solution, the stated Saudi precondition for normalization. If there isn't an expansion of the Abraham Accords to include Saudi Arabia, Israel will be denied a solid basis for cooperation with the largest and most powerful Gulf Arab state. This could be a net positive for Iran. First, continuation of a war that already has seen a staggering number of Palestinian casualties could push Saudi Arabia and Iran into closer alignment on this issue. We have already seen a subtle convergence. Saudi Arabia has been put in the position of having to condition normalization with Israel on progress toward a two-state solution, something unlikely under a Netanyahu-led coalition in Israel. While Iran has publicly opposed a two-state solution, Saudi Arabia conditioning its relations with Israel on improved conditions for the Palestinians has caused a subtle shift toward Tehran.

It is possible that once the Gaza campaign winds down, Iran's desire to maintain relations with Saudi Arabia as a hedge against possible aggression from Washington or Israel during a second Trump administration could lead it to play less of a spoiler role on the Palestinian issue, bringing it close to the position held by Riyadh. But there will be some countervailing pressures that could push Tehran in the opposite direction. Iran has been the sole country in the region to have consistently championed the cause of the Palestinians. Iran supported Hamas and Palestine Islamic Jihad in Gaza when the Arab world had largely bypassed the issue. This could give Iran, and its resistance front, some cachet with Arab masses disgruntled by their own governments' passivity.

For certain Iran will have to weigh the risks and rewards of its various options. It may find it difficult to sustain its "axis of resistance" posture while still improving its relations with its Arab neighbors given the pressures of the post-October 7 environment. Iran won't yield on supporting the various militias in its portfolio, but it could be incentivized to emphasize further its state-to-state relations and play down its substate militia strategy.[100] The incentives for this may be greater due to the weakening by Israel of Hamas and Hezbollah and the looming realities of a second Trump administration.

Story #6: The Pre-eminence of the United States in Iran's Strategy

Speaking with Iranian officials, it is evident that a disproportionate amount of their foreign policy effort and resources are directly or indirectly spent on issues related to the United States.[101] For Iran, the United States is both a regional and global actor. One could say that the United States is both a regional and global actor in almost any region of the world, and therefore this isn't particularly revelatory. But the US role as a regional actor in the Middle East is out of proportion with its presence in other regions. In the Middle East, the United States has a military presence, a history of military and political interventions, and the presence of powerful allies.

This intense focus on the United States has led to a distortion in Iran's foreign policy. While this is true with other countries in the region, with Iran it is particularly profound. On the one hand, Iran has a robust regional foreign policy with a network of militias across the Middle East, and a nascent diplomatic re-engagement with Saudi Arabia. The distortion comes in that the purpose of Iran's investments in almost all these regional initiatives has largely to do with the United States. Iran's operations in Lebanon, Syria, Iraq, and Yemen are heavily motivated by Iran's perceived need for deterrence against the United States and Israel. And while Iran's relationship with Saudi Arabia involves issues specific to the region, it too is partially derivative of Iran's desire to reduce the influence of the United States by keeping Riyadh from tilting too far toward Washington.

In many ways, the entire region has become a battleground between the competing strategies pursued by Iran and the United States. While Iran was busy building an unconventional substate shadow system of militias to buttress itself against aggression by the United States and Israel, the United States was using more conventional, Cold War-era concepts to try to contain and cajole Iran.

The US state-based strategy of containing Iran using allies in the region could be very effective if Iran and the United States ever become entangled in a direct conventional military confrontation. The United States with its overwhelming military capacity and strong state allies would have the advantage. But when direct confrontation is avoided, Iran still holds considerable advantage.[102] Iran's system for dealing with the United States has consisted of shadowy militias in the fragile states of Syria, Lebanon, Iraq, and Yemen. While these militias have sometimes attacked US positions in Syria and Iraq, for the most part the Iranian strategy has been an indirect one of just burrowing deeper into these states to frustrate American efforts to dislodge them.

This asymmetric strategy has for decades frustrated the efforts of many US presidents to contain Iran. While the United States projects power through strong states in the region, Iran's power is projected in the subterranean interstices of failed states in the region. The current region in shambles favors Iran as it allows it (and other states) to project power through the vacuum of countries at civil war.

This gets at the question of whether hostility to the United States is strategically advantageous for Iran. Given the aggressive stances taken by the United States during the Bush administration and first Trump term, and Washington's strong regional footprint, the Iranian response of a defensive crouch seems to be a strategically tenable course. But the strategic calculus is augmented by political and ideological considerations. The hostility to the United States is part of a worldview that goes back to the Iranian revolution. And in many ways, it plays to the political and economic interests of the Revolutionary Guards and other conservative and extremist parts of the regime. It also gives the regime a convenient foil for explaining away to its own population the dismal performance of the Iranian economy.

One could argue that Iran's hostile relationship with Washington has helped it cement ties with Russia and China. But there is also a strategic downside to Iran's eastward tilt. While the three countries share a common worldview about the United States, Iran is now more dependent on Russia and China because of this tilt. The Ukraine war and issues over Taiwan have mitigated the risk of this for Iran somewhat, but in the long run this could become a concern.

But there is something deeper here that often gets overlooked. The Iranians believe that the struggle with the United States is irremediable given the politics in the United States and Washington's relationship with Israel. They see US policy toward the Middle East increasingly driven by its allies rather than its hardcore vital interests. Moreover, the belief is the United States is intent on compromising Iran's sovereignty through regime change.[103]

And the Iranians buy the edict of famed Prussian military strategist Carl von Clausewitz that strategic "errors that proceed from a spirit of benevolence are the worst."[104] With Iranians I have interviewed there is a common belief that hostility toward the United States is necessary lest anything else be construed as weakness. The Iranians treat the United States as a bully that can't be placated and therefore must be resisted. The latest evidence Iran cites for this dynamic is the US withdrawal from the JCPOA agreement. The Trump administration did in fact see the deal as a sign of Iranian weakness and used maximum pressure and sanctions to get more concessions and bring Iran to its knees. Of course, this didn't work. But what is most important is that for many senior Iranians, including some of the reformists, diplomacy and accommodation with the United States is perceived to be a dead end. Only shows of strength will work with the United States, many believe. In contrast, the Iranians seem to trust the pragmatic commercial and political interests of Russia and China. These interests, the Iranians believe, act as stabilizers that can be satisfied politically and commercially without compromising Iran's sovereignty, while the United States in their eyes remains implacable.

Summation: Does Iran Have a Strategy?

The six stories in this chapter were designed to give the reader a kaleidoscopic view of the complexities of Iran's foreign policy. The stories range from the historical to the doctrinal to the conceptual. They show how Iran interpreted and adapted to a changing world and region, how it enshrined its adaptation in doctrines, and how it developed ways to maneuver around its most powerful adversary, the United States.

By distilling and synthesizing the lessons from the various stories, what composite picture appears around Iran's foreign policy strategy? At the broadest level, we can conclude that it has evolved and developed over time, but not in the traditional way we tend to think about strategy. There is little evidence to suggest that Iran wrestled with the notion of grand strategy in the way American leaders did during the early days of the Cold War. At the time of the revolution of 1979, Iranian leaders were clear that they aspired to export their revolutionary spirit to the broader region. But an aspiration is different than a strategy. While spreading the revolution beyond Iran's own sovereign borders may have been a goal, it was animated more by ideological fervor than by a clear pathway to achievement.

This shouldn't diminish the fact that the north star for the early revolutionary leaders was for Iran to serve as an inspirational engine for revolution across the Middle East. But rather than Iran having a grand design for how to shape the region in its own image, its foreign policy strategy emerged over time as an adaptation to shifting regional and global circumstances. What is paradoxical is that when the Middle East did experience paroxysms of revolution during the Arab Spring starting in 2010, Iran watched mostly from the sidelines. What was becoming clear to observers is that Iran was becoming a first-rate master adapter but only a second-rate shaper. In other words, Iran took advantage of circumstances that arose largely outside its control.

The pattern of Iran's post-revolutionary foreign policy shows that its successes were generally built on top of failed states as well as the missteps of failed leaders. Lebanon had failed as it gave way to civil war in 1975. The first real stake in the ground of Iran's strategy was the establishment of Hezbollah in Lebanon in 1982 amid the country's civil war and an Israeli occupation of the Shi'i south.

But eight years of a grinding Iran-Iraq war that commenced with an Iraqi invasion in 1980 limited Iran's capacity to build on its success with Hezbollah and spread revolution elsewhere. While it had few options in the short term, the war did lead Iran to double down on its need to build the capacity to project power and influence into the broader region. But the imperative as Iran emerged from war was different than it had been during the earlier, headier moments of the revolution. The emphasis coming out of the war was more on protecting the homeland than on exporting the revolution.

Iran believed coming out of war in 1988 that the only way to protect the homeland and preserve the sanctity of its borders was to build a buffer zone around the country. This became enshrined in a doctrine of forward defense which justified Iran's regional interventions based on a need for strategic depth. While Iran's foreign defense doctrine was partially animated by messianic, ideological motivations, this shouldn't overshadow the fact that coming out of eight years of war with Iraq, Iran prioritized protection of its borders above all else.

Only a few years after the end of Iran's war with Iraq, the Cold War ended with the collapse of the Soviet Union in 1991. Iran's threat perceptions shifted away from Iraq and toward the United States, which suddenly found itself with the capacity to operate freely in the Middle East. But the real watershed moment for Iran and the region came ten years later with 9/11. Instead of facing a threatening regional actor like Saddam Hussein, Iran now faced a reality of having a wounded and vengeful United States with occupation forces on its western border in Iraq and eastern border in Afghanistan. While initially this struck fear in the hearts of the Iranians, eventually they saw an opportunity to put into practice their forward defense doctrine. With the hated and feared Iraqi President Saddam Hussein deposed by the Americans, Iran saw a power vacuum and insinuated itself into the political, security, social, and religious structure of the country. Iran dusted off the playbook it had developed with Hezbollah in Lebanon decades earlier and applied it to the exigencies of Iraq, enabling it to create influence right under the noses of the Americans. While the Americans were concentrating power in Iraq, Iran in Sun Tzu fashion did the opposite. Rather than concentrating power, Iran instead diffused itself and extended its tentacles into the new post-Saddam Iraqi state. In other words, Iran understood that it couldn't effectively resist the American military presence, but it could insert itself into the emerging fabric of Iraq much like Sun Tzu's counsel to make oneself shapeless like water, and thereby remain impervious to the Americans. This approach of suffusing itself into the emerging structures of Iraq allowed Iran to slowly build an influence network that the Americans couldn't effectively counter.

Iran's capacity to adapt to changing circumstances was tested again in the wake of the Arab Spring protests when Syria in 2011 and Yemen in 2014 collapsed into civil war. These civil wars were laced with both threat and opportunity for the Iranians. War in Syria created a profound risk that Iran might lose its only real regional ally. And the civil war in Yemen gave Iran the opportunity to bedevil Saudi Arabia and bog it down in an unwinnable conflict.

Iran turned both civil wars to its advantage, insinuating itself into the fabric of Syria and exerting influence in the Arabian Peninsula through its support for the Houthis in Yemen, an enemy of the Saudis. The wars also allowed Iran for the first time to create a "whole of region" strategy. At the very core, the strategy tied together the failed states of Iraq, Lebanon, Syria, and Yemen into one Iranian-led network of shadowy militias, built not just to thwart and deter regional adversaries, but also the United States. While Iran knew it had little capacity to combat the United States using conventional means, it became increasingly confident that its network of militias in the region acted as a formidable deterrent.

Iran believed that its network of militias was largely impervious to the more conventional means of the United States and its allies. It used the strategy of diffusion it had developed in Lebanon in the 1980s and Iraq after 2003 to project itself into the Syrian and Yemeni civil wars, frustrating American attempts to contain Iran. In addition to thwarting American and Israeli efforts to contain it, Iran's network also served to block Saudi Arabia from reintegrating any of the failed countries of Lebanon, Iraq, Syria, and Yemen back into the Arab political orbit. Iran believed it finally had a strategy for preventing a unified Arab world from ever again threatening Iran, as it once had during the Iran-Iraq war.

What this narrative should convey is that Iran's consummate skill has been the power of adaptation. While initially Iran believed it needed to act on its forward defense doctrine to thwart its regional neighbors from attacking, over time the existential threat became the United States, a global actor. The strategic lesson Iran gleaned was that even though it couldn't thwart the United States on the global stage, it could resist it on the regional stage using its shadowy foreign policy. In other words, while Iran couldn't compete with the United States from afar, it could frustrate American efforts in Iran's own regional backyard.

The Middle East is likely undergoing a shift again, triggered by the attacks on Israel by Hamas in 2023 and the events that followed. The question is whether Iran's power of adaptation will continue working in its favor in this new environment. Iran in 2024 did what it had eschewed for decades, which was to directly confront Israel militarily. While Iran previously hid in the shadows, now with direct back-and-forth attacks with Israel, it is fully exposed. This is particularly dangerous since Iran's deterrence has been compromised with the degradation of Hezbollah and Hamas, and the potential loss of its Syrian ally in the post-Assad era.

Iran will face the horns of a vexing dilemma now that the gloves are off—will it prioritize rebuilding Hezbollah, or will it now tack more toward conventional diplomacy? Or will it make a mad dash for a nuclear weapon? At the time of writing, Iran is doing a bit of the first two and contemplating the third. Which of the approaches will be dominant will play out in subsequent years, testing out whether Iran's power of adaptation is still a core strategic capability and power skill.

7 IRAN'S STRATEGIC FUTURE

Much of this book has focused on how Iran has adapted to changes in its regional and global environments. The claim that Iran is more of an adapter than a shaper in its foreign policy may be construed by some as implying that Iran's motives are benign. This is certainly not what I have intended to convey or suggest. Iran can in fact be simultaneously adaptive and menacing. Iran has largely adapted to changes and events outside its control, but the fervor and skill with which it has turned these changes into advantages have created security threats for its neighbors and the region writ large.

This chapter will address some ways in which Iran's foreign policy might adapt and evolve in the future. Will Iran move beyond an almost totally securitized regional foreign policy toward a broader-spectrum strategy that also prioritizes economic growth? In other words, will it recalibrate its foreign policy to favor diplomacy or will it double down on support for its network of militias across the region? Niels Bohr, awarded the Nobel Prize in Physics, once said, "Prediction is very difficult, especially if it's about the future." With this tongue-in-cheek comment in mind, we won't endeavor to predict Iran's foreign policy. Instead, we will look at the factors that could influence Iran's strategic arc in the future. And we will look at a couple of possible scenarios of how Iran's foreign policy might continue to adapt.

The Future: Foreign Policy Drivers

Earlier chapters have focused on how Iran's history, great power competition, and regional dynamics have shaped its pre- and post-revolutionary foreign policy. This section will look at some of these same factors, but with a focus on how they can contribute to how Iran's future foreign policy might develop. We will look at how shifts in Iran's regional environment, including competition from rival states, could help shape the future. We will also examine great power competition and domestic politics as additional contributing drivers. These drivers will then be used to examine the different possible scenarios posited at the end of this chapter.

The battle of rival strategies

The Middle East has for decades been the scene of proxy battles. During the Cold War, the United States and Soviet Union competed with one another through their respective alliances with states in the region. Today, proxy battles continue, although they are waged not by international actors but rather regional actors. The strongest states in the region, Iran, Turkey, Saudi Arabia, Egypt, Qatar, the United Arab Emirates, and Israel, are competing with one another inside some of the weakest states, Syria, Lebanon, Libya, Iraq, and Yemen. Within this environment, Iran has distinct competitive advantages because of its militia network.

Many Gulf Arab rivals ascribe hegemonic motives to Iran because of the advantages it enjoys in the shadowy world of failed states. This view is understandable given these rivals have directly felt Iran's overwhelming influence inside these weak states, and the regional power this allows Tehran to wield. But hegemony requires one actor to be overwhelming in size, military capacity, and political and economic strength over other actors in the region. China would certainly qualify as the regional hegemon of East Asia. Unlike East Asia, though, the Middle East is more of a balance-of-power system than a hegemonic one. In the present and future Iran will face large, economically empowered states with vibrant militaries that can rival it and counterbalance its power, such as Turkey, Saudi Arabia, Egypt, the UAE, and even Israel.

This is not to downplay that Iran has plenty of advantages within the current system of failed states, giving off an aura of inevitable hegemony. But these advantages aren't likely to translate into the kind of economic, military, and political power needed to hold sway over an entire region. In other words, Iran may appear to be a hegemon in the shadowy contours of a collapsed regional order, but this is unlikely to translate into the political, military, and economic power required for true and sustainable regional hegemony.

Part of Arab frustration comes from an understanding that Iran can't be outcompeted at its own game of operating with militias in the shadowy failed states of the region. Instead, the Gulf Arab states are working to develop a different strategic model emphasizing future economic growth and diversification. One way of looking at the Middle East today is that it is a battle of different strategic models. The question is which of the two models will match up most effectively with where the Middle East is heading? And which of these actors has the most capacity to shape the direction of the Middle East going forward?

Iran's Gulf Arab rivals are not assuming that the failed states of the region will somehow stabilize with the weakening of Iran-supported militias. But they are betting on their own economies becoming vibrant economic growth engines that will spur a regional economic expansion despite the scourge of failed states dominated by Iran. In other words, by creating greater growth for themselves, they hope to shrink the overall impact of failed states on the region. As they grow larger and more prosperous, the thinking goes, the toxic effects of Syria, Lebanon, Iraq, and Yemen become diluted and proportionally smaller. And since Iran's strategy depends on these failed states, they are betting that its impact on the region could shrink as well.

The question for Iran's future is whether it will be able to compete more directly with its Arab rivals economically or simply double down on its substate militia approach. We see some strong, albeit nascent, signs that Iran is strengthening its interstate diplomatic relationships. It has re-established diplomatic relations with Saudi Arabia and has improved its relationships with Turkey and Egypt. And globally it has pivoted toward China and will likely share positions in the BRICS with the UAE and Egypt. Iranian leaders believe that membership in the Shanghai Cooperation Organization (SCO) and the BRICS will serve it well in creating more constructive relations with other states in the future.[1]

This is a promising development for Iran and possibly for the region, particularly since Tehran is likely to remain under economic sanctions by the United States for the foreseeable future. But Iran's prospects will likely be limited if it only leans toward China thinking it can circumvent its pariah status in the western-dominated global economic system. Other than Iran and Russia, none of the SCO or BRICS members are completely isolated from western economies. And it is important to keep in perspective the fact that as much as China and Iran may share antipathy toward the United States, Beijing has no desire to damage its relations within the global economic system to help Iran. While Iran's eastern tilt could potentially hitch it to Beijing's economic growth engine, Iran shouldn't overplay its hand, lest it discover the limits of China's willingness to take on the west on its behalf.

Battle of strategies: Saudi Arabia and Iran in Iraq

The battle of the strategies between Iran and its major Gulf Arab rival Saudi Arabia has already been playing out in Iraq. The competitive game in Iraq could be an indicator for what the broader regional landscape could look like for these two countries, as well as for other state relationships in the Middle East.

A focus on Iraq is important for both Iran and Saudi Arabia as each shares a long border with Iraq, making trade and other cross-border activity potentially efficient and viable. And the stakes in Iraq are high for both countries as it at least has the makings of a quasi-functioning government.

But before looking at what the prospects in the years ahead might be for competition between these two countries in Iraq, we should look at what the situation is today and how the relationship has evolved. After the American invasion in 2003, the Iranians quickly gained influence due to political and religious connections that had been forged prior to the US presence. This influence was magnified by Saudi Arabia giving Iran a huge head-start by treating Iraq as a pariah state from the beginning. The Saudis turned their worst fears of Iranian hegemony into a self-fulfilling prophesy by shunning the Iraqi government, in effect isolating it from the rest of the Arab world. Despite several entreaties by former Iraqi Prime Minister Nouri al-Malaki, King Abdullah refused to engage with Iraq on the grounds that its Shi'i leadership, including the prime minister, was seen as an Iranian proxy.[2]

However, with the passing of King Abdullah in 2015, the Saudis under the leadership of King Salman and Crown Prince Mohammed bin Salman came to believe that it had been a mistake to shun Iraq and cede control to Iran. Starting in 2016, the Saudis made amends with Iraqi Prime Minister Hayder al-Abadi, believing that notwithstanding Iranian influence, a relationship with Iraq would serve Saudi interests.[3]

The Saudis recognized that if they were going to compete with Iran in Iraq, their strategy was going to have play to their own immense financial strength and economic development finesse, rather than try to compete with Iran's militia network or its tentacle-like ties with the labyrinthine Iraqi government. In the years since 2016, the Saudis have started to operationalize their strategy by making some investments in Iraqi infrastructure.[4] In addition, since 2018, the Saudis have made investments in the energy and agriculture sectors. A Saudi-Iraqi Investment Company was established in 2023, with $3 billion allocated for major infrastructure projects.[5] But up until 2024, these investments and their impact have been relatively modest, annualized at about $1 billion.[6] There were new agreements penned in 2022 to connect Iraq to the Gulf Cooperation Council (GCC) and Saudi electricity grid.[7] And there have also been efforts to spur small business investment in Iraq. But at the time of writing, these investments have developed minimal traction.

Another competitive dynamic has been an attempt by Saudi Arabia to build soft power among the Iraqi Shi'i by visiting their shrines and developing relations in the bastions of Shi'ism, particularly in the holy cities of Karbala and Najaf.[8] At a time when Iranian soft power in the Shi'i areas has waned, as evidenced by protests in 2019 and 2020 against Iran, the Saudi approach is an interesting way for it to try to counter—or at least counterbalance—Iranian power in Iraq.

But Iran has worked behind the scenes to block Saudi investment projects out of a concern that over time Iraq could be reintegrated into the Arab fold.[9] According to Iraqi officials, Iranians have in not-so-subtle ways worked to slow down and hamper progress on Saudi infrastructure projects. But they qualified this with saying that the Iranians haven't had to do too much. The thirteen-year head start gave the Iranians a huge competitive advantage by allowing it to suffuse itself deeply into the social, political, economic, and religious fabric of the country. An additional impression gleaned from the Iraqis was that the Saudis were better at operating in the world of sovereign wealth funds in London and New York than they were at maneuvering through the "wild west" environment of Baghdad. Operating in the shadowy world of Iraq was the skill of the Iranians, not of the Saudis, I was told.[10]

The rapprochement between Saudi Arabia and Iran that came in 2023 has eased some of their tensions in Iraq, but Iran's continued hold over several Iraqi militia groups and patronage relationships inside the Iraqi government could still sabotage Saudi investments. Iraqis I interviewed for this book were skeptical about the ability of Saudi Arabia, which came late to the game in Iraq, to edge out or compete with the Iranians.[11] The only real caveat expressed came in the wake of the assassination by the

Americans of Major General Qassim Soleimani in 2020. Those who interacted with him as head of the Quds Force claimed he was a vibrant, charismatic, Arabic-speaking kingmaker in the country. Whether his successor, General Esmail Ghaani, would be as formidable a player is a question mark.

Whether Iran's first-mover advantage permanently blocks Saudi efforts in Iraq depends on several factors other than Iran's counterstrategy. One is the clarity and consistency of the Saudi Vision 2030 economic development program. Presently, the plan is mostly focused on domestic transformation of the Saudi economy.[12] Whether this ever extends to rebuilding and reintegrating Iraq and other fragile states into the Arab fold remains to be seen.

The sustainability of Iran's abundant advantages in Iraq also depends on the Iraqis themselves. If they have a stable government that is perceived by the Saudis to be less corrupt and more able to withstand Iranian pressure, Riyadh might have more confidence in making bolder investments. The other hinge factor will be the identity politics of the Iraqi people. Will Iraq move further away from sectarianism and more toward Iraqi or even Arab nationalism? In the demonstrations protesting the Iraqi government and Iran in the Shi'i majority areas in 2019 and 2020, the message was that a nascent Iraqi nationalism was stronger than a narrower sectarian identity. If this becomes a trend, then it could play well for the Saudis with whom the Iraqi people share an Arab identity. But if sectarianism prevails in the country, this will likely help cement Iran's role in Iraq through its Shi'i connections.

One way of thinking about the future is that the Iran-Saudi rivalry in Iraq is a test case for what could be a broader battle of strategies between the two countries in the region. While it is too early to ascertain what progress Saudi Arabia and other Gulf Arab states will make in trying to influence a new post-Assad government in Syria, it seems that the probability of their star rising as Iran's falls is high.[13] The same is true for Turkey, which at the time of writing seems poised to assert influence over the new regime in Damascus. The issue of timing could determine which country is best situated for the future. Iran still benefits from its first-mover advantage in the current fragile environment in Iraq and the broader region. But the Gulf Arab states, including Saudi Arabia, are making bets on a more stable future for Iraq. If this bet of greater stability in Iraq and other fragile states materializes, then the advantage could shift to Saudi Arabia in a new regional environment.

We have seen some evidence of the Gulf Arabs trying to push Iraq into more stable territory where they would have greater advantages. The UAE along with United Nations Educational, Scientific and Cultural Organization (UNESCO) is rebuilding the al-Nouri Mosque in Mosul, Iraq, in a project called "Revive the Spirit of Mosul."[14] This venerated mosque had been destroyed in the bid to liberate Iraq from ISIS. The question will be whether the Saudis and Emirates will take the long view. Reconstruction projects like the al-Nouri Mosque could ostensibly strengthen the Iraqi state, something that could redound positively to the Saudis. But there would need to be more larger-scale projects.

What could occur on the global stage that could upend a Saudi strategy and play to Iranian advantages in Iraq and beyond? A ramp-up in US-Iran tensions during a second Trump term could make Saudi efforts to compete with Iran in Iraq difficult. While the US may not actively oppose Saudi efforts in Iraq, increased tensions could worsen the investment environment in Iraq and feed Saudi skittishness. This scenario could play to Iran's strategic advantage. But should tensions between Washington and Tehran abate, the investment environment and the stability of the Iraqi government could improve, which could redound positively to the Gulf Arabs.

The balancing act will be that a Saudi strategy in Iraq will need to be less about competing with Iran and more about the development of Iraq.[15] The same could be said for Iran: Tehran's strategies for Iraq need to be looked at as benefiting Iraqis, not just hurting the Saudis. One thing I have heard consistently from Iraqis is the fear that Washington, Riyadh, and Tehran will use their country as a battleground for besting each other, which was the case during much of the first Trump administration. This only hurts the prospects for Iraqi stability and renewal. While the Iraqis could benefit from healthy competition between Saudi Arabia and Iran, they are the losers if Iraq is a battleground for hostilities between them.

Avoiding the negative effects of Saudi-Iran hostilities in Iraq helps explain the role the Iraqis played in hosting Iran-Saudi normalization talks in 2022 in Baghdad, which ultimately culminated in 2023 in a renewal of diplomatic relations between the two countries.[16] The Iraqis knew they would be the beneficiaries of a rapprochement, and conversely would be the victims should Iran-Saudi hostilities renew.

The state of the region

In thinking about possible pathways for Iran's foreign policy in the years ahead, it is important that we ponder the state of the region. Given the regional turmoil of the past decade, it is hard to remember a time of relative stability in the Middle East. But in the 1990s, Iran was seen as contained by a strong Iraq. Syria was an ally of Iran but was an independent sovereign state that had yet to fall into civil war. Yemen was inherently unstable but ruled by strongman Ali Abdullah Saleh. And while Saudi Arabia and Iran were rivals, they were not yet blood enemies. And nonstate actors weren't yet seen as existential threats.

Since Iran's current strategy developed as an adaptation to the region that emerged after the Cold War, 9/11, and the Arab Spring, if the region transitions back to a modicum of stability over the next ten to twenty years, Tehran will likely face a need to recalibrate its foreign policy. Of course, cynics will likely assert that Iran won't let the region heal, as it has an interest in the status quo. When looking at the short to medium term, they may be right. In terms of Iran's security interests, some variation of the status quo is preferable. And certainly, the major security institutions in Iran, namely the Islamic Revolutionary Guards Corps (IRGC) and its vaunted and feared Quds expeditionary force, seem to be wedded to the region as it exists today.

That having been said, Iran doesn't have complete control over how the region will unfold in the future, no more than it was responsible for the collapse of the Arab political order following the chaos of the Arab Spring. This is not to suggest that Iran won't act as a spoiler of attempts to stabilize the region, such as an Israeli-Palestinian path forward or Saudi efforts to invest in Iraq. But Iran lacks the capacity to completely control how these events and the broader region unfold.

As powerful as Iran has proven itself to be, political dynamics could militate against a continuance of the regional status quo. The protests in the Shi'i-dominated areas of Iraq and Lebanon over the past several years and Iran's countenance of brutal methods in suppressing these protests could stir up nationalist sentiment and activity. It is important not to forget that while Iran has played its Shi'i card in Iraq and Lebanon, these countries are also Arab with an inherent resistance to Persian domination.

As former Secretary of Defense James Mattis was fond of saying, "the enemy gets a vote" as to the success or failure of a strategy.[17] That is, the other powerful states in the region also have influence as to how the region unfolds in the future. Over time, the battle of strategies discussed above between Iran and its Gulf Arab state rivals will play a role in the evolution of the region. While it is possible that Iran will continue to resist Gulf Arab efforts to make significant inroads in Iraq, Lebanon, and

Syria, reconstruction imperatives in the future could nevertheless draw them into playing a bigger shaping role. Iran's ability to resist efforts by its Gulf Arab rivals to make inroads in Syria is likely to be circumscribed in the post-Assad era. Also, Turkey could become a winner in Syria given its relationship with the leadership of Hay'at Tahrir al-Sham (HTS), which at the time of writing is the dominant group in the leadership structure in Damascus.

The other factor that could determine the shape of the region is what transpires in the aftermath of the Gaza and Lebanon wars and as Iran-Israeli tensions play out. In the days before 2023, Iran was able to balance its substate shadow foreign policy of backing militias with its more conventional state-to-state diplomatic foreign policy by arguing that the former was born of necessity while the latter is where Iran wants to go in the future. But the brutal attacks on Israel by Hamas in 2023 signaled that the militias Iran supported weren't merely playing a game of defense.

With Iran's defensive claim disproven, a struggle to re-establish deterrence and set new red lines will likely continue until a new regional equilibrium is reached, which could take a lot of time. In this environment, even minor skirmishes can ratchet up quickly as the battle for escalatory dominance and the need to find new deterrent formulas take hold. In 2024, this played out with a series of direct missile and drone exchanges between Iran and Israel.

The hope would be that shifting regional dynamics causes a recalibration in Iran's foreign policy formula. While it is unlikely to give up its militia strategy, it might double down further on its diplomatic track with its Gulf Arab neighbors, Egypt, and Turkey as a hedge against aggression from Israel or the United States under a second Trump administration. Under this scenario, Iran's foreign policy could be rebalanced, maintaining its relations with the militias but in a restrained way that doesn't threaten its diplomatic track.[18]

But, of course, regional dynamics could move in a different direction, where red lines are crossed, the struggle for escalatory dominance careens out of control, and a regional war ensues. While this dark scenario of war would undermine the long-term interests of all states in the region, including Iran, it could become a reality, despite all diplomatic efforts to avoid it. Iran's foreign policy options in this kind of a scenario are limited, as both its militia strategy and its nascent diplomatic initiatives would be severely tested, with few good alternative options. If backed in a corner by further degradation of Hezbollah and more back-and-forth attacks with

Israel, actions that otherwise might seem reckless and unfathomable could appear reasonable to Iranian leaders.

Great power politics

The Middle East always confronts us with paradoxes. At a moment when global powers are busy flexing their muscles in the Middle East, smaller regional powers are asserting more independence and influence than ever before. This is not as strange or contradictory as it may seem. Regional powers like Iran, Saudi Arabia, Turkey, and Israel have more options because of, not in spite of, renewed competition between Russia, the United States, and China. Israel, Saudi Arabia, and Turkey are all hedging their bets, leveraging ties with one global power to counterbalance the influence of another. We see this with Israel, Saudi Arabia, and Turkey using relations with Russia and China to increase bargaining strength with the United States. And we see Iran acting more independently with Russia.

The other factor that accounts for regional powers having greater influence today has to do with the state of the Middle East. The collapse of four countries into civil war in the wake of the Arab Spring drew the regional powers into a regional rivalry that is uniquely their own. While the United States and Russia have intervened in Syria, Iraq, Yemen, and Libya, it is the regional powers that have shaped the civil wars in these countries and the broader region the most. Global powers have entered the fight, but rivalries on the ground in the civil wars remain largely outside the control of those global powers.

That having been said, it is important not to trivialize the role great powers play in the foreign policy formulation of regional powers. Iran's foreign policy since the revolution has largely been shaped by its interaction with the United States.[19] As of 2025, it appears that while Tehran seeks some reduction of tensions with the United States, any real rapprochement appears beyond reach. If relations between Iran and the United States spiral out of control during a second Trump administration, Tehran will be able to fall back on its old playbook of justifying its militia activity in the region based on Washington's hostility. But should there be a period of de-escalation, opportunities for broader regional diplomacy may present themselves.

This is not a sure path, as it assumes that Iran is principally driven by defensive motives. The hypothesis would be that if the threat from the

United States attenuates, Iran over time would adjust its perceptions and its actions accordingly. But what if Iran is truly ideologically committed to permanently opposing Israel and the United States, regardless of what Washington does? In this case, Iran would continue to act as a disrupter, perhaps leading to an intensified US regional role.

The tragedy of the US withdrawal from the JCPOA in 2018 is that the agreement was a test of whether Iranian behavior could be moderated over time with a less threatening posture from the United States. The US withdrawal prematurely ended the test of whether better relations with the west and a relaxation of sanctions would lead to a less aggressive regional posture and greater Iranian openness to relations with the United States and Europe. In other words, the experiment ended before the full results were in. Hopefully, there will be other opportunities to test whether Iran's behavior can be moderated with an attenuation of tensions with the United States.

It was after Washington's withdrawal from the JCPOA and the realization that pursuing relations with the United States was a dead-end that Iran decidedly tilted toward Russia and China. The question for Iran will be whether support from these two global powers yields the desired leverage and compensates for the break with the United States? In speaking with Iranians, including the late President Ibrahim Raisi and Foreign Minister Hossein Amir-Abdollahian, there was the belief that a global power shift toward the east was already underfoot, and that Iran would be the beneficiary.[20] In this same spirit, they also believed that joining the Shanghai Cooperation Council and the BRICS would further tether Tehran to China. The other conviction I heard was that Russia's isolation due to the Ukraine war would cement it more firmly to Iran. While there had been periods of Russian betrayal of Iran in the past, Iranian leaders believed that the military equipment Russia was buying from them translated into a more symmetrical power relationship.

China will likely confront Iran with greater complexity because of its size, market power, and independence. Beijing shares with Iran the sentiment that Washington needs to be resisted. But unlike Russia, China is more circumspect about taking actions that will undermine the global economic system and jeopardize its own economic interests at a time of economic fragility. Beijing believes that even with a slowing in the growth of its economy, the trend toward it assuming a future dominant global position is ineluctable. China is very comfortable that time is on its side in terms of the inevitable overtaking of the United States as the global market leader.[21]

But in the meantime, notwithstanding its friction with Washington, Beijing doesn't want to fully disrupt the international global economic system that benefits it. It sees itself dominating the global economic system, not disrupting or destroying it.

What does this mean for Iran's prospects for success in tilting toward the east? Iran's alienation from the United States in many ways was a windfall for China.[22] It cemented China's plan to project power into west Asia through its Belt and Road Initiative (BRI). And it was able to buy oil for discounted prices from an Iran under the chokehold of maximum pressure sanctions from the United States.[23]

But for Iran the impact was more mixed. China was circumspect about putting its companies at risk of secondary sanctions by the United States after Trump withdrew from the nuclear pact in 2018. In the future, we should expect China to act in concert with Tehran when convenient, but also expect it to take an independent path when broader interests are at stake. At some point in the distant future, Iran may be able to rely on its relations with East Asia to sustain it economically. But for the foreseeable future, the belief that moving toward the east will compensate for estrangement from the west is fanciful. Currently, Iran is off the hook, as there are no real prospects for the United States rejoining the nuclear deal or for sanctions to end. Iran, therefore, has few options other than to tilt toward the east. But it could be a strategic miscalculation for Iran to believe that it should reject any possible rapprochement with the west on the assumption it can forge an equal or better path with China.

The bigger question is how relations between the great powers themselves could shape Iranian behavior in the future. None of the three global powers benefits from chronic instability in the Middle East, particularly the United States and China. But the wild card will be what signals and incentives the great powers give to Iran.

If the Russia-United States relationship deteriorates further due to the Ukraine war, then Moscow may have a short-term incentive to work at cross-purposes with Washington in the Middle East, doubling down on its support for Iranian regional activities. If the Ukraine war winds down, then it is possible that Russia could act as a moderating influence on Iran.

The wildcard for 2025 and beyond will be the US-China relationship. If tensions intensify due to issues with economic tariffs, Taiwan, or North Korea, then Beijing could try to more actively oppose the United States in the Middle East, by bringing Iran closer to it. This could embolden Iran vis-à-vis the United States.

But there are perils for Iran in this equation regardless of the state of US-China relations. If Iran's conflict with Israel intensifies or widens into a broader and more sustained war, then it is possible that China will see Iran's militia activity as a liability to stability in the Middle East. Iran doubling down on its support for these militias as part of its "axis of resistance" posture will only invite more conflict and instability, something that could lead to skittishness in Beijing.

The risk for Iran in this will be that China starts to distance itself given the importance it accords to stability in the Middle East. We already have evidence of China valuing stability in the region to protect its economic interests. In 2023, China helped broker normalization between Iran and Saudi Arabia. And in 2024, China helped forge a unity deal between Hamas and the Palestinian Authority. How sustainable these deals are is unknown. But it shows that China wants to play a stabilizing role in the region, with the added value of putting Washington on the backfoot by playing a diplomatic role that was once the exclusive wheelhouse of the United States. Another test will come if there are viable prospects for a peace arrangement between Israel and the Palestinians. If Iran maintains its rigid positions and acts as a spoiler, this could further stress relations with China, which seems to prioritize regional stability.

Iran has shown skill in dealing with ambiguity in its foreign policy. It has been able to balance its shadow, subterranean militia strategy with its more conventional diplomatic strategy. It had a bit of elasticity and flexibility in simultaneously playing the role of statesman and spoiler, with beauty in the eye of the beholder. In most western eyes, the image that prevailed was of Iran as a spoiler and state sponsor of terrorism. In the eyes of Russia and China, Iran was an aggrieved party that acted as a diplomatic statesman in the nuclear talks but has since been betrayed by the United States.

The wars in Ukraine and Gaza have made Iran's strategic ambiguity approach more perilous, however. Iran supplying deadly drones to Russia and supporting Hamas and Hezbollah have reinforced the western imagery of it as a state sponsor of terror. These two wars pushed Iran further into pariah territory with European countries and have made a pathway back to Washington less likely. If it continues on this path, the question is will it be able to maintain its leverage as it sidles up to Russia and China? Or, will it find a way out of its current isolation and back to a new, albeit different, middle ground that neither brings it into complete concert with the west nor squarely in the court of China and Russia? That will depend on Iranian decision-makers but also on the diplomatic skill of the great powers.

Domestic politics

Given the events of the past few decades, it is tempting to dismiss domestic politics as a driver of Iran's foreign policy. Iranian presidents who have run popular campaigns emphasizing engagement with the west have oftentimes been stymied by conservative hardliners in their government and by a cold shoulder from the United States. Moreover, public demonstrations by Iranians protesting their country's adventurist foreign policies at the expense of domestic economic priorities have been brutally repressed. These patterns have injected many Iranians, who have repeatedly seen their hopes dashed with reform-minded presidents, with a sense of futility. They have also led to a creeping apathy among many Iranians that has been reflected in low voter turnouts during presidential elections.

President Masoud Pezeshkian ran on a platform of easing tensions with the United States and engaging with the west. Should we expect a change in the arc of Iran's foreign policy or will the new president's efforts at reform be thwarted like before by the Supreme Leader or the Revolutionary Guards?

There is no simple answer here. Iranian presidents, while they lack the ultimate authority in matters of diplomacy, can be highly influential. It seemed unfathomable that Iran would have negotiated seriously with the United States on the nuclear deal under the former firebrand president Mahmoud Ahmadinejad, who held office from 2005 to 2013. He consistently railed against the west, denied the Holocaust, and contributed to a buildup of tensions with the United States. It wasn't mere coincidence that the nuclear deal only became possible under former President Rouhani, elected in 2013. The team he selected was urbane and sophisticated in the ways of the diplomatic world. Rouhani himself attended university in Scotland. And former foreign minister Javad Zarif earned a PhD in the United States. This gave the team the bandwidth and agility to negotiate the JCPOA. Of course, the nuclear deal wouldn't have ever come about without the consent of Supreme Leader Ali

Khamenei, who has sat atop the political hierarchy in Iran for the past thirty years.

In some ways, having a reformist president like President Rouhani or today President Pezeshkian gives Ayatollah Khamenei more options. If he wants to prevent a president from pursuing engagement with the west, he can stymy the efforts directly or through the Revolutionary Guards. But if he wants to test engagement without spending his own political capital, he can give a reformist president like Pezeshkian an informal go-ahead. If successful, then Khamenei can either claim credit or yield the limelight to the president. But if it fails, as happened when Trump abandoned the JCPOA nuclear deal in 2018, he can make the president the fall guy and distance himself from it.

The question is what comes after Khamenei passes from the scene. Is it possible that the next Supreme Leader will be more pragmatic and open to a friendlier relationship with the United States and even more sensitive to the wishes of a highly educated Iranian population? While possible, it depends on what happens over the next several years. As mentioned earlier, with or without leadership changes, Iran will likely be weighing its foreign policy priorities and strategy. New leadership, though, can shift the direction of Iran's foreign policy more toward diplomacy or a continued reliance on its regional militias. While the aspirations of the Iranian people have seldom been a determinative factor in Iranian foreign policy, popular sentiment could play a more significant role in the future in which direction Iran will take. It would be a miscalculation to overly exaggerate popular sentiment as a driver of Iran's future foreign policy, but also an error to completely discount it.

Possible Foreign Policy Scenarios

Trying to predict whether Iran's foreign policy in the future will be more conflictual or cooperative is not the task at hand. The vicissitudes in the global order, the Middle East, and Iran's political scene defy attempts at forecasting. A case in point is the toppling of the Assad regime in Syria, which just a couple of weeks before it happened was not seen as a plausible scenario. The best we can do is try to identify the drivers of the future and come up with possible scenarios of how Iran's foreign policy may evolve. But which scenario materializes will depend on how the regional, global, and domestic drivers posited in the previous section interact with one another to frame choices for Iranian leaders. It will also depend on the possible emergence of new disruptive factors that we can't even anticipate sitting in 2025.

There are also contradictory trendlines that frustrate efforts to predict whether we are more likely to see a cooperative or disruptive foreign policy scenario for Iran. The need for cooperative action on climate change, health response systems, and regional security institutions is likely to weigh on Iranian leaders more urgently. But other trends we see today could pull Iran in the opposite direction. A rising global tide of authoritarianism could mean autocrats maintain power in Iran and try to distract the Iranian people with more foreign adventurism. Also, the empowerment of the main regional states in the Middle East, such as Israel, Iran, and Saudi Arabia, could make conflicts more impervious to international conflict mediation. We have already seen this trendline playing out with the difficulty international actors have had in ceasefire negotiations for Gaza and Lebanon.

Given all the factors presented, what are some of the possible scenarios for Iran's foreign policy going forward? What follows are two alternative pathways Iran's foreign policy could take. In considering these we should keep in mind that scenario construction is a heuristic exercise that never completely captures the future. It is designed to help us think through possible pathways Iran may follow, knowing full well that the future might consist of pieces of each of these scenarios.

There is a tendency among Middle East analysts, including myself, to believe that the future will be no more attractive than the present. There are career dynamics that encourage this kind of pessimism. Given the fraught history of the Middle East, the probabilities that a more pessimistic scenario will play out are greater than the prospects for a rosier one. Analysts who forecast more optimistic scenarios can be charged with naivete and wishful thinking, while pessimism is seen as a sign of gravitas and seasoned experience.

But it is important that we see a "more of the same" scenario as a possible and even perhaps most likely outcome, but not one that is predetermined. The Middle East is in a tumultuous phase of its development. As the region undergoes transformation, Iran's adaptive responses to these changes could surprise us. That is the reason for an in-depth look at the second scenario, which examines the case of Vietnam as a possible, yet perhaps unlikely, pathway for Iran. While there are some similarities between the two cases, there are also significant differences that could militate against this scenario occurring. But it is important to at least examine the prospects for this, not letting despair and pessimism dull our analytic chops.

Scenario 1: More of the same, or things get worse

Within this scenario, Iran's foreign policy would remain stuck in its current trajectory, making modest advances in diplomacy with its Arab neighbors, tilting toward the east to try to offset threats perceived from the United States and Israel, and yet still maintaining an "axis of resistance" foreign policy.

In this scenario, Iranian President Pezeshkian could try for a course correction that prioritizes diplomacy. But despite his efforts, Iran maintains its two-leveled foreign policy of working in the substate shadows with its militias and maintaining proper, albeit not warm, relations with its Gulf Arab neighbors. Within this scenario, Iran may recalibrate and rebalance its foreign policy somewhat, but there is unlikely to be a serious change in the overall policy direction.

What assumptions would we have to believe to be true for this scenario to materialize? We would need to believe that the states that have fallen prey to civil war and have served as the canvas for Iran's "axis of resistance" foreign policy will stay chronically in conflict for the foreseeable future. The challenges of Syria, Iraq, Lebanon, and Yemen climbing out of their civil conflicts and moving toward more sustainable governance prove to be insuperable in this scenario. In this scenario, the new post-Assad regime in Damascus could fail to consolidate power across the country, giving Iran a possible inroad for maintaining some presence in and influence over Syria. As part of this worst-case scenario, the Israeli-Palestinian conflict grinds on as a war of attrition with no real diplomatic solution at hand.

This scenario would also be driven by no significant change in great power relationship dynamics between Russia, China, and the United States. War in Ukraine will have perhaps entered a new phase of a war of attrition, with Russia and the United States still in a standoff against one another. And in this scenario Iran still relies on a strong relationship with Russia and growing ties with China. Because of these ties with the east, Iran feels little incentive to deal with the United States or Europe. The

United States in turn tries to contain and even deter Iran, which fuels Iran's impulse to resurrect deterrence by doubling down on its militia strategy.

Regional politics haven't improved much either in this scenario, with "bad neighborhood effects" continuing as obstacles to cooperation. Saudi Arabia's Vision 2030 program would likely continue apace but it fails to contribute significantly to robust intra-regional trade. And the efforts of the UAE to diversify beyond a hydrocarbon economy continue to show success, but the positive spillover effects to the broader region are minimal.

This scenario has a domestic politics component as well. Ayatollah Ali Khamenei is still Supreme Leader or, if he has already passed from the scene, a hardliner takes his place, equally intent on quashing internal dissent and doubling down on uncompromising stances with the west. All these factors would conspire to maintain Iran and the region on its current trajectory.

As depressing as muddling through would be, things could also unravel further with the region and Iran's foreign policy moving in a more disruptive direction. The collapse of the fragile equilibrium that kept the region and Iranian behavior in some form of check could drive a further deterioration.

The prospects of a possible constructive relationship between Iran and the west kept things in some check. Even after the United States bolted from the nuclear deal in 2018, Iran moved cautiously yet determinedly on its nuclear enrichment program, not having made the political decision to make a dash for a nuclear weapon. And even before Donald Trump started his second term, there were discussions about a possible deal between the United States and Iran. If all this completely collapses and Iran believes it has lost deterrence, particularly if there is further degradation of Hamas and Hezbollah and Syria turns hostile to Iran's interests, it could lurch toward more confrontational and dangerous behavior, including a dash for a nuclear weapon. Further fuel for this worsening scenario could be a prolonged Israeli campaign in Gaza and Lebanon or more tit-for-tat missile attacks between Israel and Iran. This could potentially lead to a wider war where Israel and Iran attack each other, but also use Syria, Iraq, Lebanon, and even Yemen as battlegrounds for confronting each other.

Early in 2023, analysts and policy-makers assuaged their fears of all-out war between Israel and Iran by claiming that neither side benefits from unbridled hostilities. While that logic is as valid today as it was then, it shouldn't dull our senses to the possibility of a wider war. With the collapse of deterrence, first for Israel after the 2023 Hamas attack, and then Iran in 2024 with Israel's assault on Hezbollah, the likelihood that both parties will continue to escalate with one another to establish dominance increases. Moreover, the security dilemma phenomenon could drive both parties to war. This dynamic comes about when either or both sides calculate that the risks of escalating to demonstrate strength are less than the risks of de-escalation that could be construed as weakness. If this drives a continual pattern of direct military attacks between Israel and Iran, the situation could careen out of control very quickly, leading to this worst-case scenario.

In addition to deterioration in Israel-Iran and US-Iran relations, further degradation of the region could drive this worst-case scenario. A continuation of the war in Gaza and Lebanon and the lack of a viable path for resolving the Israel-Palestine issue could add tinder to an already fraught situation, reinforcing the worst behavior of Iran and Israel. Saudi Arabia may be one possible mitigant, since it has a nascent relationship with Iran and holds out the prospects of normalizing relations with Israel. But this would be a thin ray of hope if the region deteriorates, and the worst instincts of Iran or Israel—or both—could be reinforced.

Aside from the regional conditions, other dynamics that can contribute to this scenario are a complete breakdown in the international consensus on the Middle East. Worsening tensions between the United States and Russia or China could lead to Iran feeling emboldened. Or just the failure of any viable de-escalatory diplomacy from the international community could allow events to get out of control.

Scenario 2: "Best case"—The Vietnam playbook

By observing more than forty years of post-revolutionary behavior, it seems more probable that Iran will stay on its current foreign policy course than radically alter its trajectory by favoring regional stability and cooperation. But if it had been suggested in 1943, while Europe was still being ravaged by the Second World War, that less than ten years later an agreement would be signed that would eventually culminate in the formation of the European Union (EU), such a prediction would have been dismissed as unrealistic, hopelessly naïve, and possibly even delusional. But in 1951, the European Coal and Steel Community (ECSC) was created through the Treaty of Paris, an agreement that integrated the coal and steel-making industries of West Germany, France, Belgium, Italy, Luxembourg, and the Netherlands. These were the industries that had helped Germany and the axis powers wage war on the European continent. This agreement proved to be the institutional cornerstone of what culminated in the formation of the EU in 1993.

Similarly, if someone in 1971 had forecast that Southeast Asia would be sufficiently peaceful over the next two decades to integrate Vietnam into a regional cooperation organization, that individual would likely have been ridiculed. In 1971, the withdrawal of the Americans from Vietnam was still two years away, and Vietnam was still engrossed in a bloody civil war, a conflict that was spilling over into the neighboring countries of Cambodia and Laos.

But by the mid-1980s, Vietnam started flirting with the Association of Southeast Asian Nations (ASEAN) and formally joined this regional organization in 1995. This momentous event occurred only a few short years after Hanoi withdrew its troops from Cambodia and had signed the Paris Accords on Cambodia in 1991.

How do these two examples relate to Iran and the Middle East? They are important in providing some perspective on the possibility that changes can occur in the future that seem highly improbable or even impossible from today's vantage point. As highly improbable as a scenario of the Middle East stabilizing and Iran shifting its foreign policy direction seems, it shouldn't be dismissed as completely fanciful either.

That having been said, it would be foolhardy to predict that the Middle East will follow the pathway of Europe or Southeast Asia, and that Iran will go through a sea change in its foreign policy. The conditions in the Middle East today are very different than those that existed in Europe in the 1950s and Southeast Asia in the 1990s. ASEAN by that time had already been a robust regional institution for several decades, having been formed on the sidelines of an armistice between Indonesia, the Philippines, and Malaysia. No comparable regional architecture exists in the Middle East today. And unlike post-war Europe in the 1950s, which had seen the complete defeat of Nazi Germany only a few years earlier, the Middle East today is in a state of suspended animation somewhere between conditions of war and peace.[24]

But there are also some interesting parallels between the cases of Iran and Vietnam that could be suggestive of a better future than might be indicated by the darker scenario outlined in the previous section. Admittedly from where we sit today, the Vietnam scenario looks like the least probable of the two. But it is important to examine the possibilities and parallels, considering the local, regional, and global conditions that might be conducive to a positive shift in Iran's foreign policy. Equally important is the follow-on question of whether there are particular policies that other states in the region and beyond might pursue to encourage those conditions.

Iran and Vietnam

The differences between the cases of Iran and Vietnam jump right out at us. Vietnam by the 1990s had already defeated the United States amid a brutal civil war inside the country followed by a withdrawal of American military forces. In contrast, Iran's struggle with the United States is taking place outside the country in the broader region with no clear resolution in sight. Also, Vietnam had been divided by civil war, while Iran has avoided such an internal conflict. On the international front, Vietnam found itself completely isolated after the collapse of the Soviet Union, while Iran has compensated for its pariah status in the west by moving closer to Russia and China. And as mentioned, Southeast Asia by the 1990s had already started to stabilize, while the Middle East remains unstable and bereft of a new equilibrium.

But there are also similarities worthy of consideration. Both countries have exhibited extreme ideological passions and rigidities. Vietnam of the 1970s embodied an ideologically potent blend of communism and nationalism, while the regime in Tehran today is committed to its own Islamic revolutionary ethos and fervor. The regional contexts of Vietnam in the 1970s and Iran of today are also similar. Vietnam was part of a dysfunctional region where state sovereignty was often violated, and border transgressions had become the norm. Iran today similarly exists in and contributes to the bad neighborhood effects of an unstable Middle East.

What is there to learn from the Vietnamese case that can help us think through future possibilities for Iran? Vietnam was able to make a transition from ideological purity to a more pragmatic set of policies, without completely shedding its set of values. Scholars on the transition that Vietnam made from the 1980s onward have cited that the country went from seeing talk of reform as "heretical thinking" to viewing it as "reality thinking," meaning that ideas that were once considered verboten became more accepted and mainstream over time.[25]

This book has argued that Iran has proven to be highly adaptive to regional and global circumstances. It has shown the ability to blend ideological and realpolitik thinking into its foreign policy decision-making process. But the question the Vietnam example begs is how far can we imagine the current government in Tehran stretching in terms of flexibility and adaptability? There was a time before the negotiations that led to the JCPOA nuclear deal when it was almost impossible to imagine Iran negotiating limits on its uranium enrichment program with the United States. But the unimaginable became reality in 2015 when Iran moved beyond a rigid ideological foreign policy to sign a deal with all permanent members of the United Nations Security Council plus Germany.

There may in fact be greater limits on how far Iran is willing or able to move off its ideologically driven positions than was the case with Vietnam. For example, it is hard to imagine Iran engaging with Israel constructively in the foreseeable future, regardless of what a realpolitik calculus would suggest. Perhaps with a different government in Tehran and a different regional climate, this taboo could be overcome as well. But it is hard to imagine this from the vantage point of today. It is important to understand, though, that the Vietnamese transition didn't occur over night, but rather came about through a complex process of domestic and international maneuvers. Similarly, any future change we might see in Iranian behavior is likely to be evolutionary rather than revolutionary.

One of the fascinating things about Vietnam was that in the lead up to joining ASEAN, it self-regulated its behavior, curbing its practices of violating the borders of other states and opening trade relationships with neighboring countries. Ten to twenty years earlier, this would have seemed unfathomable. ASEAN required flexibility on Vietnam's external behavior, such as making it commit to respecting the sovereignty and sanctity of borders of neighboring states, but didn't impose any conditions on the internal ideological orientation of the regime. Because of this, Vietnam was able to make its shift without yielding on many of its communist ideological principles.

Under what conditions, if any, would Iran give up its regional interventionist policies? It is highly improbable that Iran would ever voluntarily cut itself loose of its network of militias. But it is plausible that Iran could shift the emphasis of its foreign policy toward more conventional state-to-state diplomacy over time and away from an overly securitized, militia-based foreign policy. With the degradation of Hezbollah and Hamas, and a change in Iran's fortunes in a post-Assad Syria, this scenario could become more plausible.

Maintaining true to certain revolutionary principles was important for Vietnam as it worked through its transition, and the same would be true with Iran as well. Iran will fight to hold onto its revolutionary identity even if there is an evolution toward a different foreign policy model. One of the debates that has taken place in Iran is whether the country can open to the west without giving up the ethos of the revolution. The pragmatists in Iran, such as former presidents Rafsanjani, Khatami, Rouhani, and newly elected President Pezeshkian, didn't advocate that Iran yield on core principles that defined the revolution. But in contrast to the hardliners in Tehran, they claimed that Iran could become part of the global economy without sacrificing the integrity of the revolution or undermining the ruling regime.

Vietnam could provide a pathway for how this could be done. But what took place in Vietnam hasn't yet taken place in Iran. Vietnam saw reform as central to building domestic legitimacy for the regime, describing it as the "intellectual hegemony" of reform ideas.[26] In 1986, Vietnam launched what it called Doi Moi, which translates into English as "renovation." This involved integrating state-owned enterprises into a market economy and making other significant structural adjustments that led to profound improvements in the living standards in the country. These measures resulted in an enhancement of the legitimacy of the Vietnamese government. Later, when Vietnam formally joined ASEAN, it wore membership as a badge of honor.[27]

Iran is facing a legitimacy challenge today that has been intensifying over the past decade or more, but instead of moving toward reform and regional integration like Vietnam did, it has been moving in the opposite direction. So far, Iran has dealt with its legitimacy challenge with repression and other forms of coercion, eschewing significant reform measures. A big part of the regime legitimacy crisis in Iran is the country's dire economic performance, a condition exacerbated by international sanctions, poor economic governance, and endemic corruption. But Iranian leaders have used sanctions and hostility from the United States to try to deflect regime responsibility for the problems that impinge on their own legitimacy.

Over-analogizing the situation in Vietnam in the 1970s with conditions in Iran today would be analytically flawed. But if the argument in this book that Iran's killer-skill is adaptation holds up to scrutiny, then it is useful to explore what domestic, regional, and international conditions could someday cause Iran to adapt and evolve from an overly securitized foreign policy to a more balanced approach that gives priority to economic growth.

For Vietnam it was the end of the Cold War, threats from China, regime legitimacy challenges, and the gravitational pull of ASEAN that conspired to trigger a transformation. It is important to consider what conditions could provide Iran with some of the same dilemmas, threats, and opportunities that Vietnam faced. What stars would have to align with Iran to possibly create a change like what happened with Vietnam nearly forty years ago? There is no guarantee or even perhaps likelihood that Iran would respond at all like Vietnam, even if conditions and incentives are similar. But it is important to shed our cynicism about Iran and look at some of the conditions that favored Vietnam's transformation as possible signals to watch for and trends to reinforce in the Middle East.

Regional geopolitics

Vietnam was not a founding member of ASEAN; when it joined in 1995 as its seventh member, the organization had already existed for nearly thirty years. For most of those intervening years, the Vietnamese people and government were bystanders in witnessing the positive regional conditions that ASEAN created and the economic benefits that accrued to member states.

It is important to note that the Middle East today exhibits few of the characteristics of Southeast Asia in the 1990s. There are no real conflict mitigation institutions like ASEAN and the region in 2025 sits on the brink of war with tensions between Iran and Israel reaching a crescendo. But it is equally important to consider the perspective that Southeast Asia just two decades earlier in the 1970s was in many ways in a worse condition than the Middle East of today. It was fraught with a raging war in Vietnam, which had spilled over into Cambodia and Laos, with North Vietnamese forces having violated the borders of those two countries. And the region was economically undeveloped and unstable.

But by the 1980s and 1990s, there was a modicum of stability in Southeast Asia, with economic growth having become the priority. The formation of ASEAN in 1967 had started to solidify economic gains in some of the more stable states, like Thailand, Singapore, the Philippines, and Indonesia, even while the Vietnam war was still ongoing. Over the next several decades because of ASEAN, foreign investment increased, trade liberalization took hold, and development initiatives were undertaken, all contributing to regional stability.

Once Vietnam emerged from decades of civil war and was still struggling with reunification, the contrast between its economy and its neighbors became stark. Thailand had grown through the 1970s at an annual rate of about 7% and the Philippines at around 5%. This contrasted with Vietnam's economic stagnation and negative growth during the same decade. This regional context acted as a powerful magnet that attracted Hanoi to a different foreign policy model. ASEAN's "Open Door" policy and vision to expand membership to all Southeast Asian countries in the 1990s was also a critical factor that drew Vietnam in. This was particularly important in the post-Cold War context of regional integration concerns taking precedence over old Cold War era divisions.

Are there any prospects for a shift in Middle Eastern realities that could possibly confront Iran with a similar set of security and economic realities? Currently, there is nothing to rival ASEAN in the Middle East, but there are the Abraham Accords, signed between Israel, Bahrain, and the UAE in 2020 to normalize relations between these Gulf Arab states and Israel. Sudan and Morocco joined later, and there were some expectations that Saudi Arabia would eventually join, the prospects for which were set back by the events that ensued after the Hamas attacks on Israel in 2023.

The Abraham Accords are not a region-wide agreement, but rather a subregional pact. Moreover, the accords were conceived by the first Trump administration as a bulwark against Iran. Unlike ASEAN, which prioritized common regional interests over old Cold War divisions, the Abraham Accords shone a light on regional divisions and could sow rather than mitigate conflict with Iran. But if the accords ever develop significant economic benefits for the signatories, they could serve as a foundational stone for what could become a broader regional security and economic architecture. This is not to suggest that Iran would ever join any organization that includes Israel, but significant economic growth among Iran's immediate neighbors could serve as a powerful signal to Iran. Down the road the accords could be a facilitator of regional economic trade and growth. Iran could be watching from the sidelines and might be faced with some tough choices. Though currently Iran is making economic bets with China though the Shanghai Cooperation

Organization and BRICS, a strong regional growth engine could become a powerful influencer.

It is easy to dismiss the possibility that a subregional agreement like the Abraham Accords could ever evolve into a broader regionwide framework. And given the history of weak regional institutions in the Middle East, skepticism is warranted. But ASEAN wasn't built in a day either. While Hanoi joined ASEAN in 1995, there were informal ties starting in the mid-1980s. This "sitting on the sidelines" gave Vietnam the confidence it needed and opportunity to see the benefits that would accrue to it with formal membership. Assuming the Abraham Accords expand, and are economically successful for member states, this could put pressure on Iran.

Though perhaps a long shot, there is an informal way for the Abraham Accords to improve regional stability and subtly bring Iran into a more constructive role. In March of 2023, Iran and Saudi Arabia re-established diplomatic relations for the first time since 2016. At roughly the same time, there was talk about Saudi Arabia joining the Abraham Accords, prospects of which were killed by the Hamas attacks on Israel later that year. Should the Israeli-Palestinian situation eventually move from its current tragic trajectory toward a sustainable and acceptable solution, Saudi Arabia could become the next signatory. If that occurs, Saudi Arabia could act as an informal bridge linking together the Arab-Israeli bloc of the Abraham Accords and Arab-Iran bloc of Gulf Arab-Iran normalization, being part of both. It is hard to imagine improved relations between Iran and Israel. But what can be imagined is Saudi Arabia acting as a possible mitigant against the worst instincts of both Israel and Iran.

Iran seems to be responding more constructively, not with Israel or the United States but with its Arab neighbors. The diplomatic initiatives vis-à-vis Saudi Arabia, the UAE, and even Egypt are a tacit recognition that cooperation can provide incentives to Iran. Whether this can lead to a change as profound as what occurred in Southeast Asia with ASEAN is unknown at this time. But it is important to watch for regional conditions and trends that could weigh positively on Iranian interests and behavior. The loss of Syria as an ally of Iran could in this scenario provide an additional impetus to it moving toward a more constructive relationship with its Arab neighbors, and possibly even the United States,

There is a tendency to think of the Middle East in Manichean terms consisting of responsible actors like US allies, and disrupter actors like Iran. But it is important to keep our perspective and consider the fact that bad neighborhood effects can bring out the worst behavior in all actors. In other words, Iran isn't a complete outlier when it comes to a disrupter role in the region. Israel, Saudi Arabia, Turkey, and the UAE have also intervened in the civil wars in Syria, Iraq, Libya, Sudan, and Yemen. Today, the Gulf Arab states are more focused on economic development and diversification than on intervening in the civil war zones, but that was not always the case, with Saudi Arabia's prior military intervention in Yemen serving as a powerful example.

Leadership

It was under the dynamic leadership of Nguyen Van Linh, the General Secretary of the Communist Party from 1986 to 1991, that Vietnam's Doi Moi economic reforms took hold. There was considerable resistance from more conservative voices to making the transition from a centrally planned economy to a socialist-oriented market economy, and to opening the country to regional and global foreign direct investment (FDI). Some of the same voices we hear out of Iran today about the country risking its independence if it integrates with the global economy were heard in Hanoi in the 1980s. But ultimately the forceful leadership of General Secretary Linh, economic success, and the demonstration effect of other regional economies prevailed over these conservative voices. Vietnam ascended to ASEAN membership in 1995, just a few years after Linh's tenure ended.

One of the major lasting contributions made by Linh was to shift the overall worldview of the leadership from seeing Vietnam through a revolutionary prism where the broader region was a threat to the country and regime to seeing the regional environment as a powerful engine for generating economic growth and regime legitimacy. FDI in the country grew from $250 million in 1989 to $18 billion in 1996.[28] Also, eventually the view shifted from seeing the United States as the enemy to seeing it as a possible partner for pushing back on what it saw as China's hegemonic designs.

Could something like this happen with Iran? As unlikely as it seems today, it is possible. When Ayatollah Ali Khamenei passes from the scene as Supreme Leader, there could be a shift in direction. If it takes place at all, it is likely to be incremental and evolutionary rather than sudden. One of the obstacles is the degree to which resistance to the United States has been part of the country's governing formula since the Iranian revolution.

But with a beleaguered economy and a restive, educated population, an eventual quest for regime legitimacy could prompt a shift.

In the Vietnamese example, change came after reunification of the country and the death of the ideological father of Vietnamese communism, nationalism, and colonial resistance, Ho Chi Minh, in 1969 after nearly a quarter century in power. And even then, it took another fifteen years and the end of the war with the United States to create receptivity for change.

In the case of Iran, even though Ayatollah Ruhollah Khomeini passed away more than three decades ago, his successor Ali Khamenei has carried the revolutionary torch with little deviation from the founding ethos of the Islamic Republic. It is unlikely that significant reform will occur while he is still Supreme Leader. But when he passes from the scene, there will be opportunities for change.

It is impossible to predict how the new Iranian President Masoud Pezeshkian, elected in 2024, who ran on a reformist platform, will fare within the byzantine political system in Iran. With the current Supreme Leader, it is unlikely that he will be able to act upon his pragmatic instincts of being receptive to the west, his campaign platform notwithstanding. When I met with President Pezeshkian in September of 2024, he was still seething about the assassination of the Hamas leader Ismail Haniyeh in Tehran by Israel, right on the heels of his presidential inauguration just two months earlier. His anger came less from the killing itself and more because he viewed it as an intentional sabotage of his reform agenda at the hands of the Israelis.[29] Should the passing of Ali Khamenei occur during Pezeshkian's presidency, then the question will be whether the new Supreme Leader is receptive to a new legitimizing formula that moves beyond the now threadbare ideology of the revolution.

One of the lessons from the Vietnamese case is that leadership changes, while necessary, are woefully insufficient. In Vietnam, the rise of more progressive leadership occurred at a time when a vibrant, energetic regional institution, ASEAN, was gaining traction. Should leadership changes occur in Iran, but the regional and global conditions remain the same, we are unlikely to see a significant change in the country's foreign policy. The current regional unrest sparked by the 2023 Hamas attacks on Israel augurs poorly for the ability of the new president to make a compelling case of reaching out to the United States, even though there have been reports of a meeting between the Iranian Ambassador to the United Nations, Amir Saeid Iravani, and the Trump transition team in November 2024.[30] If war in Gaza and Lebanon continues and regional tensions remain high, there is little likelihood of significant movement. Leadership changes need to correspond with a positive regional context to imagine a Vietnam-like change in Iran's foreign policy.

Global geopolitics

One of the most critical factors that drove the transformation in Vietnam was the global geopolitical environment. With the United States having withdrawn its troops from South Vietnam in 1973, the country was able to unify under the leadership of the Viet Cong from the north. The American withdrawal signaled an end to western imperialism, which had been the dominant factor in Vietnamese politics in both the north and south since the French took control in the nineteenth century.

But the other major change was the collapse of the Soviet Union in 1991. Moscow and other East European countries had been critical sources of capital and served as the primary markets for Vietnamese goods. The end of the Cold War meant that Vietnam had to move in a new direction to secure its economic future.[31] The loss of a Soviet benefactor, the rise of China as a threat, and the welcoming culture of ASEAN all contributed to the shift in Vietnam's strategy. And, of course, the search for a legitimizing formula for the regime provided an impetus for change.

What global geopolitical factors could be conducive to a shift in Iran's foreign policy? There would need to be an attenuation of the conflict between Iran and the United States. There are analysts who suggest that the grand strategy of the United States should be to offshore balance in the Persian Gulf region against Iranian power using Israel and Saudi Arabia.[32] If the United States combines punishing sanctions with this kind of an offshore balance approach, there is little hope for a shift in the direction of Iran's foreign policy. An approach like this will just push Iran to hunker down with its support for a regional network of militias such as Hamas and Hezbollah, even though these groups have been degraded by withering Israeli bombing campaigns since 2023. But a subtle shift in American policy, encouraging growth in the Saudi-Iran relationship, taking a tougher stance on Israel's settlement policies, and reasserting that a two-state solution to the Israeli-Palestinian conflict is the official policy of the United States, could over time de-intensify the vicious cycle of Iran-US relations. Also, Washington will need to become active in bringing the Gaza and Lebanese wars to a close, as these are destabilizing to the entire region, giving Iran and its allied militias ample excuses to remain active. And US support for the Abraham Accords should be conditioned on it being a subregional agreement focused on economic development rather than a sharp cudgel against Iran.

Of course, Iran would need to do its part to deconflict relations with the United States. When the Gaza war ends, Iran would need to dial down its anti-US and anti-Israel rhetoric and the activities of the militias in its resistance axis, doing its part to break the vicious cycle.

What other global factors would be important to an Iranian transition? And does the case of Vietnam provide any clues? The rise of China in East Asia became a unifying factor for the smaller countries that joined ASEAN. When I was in Hanoi, I heard the common refrain that while America was yesterday's enemy, China is today's. Right now, there is no counterpart to this in the Middle East that could drive erstwhile enemies together. In fact, the Gulf Arabs tend to portray Iran as the China of the Middle East, even though it doesn't have the economic, political, or military heft to act as a regional hegemon. But there is no common external enemy in the Middle East to bind it together like the role China plays in East Asia.

What does stepped-up great power rivalry between the United States, Russia, and China in the Middle East mean for the direction of Iran's foreign policy? At the time of writing, Russia is preoccupied with its war in Ukraine. Moscow will also have to cope with the possibility of a hostile post-Assad Syrian government and the potential losses of its naval and air force bases in the country. China and the United States, while adversaries on the global stage, both have an interest in stability in the Middle East. Either working in parallel or in tandem, China and the United States could play a positive moderating role, with Beijing working with Iran and Washington with Israel to defuse current tensions. A few years ago, suggesting a diplomatic role for Beijing would have appeared fanciful. But China did play a pivotal role in bringing Iran and Saudi Arabia to restore diplomatic relations in 2023. And in 2024 it tried its hand in reducing tensions between Hamas in Gaza and Fatah, the dominant party in the Palestinian Authority in the West Bank. China and the United States working together toward regional stability could be a positive signal to Iran. It would also send the signal that the United States is going to play the role of a neutral global power rather than the overly partisan regional actor Iran sees it as having played.

The most constructive role for the great powers would be to encourage the development of a broad-based regional security and economic architecture, like ASEAN, but built on Middle East sensibilities. Regional institutions like ASEAN are voluntary organizations that don't always prevent conflict. But they can provide mechanisms for deconfliction and de-escalation. They can also give leaders in the region political cover for taking decisions that would otherwise be politically perilous to take.[33]

It doesn't seem feasible that a region-wide organization like ASEAN could emerge in one swallow in the Middle East. But modest steps can be taken to reinforce subregional agreements, like the Abraham Accords, or erect new ones that perhaps could be built upon later. Subregional agreements can be constructive if they are used to create positive economic traction and not used to accentuate regional tensions. Iran's new relationship with Saudi Arabia, the UAE, and Egypt could be another subregional structure that can form the foundation of a broader regional architecture. And the recently formed China-Saudi Arabia-Iran Trilateral Committee could link up great power initiatives with the growing regional ties between Iran and Saudi Arabia.

Thinking back to the example of Vietnam, ASEAN wasn't built in a day. It started with five founding members in 1967 and expanded later to include Vietnam in 1995 and other countries subsequently. Laying out a vision and fundamental principles for an organization today for the Middle East could be a first step. The initiative for this could come from regional actors, who need to have sufficient political will for cooperation to work. But regional efforts will need to be supported by the international community.[34] International actors can use their power to convene and resources to help create the conditions that play to the best, not worst instincts of all powers in the region, Iran included. Whether the Abraham Accords or the Iran-Saudi rapprochement, or both, serve as the platform, a cornerstone needs to be laid now.

In Summary

There are different variations and possibilities of how Iran might change in the future. Rather than assume only a pessimistic future, we have looked at a more optimistic one as well, examining some possible drivers and conditions that could encourage such a scenario. We have put greater emphasis on the more optimistic Vietnam scenario, not because we feel this is the most probable, but rather because it appears the least likely. If it is to move from being improbable to being remotely possible, work will need to be done by local, regional, and international actors. I believe that despite all the obstacles in this, looking at the Middle East and Iran using the historical lens of Europe after the Second World War and Southeast Asia after the Vietnam War tells us that what seems improbable today could be possible tomorrow.

Even if leadership changes in Iran converge with positive developments in the region and the international arena, there is no guarantee that Iran will go the way of Vietnam. But the utility of the Vietnam case is it points us to the possibility that leadership changes and changed regional and international contexts matter. It at least highlights that even though Iran may have a sclerotic and ideologically rigid ruling clique today, this shouldn't prejudice us or cloud our view of future possibilities. Predicting a change in Iran's foreign policy direction would be reckless. But so is dismissing the possibilities. Looking at the factors that may drive positive changes is an important analytic exercise that can give us possible windows into the future, as foggy as they might be.

Even if Iran's foreign policy does eventually make a significant course correction, it will likely not occur overnight. For that reason, the two scenarios presented shouldn't be seen as completely mutually exclusive. Things can get better and worse at the same time, particularly given the complexities of the region and Iran's worldview. We see this contradictory duality playing out today, with Iran simultaneously playing a disruptive role with the activation of its militias, and a cooperative role with its nascent diplomacy with Saudi Arabia, Egypt, and Turkey. With the particularly complex decision-making process in Iran, and overall regional dysfunction, we are likely to see both disruptive and constructive signals coming out of Tehran for some time to come. The important thing for Washington and all others who have a stake in a better future in the Middle East will be to try to reinforce the positive and not the negative.

CONCLUSION

Iran is facing a challenge today it has for decades assiduously tried to avoid. It faces the continued prospects of being drawn into direct military confrontations with Israel and possibly the United States. Iranian leaders have found themselves in this precarious position even though they are aware that their strength has not been in the capacity to use direct military force, but rather in the capability to confront Iran's enemies indirectly from the shadowy world of frail states. Iran hasn't run from the fight, but it has chosen to operate from its position of strength in the shadowy interstices of failed states rather than try to compete with the more conventional military capabilities of its adversaries. Iran in the spirit of Sun Tzu has built a "hide in plain sight" strategy of diffusion, spreading its tentacles throughout the failed states of the region, frustrating attempts by its adversaries to contain and confront it.

Now Iran is facing the reality that the useful life of this strategy of working stealthily in the shadows may be reaching its limit. Israel since the Hamas attacks of 2023 has been simultaneously waging war on Iran's regional network of militias and taking the fight to Iran directly. Instead of Iran's network of militias creating deterrence and strategic depth as intended, it has brought military attacks to the homeland.

As we have seen throughout the pages of this book, the strategic reflex to avoid fighting concentrated power directly has its roots in pre-revolutionary Iran. Over the course of its history, Iran has struggled to thwart the concentrated power of many of its adversaries. Global powers like Russia and Great Britain early in the twentieth century, and later the United States and the Soviet Union, successfully combined forces to prevent Iran from realizing its ultimate ambitions. Through this history Iran learned that even rival powers will collaborate and concentrate their resources to frustrate Iran's domestic and foreign interests. Right after the 1979 revolution, this historical lesson was reinforced with the Iraqi invasion of Iran in 1980. Almost the entire Arab world, except for Syria, and both the United States and Soviet Union concentrated their power and resources to prevent an Iranian victory.

What became clear to Iranian leaders after fighting its eight-year war with Iraq to a tie was that meeting the concentrated power of its adversaries with its own concentrated power was a losing proposition. Instead, Iran saw a winning hand in weak states that had collapsed into conflict, using a strategy of diffusing power and resources across the region to confound and frustrate its enemies who wanted to contain it. Armed with its doctrine of forward defense that came out of the war with Iraq, Iran methodically and opportunistically erected a network of militias, starting with Hezbollah in 1982, and later expanding to Hamas and Palestine Islamic Jihad (PIJ) in Gaza, the Houthis in Yemen, and the Hashd al-Sha'bi in Iraq.

Iranian leaders understood that this asymmetric strategy of diffusion didn't compensate for the lack of an effective offensive capacity against Israel or the United States, but they settled for it providing a deterrent capability that could ward off possible military assaults, as well as allowing it to conduct a low-intensity war of attrition against US forces in Iraq and Syria.

Iran in 2025 is now in the unenviable position of possibly having to compete with its adversaries on terms more favorable to them than to itself. In other words, Iran's playbook of using its stealth strategy of diffusion may no longer be as effective as it once was in coping with the more conventional strategies of concentration used by Israel and the United States. The irony is that this was brought about not by Iran's enemies, but by the actions of its own network of militias. Like the tail wagging the dog, Hamas launched a frontal assault on Israel on October 7, 2023 which was followed by missile attacks by Hezbollah on Israel the very next day. These attacks by Hamas and Hezbollah signaled that Iran's network of militias wouldn't just be used defensively for deterrence, but also for launching offensive strikes against Israel and possibly even US assets.

Israel responded to the Hamas aggression by unleashing a barrage of attacks on Hamas, Hezbollah and, in April of 2024, against Iran's consulate in Damascus. Believing it had lost deterrence, Iran retaliated by directly and unprecedently attacking Israel with drones and missiles. Then in October of 2024 after Israel killed Hamas chiefs Ismail Haniyeh in Tehran and Yahya Sinwar in Gaza, and Hezbollah head Hassan Nasrallah in

Beirut, Iran struck Israel again. Both Iranian attacks on Israel were followed by Israeli military strikes on key strategic positions in Iran.

Having crossed the Rubicon by engaging Israel in direct military conflict, having lost some of the deterrence provided by Hamas and Hezbollah, and facing future challenges of a post-Assad Syria, Tehran is at a strategic crossroads. It now confronts the possibility that its strategy of diffusion may have run its course and that it now will be compelled to compete using more conventional, concentrated means of power as it tries to re-establish deterrence. If there is a further escalation in direct hostilities with Israel, it is possible that Iran will face the impossible challenge of confronting the United States on the battlefield. The specter of this could push Iran to either pivot hard toward diplomacy with the United States or instead make a mad dash for a nuclear weapon, the ultimate deterrent.

The need for Iran to confront concentrated power may not be limited to the military domain. Iran may also be confronting the need to compete with economies that use a concentration of resources and have access to the global economy, such as those of Turkey, Saudi Arabia, and the UAE. While Iran is trying hard to escape this hard reality by sidling up to China in a tilt-east strategy, this may not be enough to propel it forward in the short to medium term.

One of the core arguments of this book has been that Iran has been a master at adapting to changing circumstances in its regional and global environments. The book has chronicled how Iran adapted skillfully to the failures of the United States and its allies in the region, and the failures of countries that fell into civil war. But Iran's luck of being able to build its strategy around the failures of others may have run out. It may now face the need to compete using its own conventional strengths rather than leaning on a militia-based strategy of diffusion.

In some ways, Iran has been moving in this direction for several years now, with renewed relations with Saudi Arabia and Egypt, and its work to tilt toward the Asian economies. But in many ways, this is a strategy of necessity, not choice. Because of hostility from Washington, but also its own preoccupation with Israel, Iran has boxed itself into an eastern strategy that may only pay off in the long term.

Iran will likely need to double down on its power skill of adaptation to generate leverage in its new environment. It is possible that Iran will face hostility from the United States and Israel, and only lukewarm support from Russia and China, countries it has relied on over the past several years. If Russian President Vladimir Putin is rehabilitated by the United States during a second Trump term, Iranian fears of duplicity and betrayal by Moscow could become a reality. The potential loss of a common cause of supporting Assad could pose new challenges for the Iran-Russia relationship. Also, Iran will need to be cautious with China, which could see it as a liability if Iran-backed militias continue to sow regional instability.

When I started on this book project, I believed that Iran would eventually face the moment when it would be forced to choose between its different priorities and competing strategies. I believed that the fact that Iran has a highly educated, nationalistic population with huge potential but a grossly underperforming economy would eventually force its leaders to make clear choices about whether to hunker down with its militia-based foreign policy or pivot to a new more conventional foreign policy model. What I didn't imagine was that the need to choose would be foisted on Iranian leaders before the book was finished.

Because of the challenge Iran is facing, I have tried to look at different scenarios of how Iran's foreign policy might respond and evolve in the future. Despite the pessimism that tends to prevail in the analytic and policy communities, I have taken the risk of looking at Vietnam as a best-case scenario of how Iran's foreign policy could evolve. But as useful as hopefully the scenarios will be to readers, the future of Iran's foreign policy can't be predicted. There are many possible wildcards that could disrupt any of the positive or negative trends we may see today. Regime change in Iran or in other countries in the region could shape Iran's foreign policy, as could a sudden downturn in the economy. Impetuous actions on the part of the United States or Israel could also throw any favorable possibilities under the bus.

A central question of the book is whether Iran has had a clear strategy. The research using primary and secondary resources and meetings with key leaders, including two Iranian presidents and three foreign ministers, has found little evidence of a planned overarching grand strategy. Instead, Iran's strategy has been emergent and adaptive to the challenges the country has faced since the revolution. But what Iran has done impressively is to consolidate its incremental successes and adaptations to its regional and global environments into a coherent pattern. While Iran may have responded tactically and opportunistically to events such as the US invasions of Iraq and Afghanistan, the civil wars in Syria and Yemen, and state failure in Lebanon, it integrated its tactical victories into something approximating an overarching strategy.

The question going forward is, if Iran's current strategic approach has emerged incrementally in response to the vagaries of a failed region, does it now need a more deliberate grand strategy going forward? It seems that the answer is yes. It will be challenged to rely on the two-track foreign policy it has had, one geared to diplomacy with states and the other oriented toward militias in the substate interstices of the Middle East. Since those two tracks have come into competition with one another, and its one state ally Syria appears potentially to be lost, the need for Iran to make a clear and deliberate bet on the future may have arrived.

Hopefully this book has provided the policy-maker, analyst, and student a framework for looking at Iran's foreign policy in a clear-eyed way that helps us respond better to a country that has the potential to alternatively be both a disruptive and constructive force in the tumultuous region of the Middle East. We have seen how the battles between Israel and Iran and between Israel and Hamas and Hezbollah have destabilized the entire region. If Iran moves in a more positive direction and tilts toward using more conventional diplomacy, the region is likely to benefit.

The United States and other global actors can't force Iran into playing a more constructive role in the Middle East. That would need to come from influences from within Iran and from the region. But Washington should follow the diplomatic counterpart to the Hippocratic Oath taken by physicians to "do no harm." We can't shape Iran's behavior, but given the outsized role the United States has played in Iran so far, we can reinforce positive behavior. The lesson of this book is that Iran has been remarkably adaptive to regional and global influences. The United States should do its part in creating an environment of diplomacy and cooperation that Iran can adapt to and bend toward.

NOTES

Preface

1 Henry Kissinger, *World Order* (Penguin Press, 2014), p. 168.

Chapter 1

1 Richard Nordquist, "What Is the Historical Present (Verb Tense) in English?," ThoughtCo (April 5, 2023), thoughtco.com/historical-present-verb-tense-1690928. While he uses this in the literary sense, I have borrowed the phrase for how history can impose itself on the present.

2 "Khomeini, 'We Shall Confront the World with Our Ideology,'" *Middle East Report*, Issue 88 (June 1980), https://merip.org/1980/06/khomeini-we-shall-confront-the-world-with-our-ideology/ and J.S. Ismael and T.Y. Ismael, "Social Change in Islamic Society: The Political Thought of Ayatollah Khomeini," *Social Problems*, Vol. 27, No. 5 (June 1980), pp. 601–619.

3 See Morteza Darabinia, Rahmatollah Marzband, and Hossein Foroughiniya, "Imam Khomeini's Foreign Policy: Conceptual Framework, Perspectives and Challenges," *Journal of International Relations and Foreign Policy*, Vol. 5, No. 2 (December 2017), pp. 32–38.

4 "Understanding Iranian Foreign Policy," Middle East Institute (April 20, 2012), https://www.mei.edu/publications/understanding-iranian-foreign-policy.

5 Anne Barnard and Andrew E. Kramer, "Iran Revokes Russia's Use of Air Base, Saying Moscow 'Betrayed Trust,'" *The New York Times* (August 22, 2016), https://www.nytimes.com/2016/08/23/world/middleeast/iran-russia-syria.html.

6 See Mark N. Katz, "Russia and Iran," *Middle East Policy*, Vol. XIX, No. 3 (Fall 2012), pp. 54–64.

7 Ahmad Fazli Nejad, Abdol Rasul Kheir Andish, and Abed Akbari, "The Role of Germany as a Third Power in Qajar Foreign Policy in Competition with Britain and Russia," *International Journal of Scientific Study*, Vol. 5, No. 3 (June 2017), pp. 342–349 and Mansour Bonakdarian, *U.S.-Iranian Relations: 1911–1951*, https://www.files.ethz.ch/isn/58235/MESV3-2.pdf.

8 For reference to Iranian "memory" of historical events, see Reza Zia-Ebrahimi, "Better a Warm Hug than a Cold Bath: Nationalist Memory and the Failures of Iranian Historiography," *Iranian Studies*, Vol. 49, No. 5 (September 2016), pp. 837–854.
9 "Khomeini, 'We Shall Confront the World with Our Ideology.'"
10 See Sandra Mackey, *The Iranians: Persia, Islam and the Soul of a Nation* (Dutton, an imprint of Penguin Group, 1996), pp. 83–90.
11 Mackey, *The Iranians*, pp. 83–90.
12 Mackey, *The Iranians*, p. 82.
13 Rouhollah K. Ramazani, *The Foreign Policy of Iran: A Developing Nation in World Affairs, 1500–1943* (University Press of Virginia, 1966), p. 16.
14 Ramazani, *The Foreign Policy of Iran*, p. 14.
15 For a description of the thinking of west-toxification, see Hassan Abbas, "'Islam versus the West' and the Political Thought of AbdolKarim Saroush," *Al Nakhlah: The Fletcher School Online Journal for issues related to Southwest Asia and Islamic Civilization* (Spring 2006), https://ciaotest.cc.columbia.edu/olj/aln/aln_spring06/aln_spring06a.pdf.
16 Ramazani, *The Foreign Policy of Iran*, pp. 18–19.
17 "Iran: Consolidation and Repression," *Strategic Survey*, Vol. 83, No. 1 (1982), pp. 79–84.
18 See L. Lockhart, *The Fall of the Safavi Dynasty and the Afghan Occupation of Persia* (Cambridge University Press, 1958), p. 20.
19 For an account of the hostage crisis itself and some of the Iranian political ramifications, see Mark Bowden, *Guests of the Ayatollah: The First Battle in America's War with Militant Islam* (Grove Press, 2006).
20 See Jonas Hanway, *Revolutions of Persia* (London, 1754), pp. 10–22.
21 See Ramazani, *The Foreign Policy of Iran*, pp. 14–15.
22 Afshin Molavi, "The Disenchantment," *Wilson Quarterly*, Vol. 27, No. 1 (Winter 2003), pp. 48–55.
23 Ramazani, *The Foreign Policy of Iran*, pp. 18–19.
24 See R.K. Ramazani, "Ideology and Pragmatism in Iran's Foreign Policy," *Middle East Journal*, Vol. 58, No. 4 (Autumn 2004), pp. 549–559.
25 Ramazani, *The Foreign Policy of Iran*, p. 14.
26 Seyed Mohammad Houshisadat, "Foreign Policy of Modern Persia (Iran) and the Middle East," *Journal of International and Global Studies*, Vol. 10, No. 1 (2018), p. 135, https://digitalcommons.lindenwood.edu/cgi/viewcontent.cgi?article=1441&context=jigs.
27 Houshisadat, "Foreign Policy of Modern Persia (Iran) and the Middle East," p. 137.
28 Ramazani, *The Foreign Policy of Iran*, pp. 13–30.

29 Andrew J. Newman, "'Great Men', 'Decline' and Empire: Safavid Studies and a Way Forward?," *Medieval Worlds*, No. 2 (2015), p. 47.
30 Ramazani, *The Foreign Policy of Iran*, p. 32.
31 See Ariane M. Tabatabai, *No Conquest, No Defeat: Iran's National Security Strategy* (Oxford University Press, 2020), pp. 29–31.
32 Ramazani, *The Foreign Policy of Iran*, pp. 38–40.
33 See the account of this by W. Morgan Shuster, *The Strangling of Persia: A Personal Narrative* (Higgins Press, 2008).
34 Shuster, *The Strangling of Persia*, p. 114.
35 Ramazani, *The Foreign Policy of Iran* pp. 106–107.
36 Nikki R. Keddie, *Modern Iran: Roots and Results of Revolution* (Yale University Press, 2003), pp. 38–45.
37 Richard W. Cottam, *Nationalism in Iran* (University of Pittsburgh Press, 1979), pp. 164–168.
38 Ramazani, *The Foreign Policy of Iran*, pp. 61–62.
39 Ramazani, *The Foreign Policy of Iran*, pp. 82–88.
40 Cottam, *Nationalism in Iran*, pp. 18–20.
41 Cottam, *Nationalism in Iran*, pp. 172, 257.
42 Cottam, *Nationalism in Iran*, pp. 20–22.
43 Ramazani, *The Foreign Policy of Iran*, pp. 209–221.
44 I discussed this with the late President Raisi and late Foreign Minister Abdollahian both in September of 2022 and 2023. They were bullish on Iran's leverage due to these factors.
45 Arash Reisinezhad, *The Shah of Iran, the Iraqi Kurds, and the Lebanese Shia* (Palgrave Macmillan, 2019), chapter 2.
46 April R. Summitt, "For a White Revolution: John F. Kennedy and the Shah of Iran," *The Middle East Journal*, Vol. 58, No. 4 (Autumn, 2004), pp. 560–575.
47 Summitt, "For a White Revolution."
48 Cottam, *Nationalism in Iran*, pp. 323–337.
49 Ramazani, *Independence Without Freedom: Iran's Foreign Policy* (University of Virginia Press, 2013, pp. 83–84.

Chapter 2

1 Leonard C. Sebastian, *Realpolitik Ideology: Indonesia's Use of Military Force* (ISEAS-Yusof Ishak Institute, 2005), chapter 1.
2 See Seyed Mahdi Hosseini Matin, "Iran's Desired Power Status," *Iranian Review of Foreign Affairs*, Vol. 3, No. 1 (Spring 2012), pp. 183–206. Also, see Richard Herrmann, "The Power of Perceptions in Foreign-Policy Decision

Making: Do Views of the Soviet Union Determine the Policy Choices of American Leaders?," *American Journal of Political Science*, Vol. 30, No. 4 (November 1986), pp. 841–875 for a discussion of how schemas work to prejudice foreign policy decisions.

3   See *Britain in Egypt* (University of Cambridge), https://www.whipplelib.hps.cam.ac.uk/special/exhibitions-and-displays/conflicting-chronologies/britain-egypt.

4   See Richard W. Cottam, *Foreign Policy Motivation: A General Theory and Case Study* (University of Pittsburgh Press, 1977), pp. 62–80 for a general theory involving seeing the opponent in either complex or simplified terms.

5   Umut Aydin, "Emerging Middle Powers and the Liberal International Order," *International Affairs*, Vol. 97, No. 5 (September 2021), pp. 1377–1394.

6   For an excellent analysis of Saddam Hussein's decision-making process, see Steve Coll, *The Achilles Trap: Saddam Hussein, the C.I.A., and the Origins of America's Invasion of Iraq* (Penguin Press, 2024).

7   Jonathan C. Randal, "Iran Warns of Threat by Soviets," *The Washington Post* (March 21, 1980), https://www.washingtonpost.com/archive/politics/1980/03/22/iran-warns-of-threat-by-soviets/7f59c11e-8076-4ad7-87a9-b61e21270c53/.

8   Shahram Chubin and Charles Tripp, *Iran and Iraq at War* (Westview Press, 1988), p. 238.

9   Ole R. Holsti, "Cognitive Process Approaches to Decision-Making: Foreign Policy Actors Viewed Psychologically," *American Behavioral Scientist*, Vol. 20, No. 1 (September/October 1976), 11–32.

10 See Paige Johnson Tan, "Navigating a Turbulent Ocean: Indonesia's Worldview and Foreign Policy," *Asian Perspectives*, Vol. 31, No. 3 (2007), 147–181.

11 Khamenei 1390/2011-20012: 43, taken from Seyed Mohammed Marandi and Raffaele Mauriello, "The Khamenei Doctrine: Iran's Leader on Diplomacy, Foreign Policy and International Relations," in Nassef Manabilang Adiong, Raffaele Mauriello, and Deina Abdelkader (Eds.), *Islam in International Relations: Politics and Paradigms* (Routledge, 2019), pp. 18–38.

12 Thomas S. Mowle, "Worldviews in Foreign Policy: Realism, Liberalism, and External Conflict," *Political Psychology*, Vol. 4, No. 23 (September 2003), pp. 561–592.

13 Ali M. Ansari, "Iran and the U.S. in the Shadow of 9/11: Persia and the Persian Question Revisited," *Iranian Studies*, Vol. 39, No. 2 (June 2006), p. 160.

14 John Ghazvinian, *America and Iran: A History 1720 to the Present* (Knopf, 2021), p. 149.

15 The historical message of Imam Khomeini addressed to the pilgrims of the Sacred House of Allah in 1408 A.H., first edition, Tehran, Iran, Foundation of Islamic Thought, Zul-Hajjah 1408 (1987).

16 "Khomeini Called 'a Lunatic'" [by Anwar Sadat], *The New York Times* (November 10, 1979), https://www.nytimes.com/1979/11/10/archives/khomeini-called-a-lunatic.html.

17 See Ray Takeyh, *Guardians of the Revolution: Iran and the World in the Age of the Ayatollahs* (Oxford University Press, 2009), pp. 18–22.

18 See Shireen T. Hunter, *Iran and the World: Continuity in a Revolutionary Decade* (Indiana University Press, 1990), chapter 3.

19 See Nikki R. Keddie, *An Islamic Response to Imperialism: Political and Religious Writings of Sayyid Jamal ad-Din "al-Afghani"* (University of California Press, 1983)

20 Rouhollah K. Ramazani, *The Foreign Policy of Iran: A Developing Nation in World Affairs, 1500–1941* (University Press of Virginia, 1966), pp. 88–95.

21 See R.K. Ramazani, *Revolutionary Iran: Challenge and Response in the Middle East* (Johns Hopkins University Press, 1988), pp. 21–22.

22 See Hunter, *Iran and the World*, pp. 37–40.

23 See Richard W. Cottam, "Iran's Perception of the Superpowers," in Barry M. Rosen (Ed.), *Iran Since the Revolution: Internal Dynamics, Regional Conflicts and the Superpowers* (Columbia University Press, 1985), pp. 133–147. Also see Ali Akbar Hojatoleslam Hashemi Rafsanjani, February 25, 1983 in a speech to the Majlis.

24 Khomeini, February 10, 1986, in BBC/SWB/ME (February 12, 1986), Tehran Radio Commentary, Home Service.

25 Shane Harris and Matthew M. Aid, "Exclusive: CIA Files Prove America Helped Saddam as He Gassed Iran," *Foreign Policy* (August 26, 2013), https://foreignpolicy.com/2013/08/26/exclusive-cia-files-prove-america-helped-saddam-as-he-gassed-iran/.

26 Tehran, Home Service, June 14, 15, 1987, in BBC/SWB/ME (May 15, 1987), A/6-7.

27 Chubin and Tripp, *Iran and Iraq at War*, p. 222.

28 See Michael H. Armacost (Undersecretary of State for Political Affairs), "U.S. Policy in the Persian Gulf and Kuwaiti Reflagging," statement to US Senate Foreign Relations Committee (June 16, 1987), Bureau of Public Affairs- U.S. Department of State.

29 See letter by Iranian Foreign Minister Ali Akbar Velayati to UN Secretary General (February 14, 1984), https://nsarchive.gwu.edu/document/28045-document-05-ali-akbar-velayati-message-minister-foreign-affairs-islamic-republic.

30 Chubin and Tripp, *Iran and Iraq at War*, p. 222.

31 Chubin and Tripp, *Iran and Iraq at War*, pp. 238–239.

32 See Ariane M. Tabatabai and Annie Tracy Samuel, "What the Iran-Iraq War Tells Us About the Future of the Iran-Nuclear Deal," *International Security*, Vol. 42, No. 1 (Summer 2017), 152–185.

33 President Ali Khamenei at the UN General Assembly Meeting (September 22, 1987), https://english.khamenei.ir/news/1413/Leader-s-Speech-at-UN-General-Assembly
34 Cottam, "Iran's Perception of the Superpowers," pp. 133–147.
35 Adam Tarock, *The Superpowers' Involvement in the Iran-Iraq War* (Nova Science Publishers, 1998).
36 Ayatollah Khomeini, *Kayhan*, 30th Farvardin 1359 (April 19, 1980). Also, see Oriana Fallaci, "An Interview with Khomeini," *The New York Times Magazine* (October 7, 1979), https://www.nytimes.com/1979/10/07/archives/an-interview-with-khomeini.html.
37 R.K. Ramazani, "Iran's Foreign Policy: Contending Orientations," *Middle East Journal*, Vol. 43, No. 2 (Spring, 1989), pp. 202–217.
38 See Mohiaddin Mesbahi, "Free and Confined: Iran and the International System," *Iranian Review of Foreign Affairs*, Vol. 2, No. 5 (Spring 2011), pp. 9–34 for the concept of strategic loneliness.
39 Ayatollah Khamenei, "Seven Realities of the 8-Year War the Enemy Seeks to Distort," Video Conference (September 21, 2020), https://english.khamenei.ir/news/8001/Seven-realities-of-the-8-year-war-the-enemy-seeks-to-distort.
40 Ali Fathollah-Nejad, "Iranians Respond to the Regime: 'Leave Syria Alone'", *Al-Jazeera* (May 2, 2018), https://www.aljazeera.com/opinions/2018/5/2/iranians-respond-to-the-regime-leave-syria-alone.
41 Robert Pear, "Khomeini Accepts 'Poison' of Ending the War with Iraq: U.S. Sending Mission," *The New York Times* (July 21, 1988), https://www.nytimes.com/1988/07/21/us/khomeini-accepts-poison-of-ending-the-war-with-iraq-un-sending-mission.html.
42 "Iran under Rafsanjani: Seeking a New Role in the World Community," *Director of Central Intelligence: National Intelligence Estimate* (Washington, DC, October 17, 1991).
43 See Ross Harrison, "Iran, Russia, China: A Triple Alliance Under the Strain of War", in *Expert Views: How Should We Navigate the New Rules of the Game in the Israel-Iran Conflict* (The Middle East Institute, April 25, 2024), https://www.mei.edu/publications/expert-views-how-should-we-navigate-new-rules-game-israel-iran-conflict.
44 H. Rastgoo, "Decoding Iran's Politics: What Was Tehran's Share of the Responsibility for the Iran-Iraq War?," *Iran Wire* (August 16, 2019), https://iranwire.com/en/features/66239/.
45 Richard W. Cottam, *Iran and the United States: A Cold War Case Study* (University of Pittsburgh Press, 1988), p. 255.
46 For an excellent analysis of the political wrangling among revolutionary elites in Iran that formed the backdrop for the hostage crisis, see Alex Vatanka, *The Battle of the Ayatollahs: The United States, Foreign Policy, and Political Rivalry Since 1979* (IB Tauris, 2021), chapter 2.

47 Mark Bowden, *Guest of the Ayatollah: The Iran Hostage Crisis* (Grove Atlantic, 2006).

48 This was recounted to me directly by Richard Cottam in Pittsburgh and on a trip we took together to the Middle East in May of 1988. My conversations with Dick were private but some of the conversations he had with Iranians are part of the public record. See https://history.state.gov/historicaldocuments/frus1977-80v11p1/d145.

49 Nasser Karimi and Aron Heller, "40 Years On, Iranians Recall 1979 US Embassy Hostage Crisis," *Associated Press* (November 1, 2019), https://apnews.com/article/iran-revolution-anniversary-ap-top-news-tehran-international-news-iran-352409d3e9c34179a0fe9402a7254014.

50 "Key Moments in the 1979 Iran Hostage Crisis at U.S. Embassy," *Associated Press* (November 4, 2019), https://apnews.com/article/6149da2418b140c2b1d5b0ca5779bac5.

51 Speech of Ayatollah Khamenei (December 27, 2017) in a meeting with the members of the Coordination Council of Islamic Propagation, https://english.khamenei.ir/news/5370/We-must-develop-our-economy-from-inside-to-combat-sanctions.

52 Interview with Ali Javadi, "Gulf War: An Iranian Perspective," *Marxists.org* (March/April 1991), ATC 31, https://www.marxists.org/history/etol/newspape/atc/6967.html.

53 Patrick J. Garrity, "Why the Gulf War Still Matters: Foreign Perspectives on the War and the Future of International Security," Center for National Security Studies, Los Alamos National Laboratory, Report No. 16 (July 1993), https://www.osti.gov/biblio/10178236.

54 Reza Ekktiari Amiri and Fakhreddin Soltani, "Iraqi Invasion of Kuwait as Turning Point in Iran-Saudi Relationship," *Journal of Politics and Law*, Vol. 4, No. 1 (March 11, 2011), p. 191.

55 Vatanka, *The Battle of the Ayatollahs*, pp. 94–98.

56 Vatanka, *The Battle of the Ayatollahs*, pp. 98–100.

57 Kashif Mumtaz Ghumman, "Iran-US Relations in the Post-9/11 Days: Problems and Prospects," *Strategic Studies*, Vol. 22, No. 3 (2002), 170–186.

58 Takeyh, *Guardians of the Revolution*, chapter 9.

59 This was evident in discussions the author had with Iran's President Raisi in 2022 and 2023, and with Foreign Minister Hossein Abdollahian in 2021, 2022, and 2023. These impressions haven't been tested since the October 7, 2023 attacks on Israel by Hamas or since the deaths of President Raisi or Foreign Minister Abdollahian.

60 See Gary Sick, "Rethinking Dual Containment," *Survival*, Vol. 40, No. 1 (Spring 1998), pp. 5–32.

61 See Ross Harrison, "U.S.-Iran Showdown: Clashing Strategic Universes Amid a Changing Region," *Al Jazeera Center for Studies* (April 16, 2020).

62 Elaine Sciolino, "Condemning Iranian Oil Deal, U.S. May Tighten Trade Ban," *The New York Times* (March 10, 1995), https://www.nytimes.com/1995/03/10/world/condemning-iranian-oil-deal-us-may-tighten-trade-ban.html.

63 Elaine Sciolino, "Iranian Leader says U.S. Move on Oil Deal Wrecked Chance to Improve Ties," *The New York Times* (May 16, 1995), https://www.nytimes.com/1995/05/16/world/iranian-leader-says-us-move-on-oil-deal-wrecked-chance-to-improve-ties.html.

64 Ansari, "Iran and the U.S. in the Shadow of 9/11," p. 159.

65 Mike Wallace Interview on 60 Minutes (March 8, 1997) with Akbar Hashemi Rafsanjani in Tehran, https://www.c-span.org/program/interview/president-rafsanjani-interview/162036.

66 See Robin Wright, "New U.S. Sanctions will Backfire, Iranians Say: Embargo: President Rafsanjani, Opposition Leader Warn that Move Will Unify People Behind Tehran Government," *Los Angeles Times* (May 16, 1995), https://www.latimes.com/archives/la-xpm-1995-05-16-mn-2535-story.html.

67 (Author Redacted) *Iran: U.S. Policy and Options*, Congressional Research Service (CRS) Report for Congress (Updated January 14, 2000), https://www.everycrsreport.com/reports/97-231.html.

68 Ansari, "Iran and the U.S. in the Shadow of 9/11," p. 162.

69 Ansari, "Iran and the U.S. in the Shadow of 9/11," pp. 158–159.

70 In addition to private conversations I had with Feith, see Douglas J. Feith, *War and Decision: Inside the Pentagon at the Dawn of the War on Terror* (Harper, 2008).

71 Ghumman, "Iran-US Relations in the Post-9/11 Days," 170–186.

72 Amin Tarzi, "Proliferation Assessment: Iran's Strategic Environment After 9/11," James Martin Center for Non-Proliferation Studies (CNS) (2002), p. 32, https://www.jstor.org/stable/pdf/resrep09902.10.pdf.

73 Ghumman, "Iran-US Relations in the Post-9/11 Days," 170–186. Also Andrew Glass, "President Bush Cites 'Axis of Evil', January 29th 2002," *Politico* (January 29, 2019), https://www.politico.com/story/2019/01/29/bush-axis-of-evil-2002-1127725.

74 Alex Horton, "Soleimani's Legacy: The Gruesome, Advanced IEDs that Haunted U.S. Troops in Iraq," *The Washington Post* (January 3, 2020), https://www.washingtonpost.com/national-security/2020/01/03/soleimanis-legacy-gruesome-high-tech-ieds-that-haunted-us-troops-iraq/.

75 "David Petraeus on Soleimani," *National Public Radio (NPR)* (January 5, 2020), https://www.npr.org/2020/01/05/793722592/david-petraeus-on-soleimani.

76 Takeyh, *Guardians of the Revolution*, pp. 216–218.

77 Ansari, "Iran and the U.S. in the Shadow of 9/11," p. 156.

78 Ali Ansari, "Persian Summer vs. Arab Spring," *Al Jazeera* (December 22, 2013), https://www.aljazeera.com/opinions/2013/12/22/persian-summer-vs-arab-spring.

79 Dina Esfandiary and Ariana Tabatabai, "Iran's ISIS Policy," *International Affairs*, Vol. 91, No. 1 (2015), pp.1–15, https://www.chathamhouse.org/sites/default/files/field/field_publication_docs/INTA91_1_01_Esfandiary_Tabatabai.pdf.

80 See Dina Esfandiary and Ariane Tabatabai, *Triple Axis: Iran's Relations with Russia and China* (IB Tauris, 2018).

81 Esfandiary and Tabatabai, *Triple Axis*, pp. 142–146.

82 "Russian Declaration Was Kind of a Show-Off and Disloyalty," *Iran's National TV* (August 22, 2016), https://www.yjc.ir/fa/news/5747571, as reported in Hamed Mousavi and Amin Naeni, "Iran and Russia Pivot to the East: Was it U.S. Pressure?," *Middle East Policy*, Vol. XXVI, No. 3 (Fall 2019), p. 112.

83 Sediqeh Zamanian, "'Russia Day' Banquet in Tehran Embassy Astounds Iranians," *Iran International* (June 8, 2022).

84 E. Koolaee, H. Mousavi, and A. Abedi, "Fluctuations in Iran-Russia Relations During the Past Four Decades," *Iran and the Caucasus*, Vol. 24, No. 2 (2020), pp. 216–232.

85 Najmeh Bozorgmehr, "Zarif Leak Reveals Who Really Wields Power in Iran Nuclear Deal," *Financial Times* (April 28, 2021), https://www.ft.com/content/7266aa0c-d9e2-4f5d-8dc5-d2e00ee0b4ad.

86 The author met with President Raisi in New York City in both 2022 and 2023 on the sidelines of his attendance of the United Nations General Assembly meetings.

87 Mohiaddin Mesbahi, "Free and Confined," pp. 9–34.

88 Matthew Karnitschnig, "Russia Eyes Iran as Sanctions-Busting Backdoor for Oil Sales," *Politico* (August 23, 2022), https://www.politico.eu/article/russia-eyes-iran-as-sanctions-busting-backdoor-for-oil-sales/.

89 Omer Behram Ozdemir, "Russia's War in Ukraine Gives Iran the Upper Hand in Syria," *Politics Today* (May 26, 2022), https://politicstoday.org/russia-war-in-ukraine-gives-iran-the-upper-hand-in-syria/. Also "The Cultural Frontlines for Russia and Iran in Syria," *The Syrian Observer* (August 9, 2018), https://syrianobserver.com/foreign-actors/the_cultural_frontlines_russia_iran_syria.html.

90 See Esfandiary and Tabatabai, *Triple Axis* for an overview of this relationship.

91 See Mohammad Kazem Sajaddpour, Deputy Foreign Minister of Iran, in *Russia-Iran Partnership: An Overview and Prospects for the Future*. Russian International Affairs Council and The Institute for Iran-Eurasia Studies, Report No. 29 (2016), pp. 34–36.

92 *Russia in the Middle East: National Security Challenges for the United States and Israel in the Biden Era*. Wilson Center's Kennan Institute and Institute for Policy and Strategy (2021), https://www.wilsoncenter.org/publication/report-russia-middle-east-national-security-challenges-united-states-and-israel-biden.

93 "Foreign Ministry: China Appreciates Iranian President-Elects's Remarks on Bilateral Relation," *CGTN* (July 15, 2024), https://news.cgtn.com/news/2024-07-15/China-appreciates-Iranian-president-elect-s-remarks-on-bilateral-ties-1vgjHkCJjsQ.

94 Erzsebet N. Rozna, "Iran and China: Looking for an Alliance and Regional Power Status," *Iranian Review of Foreign Affairs*, Vol. 2, No. 5 (Spring 2011), p. 133.

95 Hunter, *Iran and the World*, p. 160.

96 The author has had several meetings in Track 1.5 meeting with senior Chinese influencers who were clear that they would remain neutral, explaining that the US approach of taking sides in regional conflicts neither served US interests nor quelled hostilities.

97 Author's discussions with Iranian diplomats and Chinese influencers in Track 1.5 talks held at the Hofburg Palace in Vienna, Austria (December 2018).

98 Anoushiravan Ehteshami, Niv Horesh, and Ruike Xu, "Chinese-Iranian Mutual Strategic Perceptions," *The China Journal*, No. 79 (August 9, 2017), pp. 1–20.

99 "China and Iran Sign 25-year Cooperation Agreement", *Reuters* (March 29, 2021), https://www.reuters.com/article/world/iran-and-china-sign-25-year-cooperation-agreement-idUSKBN2BJ0HG/.

100 Susan Maloney, "1979: Iran and America," *Brookings* (January 24, 2019), https://www.brookings.edu/articles/1979-iran-and-america/.

101 See Harrison, "The U.S.-Iran Showdown."

102 From the statement made by the President of the Islamic Republic of Iran at the UNGA, H.E. Ayatollah Dr. Seyyed Ebrahim Raisi, President of the Islamic Republic of Iran. Before the United Nations General Assembly, New York (September 2022), https://netherlands.mfa.ir/en/newsview/694250/The-full-transcript-of-HE-Ebrahim-Raisis-speech-at-the-77th-session-of-the-United-Nations-General-Assembly.

103 Farideh Farhi and Saideh Lotfian, "Iran's Post-Revolution Foreign Policy Puzzle," in Henry R. Nau and Deepa Ollapally (eds.), *Worldviews of Aspiring Powers:Domestic Foreign Policy Debates in China, India, Iran, Japan and Russia* (Oxford Academic, 2012), pp. 114–140.

104 Takeyh, *Guardians of the Revolution*, pp. 35–36.

105 See Ahmed Aboudouh, "Yes China Pressured Iran on Red Sea Attacks, But Only to Protect Its Own Ships," Expert Comment, Chatham House

(February 27, 2024), https://www.chathamhouse.org/2024/02/yes-china-pressured-iran-red-sea-attacks-only-protect-its-own-ships.

Chapter 3

1   John Simpson, "The Plane Journey that Set Iran's Revolution in Motion," *BBC* (February 1, 2019), https://www.bbc.com/news/world-middle-east-47043561.
2   "Khomeini, 'We Shall Confront the World with Our Ideology,'" *Middle East Report*, Issue 88 (June 1980), https://merip.org/1980/06/khomeini-we-shall-confront-the-world-with-our-ideology/.
3   See Henry A. Kissinger, "The Next Steps with Iran", *The Washington Post* (July 31, 2006), https://www.henryakissinger.com/articles/the-next-steps-with-iran/.
4   Alex Vatanka, "Whither the IRGC of the 2020s? Is Iran's Proxy Warfare Strategy of Forward Defense Sustainable?," *New America* (January 15, 2021), https://www.newamerica.org/future-security/reports/whither-irgc-2020s/.
5   "The Graphics of Revolution and War: Iranian Poster Arts," University of Chicago Library (October 15, 2011), https://www.lib.uchicago.edu/collex/exhibits/graphics-revolution-and-war-iranian-poster-arts/demonizing-enemy/.
6   Kourosh Ziabari, "Iranians Have Become Desensitized to the Question of Palestine", *New Lines Magazine* (November 17, 2023), https://newlinesmag.com/spotlight/iranians-have-become-desensitized-to-the-question-of-palestine/.
7   The late President Raisi reiterated this both in my 2022 and 2023 sessions with him.
8   See Jason BeDuhn, "The Co-formation of the Manichean and Zoroastrian Religions in Third Century Iran," *Entangled Religions*, Vol. 11, No. 2 (2020), https://er.ceres.rub.de/index.php/ER/article/view/8414/7832
9   See "Khomeini, 'We Shall Confront the World with Our Ideology."
10 Kayhan Barzegar and Abdolrasool Divsallar, "Political Rationality in Iranian Foreign Policy," *The Washington Quarterly*, Vol. 40, No. 1 (2017), 39–53.
11 See Ross Harrison, "U.S. Foreign Policy Towards the Middle East: Pumping Air Into a Punctured Tire," Research Paper, Arab Center for Research and Policy Studies, Doha, Qatar (March 7, 2019), https://www.dohainstitute.org/en/Lists/ACRPS-PDFDocumentLibrary/US-Foreign-Policy-Towards-the-Middle-East-Pumping-Air-into-a-Punctured-Tire.pdf.
12 Ali Fathollah, "Iranian Respond to the Regime: Leave Syria Alone," *Al Jazeera* (May 2, 2018), https://www.aljazeera.com/opinions/2018/5/2/iranians-respond-to-the-regime-leave-syria-alone.

13 "Iran's Raisi Lands in Saudi Arabia for Gaza Summit," *Al Arabiya News* (November 11, 2023), https://english.alarabiya.net/News/saudi-arabia/2023/11/11/Iran-President-lands-in-Saudi-Arabia-for-Gaza-summit-Reports-.

14 The meeting with Iranian President Ibrahim Raisi was held as "off the record" on September 22, 2022 but reported by his office as follows: https://www.president.ir/en/139734.

15 The author met with President Masoud Pezeshkian in New York City on September 25, 2024, as well as with Foreign Minister Abbas Araghchi, Vice President (and former Foreign Minister) Javad Zarif, and the Permanent Representative of Iran to the United Nations Amir Saeed Iravani.

16 See Iranian President Pezeshkian' speech to the UN General Assembly on September 24, 2024: https://www.youtube.com/watch?v=-YPEYKYzaZI. He reiterated his comments in my closed-door meeting with him the next day.

17 The author was part of Track 1.5 discussions between Iran, Saudi Arabia, and the UEA, and Turkey, Russia, and China that took place in Malta and Oman, and Vienna. In Baghdad (December 15–16, 2017), the parties agreed to a series of good neighborhood principles for the Middle East: https://www.mei.edu/publications/baghdad-declaration-good-neighborhood-principles-middle-east.

18 Barzegar and Divsallar, "Political Rationality in Iranian Foreign Policy," pp. 39–53.

19 "Iran Military Power: Ensuring Regime Survival and Securing Regional Dominance," Defense Intelligence Agency (2019), https://www.dia.mil/Portals/110/Images/News/Military_Powers_Publications/Iran_Military_Power_LR.pdf.

20 *France 24* (April 11, 2024), https://www.france24.com/en/middle-east/20240411-%F0%9F%94%B4-live-biden-vows-ironclad-support-for-israel-against-iran-reprisals.

21 Stephen M. Walt, "Alliance Formation and the Balance of World Power," *International Security*, Vol. 9, No. 4 (Spring 1985), pp. 3–43.

22 Kayhan Barzegar, "Roles at Odds: The Roots of Increased Iran-U.S. Tension in the Post 9/11 Middle East," *Iranian Review of Foreign Affairs*, Vol. 1, No. 3 (Fall 2010), p. 86.

23 Ray Takeyh, *The Guardians of the Revolution: Iran and the World in the Age of the Ayatollahs* (Oxford University Press, 2009), p. 18.

24 Elliot C. McLaughlin, "Iran's Supreme Leader: There Will Be No Such Thing as Israel in 25 Years," *CNN* (September 11, 2015), https://edition.cnn.com/2015/09/10/middleeast/iran-khamenei-israel-will-not-exist-25-years/index.html. Also see speech by Supreme Leader Ayatollah Ali Khamenei in a meeting with reciters of Holy Koran, "The Unique Steadfastness of Palestinians and the Crimes of Zionists and Western Civilization" (March 12 2024), https://english.khamenei.ir/news/10636/The-unique-steadfastness-

of-Palestinians-the-crimes-of-Zionists. Also, in meetings with the late President Raisi, he didn't use the word Israel, but instead referred to the Zionist entity. Krishnadev Calamur, "In a Speech to Congress, Netanyahu Blasts 'a Very Bad deal' with Iran," *National Public Radio* (March 3, 2015), https://www.npr.org/sections/thetwo-way/2015/03/03/390250986/netanyahu-to-outline-iran-threats-in-much-anticipated-speech-to-congress.

25 Meetings in New York City with President Raisi, September 2022 and 2023.

26 Arash Azizi "What Do Iranians Think of Israel? Their Views Might Surprise You," *IranSource*, Atlantic Council (October 13, 2023), https://www.atlanticcouncil.org/blogs/iransource/israel-hamas-iran-views/.

27 Dalia Dassa Kaye, Alireza Nader, and Parisa Roshan, *Israel and Iran: A Dangerous Rivalry* (Rand Corporation, 2011), p. 66, https://www.rand.org/content/dam/rand/pubs/monographs/2011/RAND_MG1143.pdf.

28 Kaye, Nader, and Roshan, *Israel and Iran*, p. 61.

29 Calamur, "In a Speech to Congress."

30 Interview with President Mohammed Khatami, *CNN.com* (January 7, 1998).

31 Ali Khamenei, "Conspiracy After the Elections", Iran International.Org (September 2009).

32 Ross Harrison, "After the Gaza War: The Risks of Deterrence and the Chances of Peace," *The National Interest* (November 20, 2023), https://nationalinterest.org/feature/after-gaza-war-risks-deterrence-and-chances-peace-207379?page=0%2C1. Also see Alex Vatanka, "An Israeli-Palestinian Peace Process would Present Iran with a Difficult Choice," The Middle East Institute (December 1, 2023), https://www.mei.edu/publications/israeli-palestinian-peace-process-would-present-iran-difficult-choice.

33 International Press, "The Israel-Iran Connection," *Journal of Palestine Studies*, Vol. 16, No. 3 (1987), 210–212.

34 See Trita Parsi, *Treacherous Alliance: The Secret Dealings of Israel, Iran and the U.S.* (Yale University Press, 2007), p. 106.

35 Garrett Nada, Thomas Neal, Cameron Glenn, and Others, "Flashpoints: Iran and Saudi Arabia," *The Iran Primer* (September 18, 2019), https://iranprimer.usip.org/blog/2019/sep/18/flashpoints-iran-and-saudi-arabia.

36 See Richard W. Cottam, *Iran and the United States: A Cold War Case Study* (University of Pittsburgh Press, 1988), pp. 146–147.

37 Shireen T. Hunter, *Arab-Iranian Relations: Dynamics of Conflict and Accommodation* (Rowman & Littlefield, 2019), pp. 218–219.

38 Banafsheh Keynoush, *Saudi Arabia and Iran: Friends or Foes?* (Palgrave Macmillan, 2016), part 4, pp. 114–116.

39 Hunter, *Arab-Iranian Relations*, pp. 224–225.

40 See Paul Salem and Ross Harrison, *Escaping the Conflict Trap: Toward Ending Civil Wars in the Middle East*, 2nd edition (IB Tauris, 2022).

41 Ali Afshari "Why Are So Many Iranians Seemingly Indifferent to the War in Gaza," *Stimson* (May 13, 2024), https://www.stimson.org/2024/why-are-so-many-iranians-seemingly-indifferent-to-the-war-in-gaza/.
42 "Iran on New Middle East Peace Deals," *Iran Primer* (September 15, 2020), https://iranprimer.usip.org/blog/2020/sep/15/iran-new-middle-east-peace-deals.
43 The author had meetings with Iranian Foreign Minister Javad Zarif in April 2019, where he was clear about the strategy of using fear to bring the Saudis to the table. While he didn't lay out the specifics of the strategy, he did say that the UAE would be a reprisal target should Iran be attacked. And he said that we would likely see an escalation of Iranian resistance to the American maximum pressure campaign of the Trump administration. While he didn't say directly that this was a strategy to bring the Saudis to the table, he did imply that Iran showing it could counter the US with "maximum resistance" would impose costs on the US and also on Riyadh.
44 In conversations with the Late President Raisi in September 2022, he explicitly said that relations with regional rivals such as Saudi Arabia would be healthier without the distortions created by US policy in the region.
45 "Tensions Rise in the World's Most Strategic Choke Point," *Reuters Graphics* (July 19, 2019), https://www.reuters.com/graphics/MIDEAST-ATTACKS-HORMUZ/0100B0B50N3/.
46 Farhad Rezaei, *Iran's Foreign Policy After the Nuclear Agreement* (Palgrave Macmillan, 2019), p. 190.
47 Shahram Chubin, *Iran's National Security Policy: Intentions, Capabilities, and Impact* (The Carnegie Endowment for International Peace, 1994), pp. 8–10.
48 Rezaei, *Iran's Foreign Policy After the Nuclear Agreement*, p. 194.
49 "Turkey and Saudi Arabia Ominous Plan for Yemen," *Fars News Agency* (March 21, 2015) and "Turkey-Saudi Arabia New Sedition is Forthcoming: Meeting of ISIS Supporters in Riyadh," *Mehr News Agency* (December 20, 2015).
50 Ahmad Majidyar, "Iran-Backed Iraqi Mobilization Forces Urge Baghdad to Expel Turkish Ambassador," *Iran Observed*, The Middle East Institute (April 24, 2017), https://www.mei.edu/publications/iran-backed-iraqi-mobilization-forces-urge-baghdad-expel-turkish-ambassador.
51 "Iran Report: March 20, 2003," *Radio Free Europe and Radio Liberty*, Vol. 6, No. 12 (March 20, 2003), https://www.rferl.org/amp/1342725.html.
52 This came through in a meeting with former Prime Minister of Iraq, Haidar al Abadi on May 7, 2022.
53 Mustak El-Hilo, "The Prominent Figure as al-Sistani's Potential Successor: al-Irvani," *Iram*, Center for Iranian Studies (December 14, 2021), https://iramcenter.org/en/the-prominent-figure-as-al-sistanis-potential-successor-al-irvani_en-642.

54 "Iraqi Tomato Farmers Find it Difficult to Compete with Imported Goods," *Horti Daily* (July 8, 2022), https://www.hortidaily.com/article/9442807/iraqi-tomato-farmers-find-it-difficult-to-compete-with-imported-goods/.

55 Interview with former Prime Minister Haidar al-Abadi on May 7, 2022.

56 "Iraq Unrest: Protesters set Fire to Iranian Consulate in Najaf," *BBC* (November 28, 2019), https://www.bbc.com/news/world-middle-east-50580940.

57 Interview with Professor Seyed Hamzeh Safavi, University of Tehran, the son of former Revolutionary Guard Commander Yahya Rahim Safavi, on July 13, 2022.

58 Mohammad al-Sayyad, "The Supreme Marjayya: The Post-Sistani Era and the Future of the Hawza," *Rasanah* (April 18, 2022), https://rasanah-iiis.org/english/centre-for-researches-and-studies/the-supreme-marjayya-the-post-sistani-era-and-the-future-of-the-hawza/.

59 Khalil Sardarnia and Mohammed Reza Chitsazian, "The Future of Iran-Iraq Relations: Possible Scenarios," *Iranian Political Studies*, Vol. 1, No. 1 (May 2019), pp. 43–59.

60 See Jubin M. Goodarzi, *Syria and Iran: Diplomatic Alliance and Power Politics in the Middle East* (IB Tauris, 2009), pp. 11–28.

61 Hunter, *Arab-Iranian Relations*, pp. 198–200.

62 Quoted in Ashfon Ostovar, *Vanguard of the Imam: Religion, Politics, and Iran's Revolutionary Guards* (Oxford University Press, 2016). Khuzestan, in southwestern Iran, is the site of a decades-long separatist movement and drawn from Oula A. Alrifai, "In the Service of Ideology: Iran's Religious and Socioeconomic Activities in Syria", *Policy Notes*, No. 100, The Washington Institute for Near East Policy (March 2021), https://www.washingtoninstitute.org/policy-analysis/service-ideology-irans-religious-and-socioeconomic-activities-syria.

63 Michael B. Bishku, "Egyptian-Iranian Relations and the Politics of the Middle East During the Cold War," *The Maghreb Review*, Vol. 36, No. 1 (2011), pp. 3–21.

64 "Iran, Syria discuss expansion of monetary, banking relations," *Tehran Times* (November 29, 2023).

65 Parisa Hafezi, "Syria's Bashar al-Assad Meets Ayatollah Ali Khamenei in Tehran," *Reuters* (May 8, 2022), https://www.reuters.com/world/middle-east/syrian-president-meets-iranian-leader-tehran-nour-news-reports-2022-05-08/.

66 Alrifai, "In the Service of Ideology."

67 Barzegar and Divsallar, "Political Rationality in Iranian Foreign Policy," p. 47.

68 Insights from Lebanese political analyst Khaldoun El-Charif in an interview of May 2022.

69 Michael Horovitz, "Report: Iran Cautioned Hezbollah Not to Spark Full-Scale War with Israel," *The Times of Israel* (February 18, 2024), https://www.timesofisrael.com/report-iran-cautioned-hezbollah-not-to-spark-full-scale-war-with-israel/. This was first reported in *The Washington Post*.

70 I got this view from several Saudi and Emirati sources. One is from conversations with Ali Shahabi, a close confident of Mohammed bin Salman. Another is with several key leaders at the King Faisal Center for Research and Islamic Studies in Riyadh, Saudi Arabia. Also, from key Emirati decision-makers during back-channel Track 1.5 discussions between 2016 and 2019 in Muscat, Oman and in Valletta, Malta.

Chapter 4

1 R.K. Ramazani, "Reflections on Iran's Foreign Policy: Defining the 'National Interest,'" in *Independence without Freedom: Iran's Foreign Policy* (University of Virginia Press, Charlottesville, 2013).

2 See Foad Izadi, Professor at Tehran University, *Hawza News*, https://www.hawzahnews.com/news/872053/.

3 This came through discussions I had with the late Iranian President Raisi and Foreign Minister Abdollahian in September of 2022 and 2023.

4 See Javad Heirnan-Nia, "How Iran's Interpretation of the World Order Affects its Foreign Policy," *IranSource*, Atlantic Council (May 11, 2022), https://www.atlanticcouncil.org/blogs/iransource/how-irans-interpretation-of-the-world-order-affects-its-foreign-policy/.

5 Mahdi Ahouie, "The Implications of 'Strategic Loneliness' for Iran's Geopolitics: Inevitable or Constructed?," *Journal of World Sociopolitical Studies*, Vol. 5, No. 3 (July 2021), pp. 507–544.

6 Lt. Colonel John P. Baker, "Maslow, Needs and War," *U.S. Army War College Strategy Research Project* (February 28, 2012), https://apps.dtic.mil/sti/tr/pdf/ADA560680.pdf.

7 Ross Harrison, "After the Gaza War: The Risks of Deterrence and the Chances of Peace," *The National Interest* (November 20, 2023), https://nationalinterest.org/feature/after-gaza-war-risks-deterrence-and-chances-peace-207379?page=0%2C1.

8 See Paul Salem and Ross Harrison (eds.), *Escaping the Conflict Trap: Toward Ending Civil War in the Middle East*, 2nd edition (IB Tauris, 2023), pp. 73–75.

9 "'Never Threaten an Iranian': How One Diplomat's Outburst Blew Up," *BBC* (July 10, 2015), https://www.bbc.com/news/blogs-trending-33464560.

10 See Trita Parsi, *Losing an Enemy: Obama, Iran and the Triumph of Diplomacy* (Yale University Press, 2017) for his analysis of Iranian calculations and US policy responses.

11 For the best work on Iranian nationalism, see Richard W. Cottam, *Nationalism in Iran, Updated through 1978* (University of Pittsburgh Press, 1979), pp. 1–11.
12 K. J. Holsti, "National Role Conceptions in the Study of Foreign Policy," *International Studies Quarterly*, Vol. 14, No. 3 (September 1970), pp. 233–309.
13 From meetings with late President Raisi in September of 2022 and 2023.
14 President Masoud Pezeshkian in front of the 79th Session of the United Nations General Assembly in New York on September 24, 2024, https://gadebate.un.org/sites/default/files/gastatements/79/ir_en.pdf. Also, the author met with President Pezeshkian on September 25.
15 See types of roles in Holsti, "National Role Conceptions in the Study of Foreign Policy," p. 255. Also see Dina Esfandiary and Ariane Tabatabai, *Triple Axis: Iran's Relations with Russia and China* (I.B. Tauris, 2018).
16 "Iranian Press Review: China and Russia Criticized over Response to Israeli Strikes," *Middle East Eye: Iranian Press Review* (November 2, 2024), https://www.middleeasteye.net/news/iranian-press-review-china-and-russia-criticised-over-response-israeli-strikes.
17 Conversations with Ali Shihabi, former head of the Arabia Foundation in DC and someone closely tied to the government of Crown Prince Mohammed bin Salman reflected the view that Iran's strategic orientation was offensive in nature. I got some of the same impressions, but more nuanced from many conversations with the late Jamal Khashoggi, who had close ties to the Saudi government during the reign of King Abdallah. And also conversations I had with senior Saudi officials in 2013 in Riyadh, Dammam, and Dhahran, Saudi Arabia reflected this view and skepticism. Also, similar impressions were gleaned during several Track 1.5 meetings with Saudis and Emiratis in Muscat, Abu Dhabi, Malta, and Vienna between 2015 and 2018 reflected the same views.
18 Maziar Motamedi, "Why is the Shalamcheh-Basra Railroad so Important to Iran and Iraq," *Al Jazeera* (September 6, 2023), https://www.aljazeera.com/news/2023/9/6/why-is-the-shalamcheh-basra-railroad-so-important-to-iran-and-iraq.
19 Discussions in 2022 with Dr Hamze Safavi, professor at Tehran University and son of former IRGC commander Yahya Rahim Safavi and Ghadir Nasri, Director of the Center for Middle East Strategic Studies (CMESS), both close to the Beit of Supreme Leader Ayatollah Ali Khamenei revealed these views.
20 This was evident in discussions with the then foreign minister of Iran, Javad Zarif, in April 2019. And after the killing of Major General Qassim Soleimani by the United States in 2020, finding Iranian political elites to publicly favor further engagement was nearly impossible.
21 Discussions with the late President Raisi in September 2022 and 2023 yielded this answer. A similar response came from the late Foreign Minister Abdollahian during that same twelve-month period.
22 See Harrison, "After the Gaza War."

Chapter 5

1. Richard K. Betts, "Is Strategy an Illusion," *International Security*, Vol. 25, No. 2 (Autumn 2000), p. 6.
2. See Ross Harrison, *Strategic Thinking in 3D: A Guide for National Security, Foreign Policy, and Business Professionals* (Potomac Books, 2013), pp. 35–50.
3. See Harrison, *Strategic Thinking in 3D*, pp. 35–50.
4. Andre Beaufre, *Introduction to Strategy: With Particular Reference to Problems of Defense, Politics, Economics and Diplomacy in the Nuclear Age* (Praeger, 1965), p. 38.
5. W. Morgan Shuster, *The Strangling of Persia: A Record of European Diplomacy and Oriental Intrigue* (Mage Publishing, 1912).
6. Speech by Ayatollah Khomeini, *Radio Tehran* (March 21, 1980). Also, "Khomeini, 'We Shall Confront the World with Our Ideology,'" *Middle East Report*, Issue 88 (June 1980), https://merip.org/1980/06/khomeini-we-shall-confront-the-world-with-our-ideology/.
7. Itamar Rabinovich, "How Iran's Regional Ambitions Have Developed Since 1979," *Brookings* (January 24, 2019), https://www.brookings.edu/blog/order-from-chaos/2019/01/24/how-irans-regional-ambitions-have-developed-since-1979/.
8. Ahmad Majidyar, "Khamenei Defends Increasingly Unpopular Syrian Military Intervention," *News Brief*, Middle East Institute (January 6, 2017), https://mei.edu/publications/khamenei-defends-increasingly-unpopular-syrian-military-intervention.
9. John Lewis Gaddis, *On Grand Strategy* (Penguin Press, 2018), p. 12.
10. Colleague and Iranian Scholar Abdolrasool Divsallar calls this a "salt water" strategy, of Iran investing in capabilities that might not become central to its strategy until later on as a kind of "dry-powder."
11. One of the best in this regard is from Anthony H. Cordesman, "Iran and the Changing Military Balance in the Gulf—Net Assessment Indicators, Full Report," Center for Strategic and International Studies (CSIS) (March 26, 2020), https://www.csis.org/analysis/iran-and-changing-military-balance-gulf-net-assessment-indicators.
12. See Joseph S. Nye, Jr.'s treatment of soft power in *Soft Power: The Means to Success in World Politics* (Public Affairs, 2009)
13. Hanin Ghaddar, "Iran is Losing the Middle East, Protests in Iraq and Lebanon Show," *Foreign Policy* (October 22, 2019), https://foreignpolicy.com/2019/10/22/iran-losing-middle-east-iraq-lebanon-protests-bad-governance/.
14. Stephanie Radi, "Protest Held in Beirut Against Visit by Iran's Foreign Minister," *AA Turkey* (October 7, 2021), https://www.aa.com.tr/en/middle-east/protest-held-in-beirut-against-visit-by-iran-s-foreign-minister/2384980.

15 Richard Burkholder, "Lebanese See Hezbollah as Politically Stronger after Conflict with Israel," *Gallup* (November 17, 2006), https://news.gallup.com/poll/25489/lebanese-see-hezbollah-politically-stronger-after-conflict-israel.aspx.

16 Vivian Yee and Hwaida Saad, "For Lebanon's Shi'ites, a Dilemma: Stay Loyal to Hezbollah or Keep Protesting?," *The New York Times* (February 4, 2020), https://www.nytimes.com/2020/02/04/world/middleeast/lebanon-protests-shiites-hezbollah.html?searchResultPosition=1.

17 See Hamid Reza and Julien Barnes-Dacey, "Beyond Proxies: Iran's Deeper Strategy in Syria and Lebanon," *Policy Brief*, European Council on Foreign Relations (June 2024), https://ecfr.eu/wp-content/uploads/2024/06/Beyond-proxies-Irans-deeper-strategy-in-Syria-and-Lebanon-v2.pdf.

18 Sebastian Casteliar and Azhar Al-Rubaie, "Iranian Imports Overtake Local Produce in Iraq's Basra," *The New Arab* (November 15, 2018), https://www.newarab.com/analysis/iranian-imports-overtake-local-produce-iraqs-basra.

19 Kareem Chehayeb and Abdulrahman Zeyad, "Iraqi Officials are Defending a Barter Deal with Iran, Say it Doesn't Violate US Sanctions on Tehran," *Associated Press* (July 13, 2023), https://apnews.com/article/iraq-iran-electricity-sanctions-oil-gas-e0bd5674c5b70020eb564fe7c9ff1446.

20 Alissa J. Rubin and Falih Hassan, "Iraq Protestors Burn Down Iran Consulate in Night of Anger," *The New York Times* (November 27, 2019), https://www.nytimes.com/2019/11/27/world/middleeast/iraqi-protest-najaf-iran-burn.html?searchResultPosition=2.

21 Kenneth M. Pollack, "Iran in Iraq," *Issue Brief*, Atlantic Council (December 2017), https://www.atlanticcouncil.org/in-depth-research-reports/issue-brief/iran-in-iraq/.

22 I met with former Iraqi Prime Minister Haydar al-Abadi on May 7, 2022 and he said that after the protests and after the 2020 killing of Iranian Major General Qassim Soleimani, Iran has become less heavy-handed and less visible at the national level. I also met with Farhad Alaaldin, head of the Iraqi Advisory Council, formerly political advisor to the former president of Iraq Fuad Masum.

23 Giorgio Cafiero, "Analysis: Iran's Influence Prevents Iraq's Arab Reintegration," *Al Jazeera* (March 20, 2023), https://aje.io/6bw2xk.

24 Timour Azhari and Andrew Mills, "Gulf Arab States Test Waters with Iraq Investment," *Reuters* (April 3, 2024), https://www.reuters.com/world/middle-east/gulf-arab-states-test-waters-with-iraq-investment-2024-04-03/.

25 See Nadia Von Maltzahn, *The Syria-Iran Axis: Cultural Diplomacy and International Relations in the Middle East* (I.B. Tauris, 2013).

26 Matthew D. Crosston, "Cold War and Ayatollah Residues: Syria as a Chessboard for Russia, Iran and the United States," *Strategic Studies Quarterly*, Vol. 8, No. 4 (Winter 2014), pp. 94–111. Also, see Oula A. Alrifai, "In the Service of Ideology: Iran's Religious and Socioeconomic Activities in

Syria", *Policy Notes*, No. 100, The Washington Institute for Near East Policy (March 2021), https://www.washingtoninstitute.org/policy-analysis/service-ideology-irans-religious-and-socioeconomic-activities-syria.

27 Ali Akbar, "Iran's Soft Power in Syria after the Syrian Civil War," *Mediterranean Politics*, Vol. 28, No. 2 (2023), pp. 227–249.

28 James M. Markham, "Arafat, in Iran, Reports Khomeini Pledges Aid for Victory Over Israel," *The New York Times* (February 19, 1979), https://www.nytimes.com/1979/02/19/archives/arafat-in-iran-reports-khomeini-pledges-aid-for-victory-over-israel.html.

29 Frederic Wehrey, David E. Thaler, Nora Bensahel, Kim Cragin, Jerrold D. Green, Dalia Dassa Kaye, Nadia Oweidat, and Jennifer J. Li, *Dangerous but Not Omnipotent: Exploring the Reach and Limitations of Iranian Power in the Middle East* (The Rand Corporation, 2009).

30 Wehrey, Thaler, Bensahel, Cragin, Green, Kaye, Oweidat, and Li, *Dangerous but Not Omnipotent*, p. 36.

31 Arab Barometer Wave VIII, *Tunisia Report* (2023–2024), https://www.arabbarometer.org/surveys/arab-barometer-wave-viii/.

32 Seth G. Jones and Danika Newlee, "The United States' Soft War with Iran," *CSIS Brief* (June 2019), https://www.csis.org/analysis/united-states-soft-war-iran.

33 Jones and Newlee "The United States' Soft War with Iran."

34 Jones and Newlee "The United States' Soft War with Iran."

35 Joseph S. Nye, Jr., "American Soft Power After Trump," in *The Soft Power 30: A Global Ranking of Soft Power 2019* (USC Center on Public Diplomacy, 2019), pp. 49–53.

36 Ladan Boroumand, "Iranians Turn Away from the Islamic Republic," *Journal of Democracy*, Vol. 31, No. 1 (January 2020), pp. 169–181. Also, see Jones and Newlee "The United States' Soft War with Iran."

37 Arron Merat, "Terrorists, Cultists—or Champions of Iranian Democracy? The Wild, Wild Story of the MEK," *The Guardian* (November 9, 2018), https://www.theguardian.com/news/2018/nov/09/mek-iran-revolution-regime-trump-rajavi.

38 Ali Fathollah-Nejad, "Iranians Respond to the Regime: 'Leave Syria Alone,'" *Al-Jazeera* (May 2, 2018), https://www.aljazeera.com/opinions/2018/5/2/iranians-respond-to-the-regime-leave-syria-alone.

39 Raz Zimmt, "The Gasoline Protests in Iran: Initial Assessments and Implications," *INSS Insight*, No. 1228 (November 18, 2019), https://www.inss.org.il/wp-content/uploads/2019/11/No.-1228.pdf.

40 See Nan Tian, Diego Lopes da Silva, Xiao Liang, and Lorenzo Scarazzato, "Trends in World Military Expenditure 2023," *SIPRI Fact Sheet*, Stockholm International Peace Research Institute (SIPRI) (April 2024), https://www.sipri.org/publications/2024/sipri-fact-sheets/trends-world-military-

expenditure-2023. The $10 billion in expenditures shown are lower than other reports, such as from CSIS, but I believe the difference is the $10 billion listed is a measure of Iran's conventional military capability, while it doesn't include Iran's asymmetric expenditures, such as its support for and establishment of militias across the Arab world.

41 Sanam Vakil and Bilal Y. Saab, "Iran's Attack on Israel Was Not the Failure Many Claim but It Has Ended Israel's Isolation," *Expert Comment*, Chatham House (April 16, 2024), https://www.chathamhouse.org/2024/04/irans-attack-israel-was-not-failure-many-claim-it-has-ended-israels-isolation.

42 Ross Harrison "After the Gaza War: The Risks of Deterrence and the Chances of Peace," *The National Interest* (November 20, 2023), https://nationalinterest.org/feature/after-gaza-war-risks-deterrence-and-chances-peace-207379?page=0—C1.

43 US Defense Intelligence Agency, *Iran: Military Power: Ensuring Regime Survival and Securing Regional Dominance* (US Government Publishing Office, 2019), https://www.dia.mil/portals/110/images/news/military_powers_publications/iran_military_power_lr.pdf.

44 Javad Heiran-Nia, "Iranians Debate Whether It's Time to Develop Nuclear Weapons," *Stimson* (November 8, 2024), https://www.stimson.org/2024/iranians-debate-whether-its-time-to-develop-nuclear-weapons/.

45 World Bank, *World Development Indicators* (last updated December 18, 2024), https://datacatalog.worldbank.org/search/dataset/0037712/World-Development-Indicators.

46 https://data.worldbank.org/indicator/SP.POP.1564.TO.ZS.

47 See https://www.eia.gov/international/content/analysis/countries_long/Iran/pdf/Iran%20CAB%202024.pdf.

48 See Massoud Karshenas and Hassan Hakimian, "Oil, Economic Diversification and the Democratic Process in Iran," *Iranian Studies*, Vol. 38, No. 1 (March 2005), pp. 67–90 for analysis of the problems with diversification of Iran's economy.

49 https://iranprimer.usip.org/blog/2021/mar/03/sanctions-5-trumps-maximum-pressure-targets.

50 https://www.cfr.org/backgrounder/irans-revolutionary-guards.

51 https://genderdata.worldbank.org/en/economies/iran-islamic-rep#:~:text=In%20the%20Islamic%20Republic%20of%20Iran%2C%20the%20labor%20force%20participation,older%20that%20is%20economically%20active.

52 https://www.ilo.org/sites/default/files/2024-10/GEDI-STAT%20brief_formatted_28.10.24_final.pdf.

53 See World Bank, *Iran Economic Monitor: Sustaining Growth Amid Rising Geopolitical Tensions* (World Bank, Spring 2024), https://documents.worldbank.org/en/publication/documents-reports/

documentdetail/099051007102421530/idu1398008291628d14b5a1a9f91728b946987e4.

54 See Karshenas and Hakimian, "Oil, Economic Diversification and the Democratic Process in Iran," p. 67–90.

55 https://www.atlanticcouncil.org/blogs/iransource/iran-drone-uavs-russia/ https://isis-online.org/uploads/isis-reports/documents/Iran-Russia_Military_Technology_Axis_June_25_2024_Final.pdf.

56 Interview with economist Djavad Salehi-Isfahani, Professor of Economics at Virginia Tech, on July 1, 2022.

57 Kelly Skinner, "Gaza War Helps Iran Repair Image in Region—But for How Long?," *Amwaj.Media* (March 29, 2024), https://amwaj.media/article/gaza-war-helps-iran-repair-image-in-region-but-for-how-long.

58 Kenneth M. Pollack "Iran's Grand Strategy Has Fundamentally Shifted," *Foreign Policy* (August 15, 2023), https://foreignpolicy.com/2023/08/15/irans-grand-strategy-has-fundamentally-shifted/.

Chapter 6

1 See Henry Mintzberg and James A. Waters, "Of Strategies, Deliberate and Emergent," *Strategic Management Journal*, Vol. 6, No. 3 (July–September 1985), pp. 257–272.

2 Daniel Schorr, "1975 Background to Betrayal," *The Washington Post* (April 7, 1991), https://www.washingtonpost.com/archive/opinions/1991/04/07/1975-background-to-betrayal/aa973065-ea5e-4270-8cf9-02361307073c/.

3 Geraint Hughes, "All the Shah's Men: Imperial Iranian Brigade Group in the Dhofar War," *Defence-In-Depth*, Defence Studies Department, King's College London (July 13, 2016), https://defenceindepth.co/2016/06/06/all-the-shahs-men-the-imperial-iranian-brigade-group-in-the-dhofar-war/.

4 Garrett Nada with Thomas Neal, Cameron Glenn and others, "Flashpoints: Iran and Saudi Arabia," *The Iran Primer*, United States Institute of Peace (September 18, 2019), https://iranprimer.usip.org/blog/2019/sep/18/flashpoints-iran-and-saudi-arabia, and Bruce Riedel, "What Iran's Revolution Meant for Iraq," *Brookings* (January 24, 2019), https://www.brookings.edu/articles/what-irans-revolution-meant-for-iraq/.

5 National Foreign Assessment Center, *Iran: Exporting the Revolution—An Intelligence Assessment*, Secret PA 80-10121 (March 1980), p. 1, https://www.cia.gov/readingroom/docs/CIA-RDP81B00401R000500100001-8.pdf.

6 National Foreign Assessment Center, *Iran: Exporting the Revolution*, p. 1.

7 I first heard preclusion as part of a strategy lexicon by colleague and friend Marc Grossman, former US Undersecretary of State for Political Affairs. Also see Jakub Grygiel and A. Wes Mitchell, "A Preclusive Strategy to Defend

the NATO Frontier," *The American Interest* (December 2, 2014), https://www.the-american-interest.com/2014/12/02/a-preclusive-strategy-to-defend-the-nato-frontier/.

8 David Daoud, "The Arab League Thinks Readmitting Syria Will Push Out Iran: They're Wrong," *IranSource*, Atlantic Council (May 16, 2023), https://www.atlanticcouncil.org/blogs/iransource/the-arab-league-thinks-readmitting-syria-will-push-out-iran-theyre-wrong/.

9 "Saudi Arabia Halts $3 Billion Aid Package to Lebanese Army, Security Aid," *Reuters* (February 19, 2016), https://www.reuters.com/article/idUSKCN0VS1K7/.

10 In May of 2022 I met with former Prime Minister Haidar al Abadi who explained how he had engaged with Saudi Arabia and both the successes and failures of Saudi attempts to reintegrate Iraq into the Arab fold.

11 For a comparison of Iran's military capabilities with those of the GCC, see Anthony H. Cordesman, *Iran and the Changing Military Balance in the Gulf—Net Assessment Indicators*, Full Report," Center for Strategic and International Studies (CSIS) (March 26, 2020), https://www.csis.org/analysis/iran-and-changing-military-balance-gulf-net-assessment-indicators.

12 "Comparison of Iran and Turkiye Military Strengths (2024)," *GFP*, https://www.globalfirepower.com/countries-comparison-detail.php?country1=iran&country2=turkey. Also see Anthony H. Cordesman and Nicholas Harrington, *The Arab Gulf States and Iran: Military Spending, Modernization, and the Shifting Military Balance*, Center for Strategic and International Studies (CSIS) (December 12, 2018), https://www.csis.org/analysis/arab-gulf-states-and-iran-military-spending-modernization-and-shifting-military-balance.

13 See Ross Harrison, *Strategic Thinking in 3D: A Guide for National Security, Foreign Policy and Business Professionals* (Potomac Books, 2013), pp. 108–109.

14 "Iraqis Helping Iran Skirt Sanctions: NY Times," *Reuters* (August 18, 2012). Also see "Iranian Goods Spread in Syria's Idlib Markets," *North Press Agency* (December 25, 2021), https://npasyria.com/en/69755/.

15 General Carl Von Clausewitz, *On War* (CreateSpace Independent Publishing, 2010).

16 Cordesman, *Iran and the Changing Military Balance in the Gulf*, p. 115.

17 Abdolrasool Divsallar, in "Understanding the Role of Iran in Regional Escalation," *Webinar*, Chatham House (January 25, 2024), https://www.chathamhouse.org/events/all/open-event/understanding-role-iran-regional-escalation.

18 Sun Tzu, *The Art of War*, chapter 3 (widely available).

19 Lieutenant Colonel Ronald F. Rokosz, *Clausewitz and the Iran-Iraq War*, Study Project, US Army War College (March 6, 1989), https://apps.dtic.mil/sti/tr/pdf/ADA207262.pdf.

20 Derek M.C. Yuen, *Deciphering Sun Tzu: How to Read the Art of War* (Oxford University Press, 2014), p. 14.
21 "Saudi Oil Attacks: Drones and Missiles Launched from Iran—U.S.," *BBC* (September 17, 2019), https://www.bbc.com/news/world-middle-east-49733558.
22 Sun Tzu, *The Art of War*. Also Yuen, *Deciphering Sun Tzu*, p. 80.
23 See von Clausewitz, *On War*.
24 Ben Hubbard, Isabele Kerschner, and Anne Barnard, "Iran, Deeply Embedded in Syria, Expands Axis of Resistance," *The New York Times* (February 19, 2018), https://www.nytimes.com/2018/02/19/world/middleeast/iran-syria-israel.html.
25 Kashif Mumtaz Ghumman, "Iran-US Relations in the Post-9/11 Days: Problems and Prospects," *Strategic Studies*, Vol. 22, No. 3 (2002), pp. 170–186.
26 Andrew Glass, "President Bush Cites 'Axis of Evil,' Jan. 29 2002," *Politico* (January 29, 2019), https://www.politico.com/story/2019/01/29/bush-axis-of-evil-2002-1127725.
27 Ayatollah Khamenei, "Leader's Speech to Government Officials," *Khamenei.ir* (July 24, 2012), https://english.khamenei.ir/news/1655/Leader-s-Speech-to-Government-Officials.
28 Ross Harrison, "After the Gaza War: The Risks of Deterrence and Chances of Peace," *The National Interest* (November 20, 2023), https://nationalinterest.org/feature/after-gaza-war-risks-deterrence-and-chances-peace-207379?page=0%2C1.
29 Yuen, *Deciphering Sun Tzu*, pp. 105–106.
30 See Ayatollah Khamenei's speech at the Imam Reza Shrine, March 21, 2007, in which he talks about knowing the enemy and uncovering its plot and strategy: https://english.khamenei.ir/news/1609/Leader-s-Speech-at-Imam-Reza-s-a-s-Shrine.
31 Meetings where this was revealed took place with then Foreign Minister Javad Zarif in April 2019.
32 See Yuen, *Deciphering Sun Tzu*, p. 107. The author looks at Sun Tzu's assigned importance of disrupting the enemy's plans but also draws from B.H. Liddell Hart, *Strategy*, 2nd revised edition (Praeger Publioshers, 1967), p. 349.
33 See Cordesman, *Iran and the Changing Military Balance in the Gulf*.
34 See Harrison, *Strategic Thinking in 3D*, chapter 3, as well as Yuen, *Deciphering Sun Tzu*, p. 107. The author looks at Sun Tzu's assigned importance of disrupting the enemy's plans but also draws from Liddell Hart, *Strategy*, p. 349.
35 See Ofira Seliktar and Farhad Rezaei, "Exporting the Revolution and Building Hegemony," in *Iran, Revolution and Proxy Wars* (Palgrave Macmillan, 2020), chapter 1; S.K. Malik, *Quranic Concept of War* (Himalayan

Books, 2020); and J. G. Eaton, "The Beauty of Asymmetry: An Examination of the Context and Practice of Asymmetric and Unconventional Warfare from a Western/Centrist Perspective," *Defence Studies*, Vol 2. No. 1 (Spring 2002), pp. 51–82.

36 "The Importance of Strategic Depth," *International Strategic Analysis* (October 24, 2018), https://www.isa-world.com/news/?tx_ttnews%5Btt_news%5D=442&tx_ttnews%5BbackPid%5D=1&cHash=2fab7c50561ded287453afb408a82901.

37 Charles W. Freeman, *Arts of Power: Statecraft and Diplomacy* (United States Institute of Peace Press, 1997), p. 71.

38 Hamidreza Azizi, *The Concept of "Forward Defence": How Has the Syrian Crisis Shaped the Evolution of Iran's Military Strategy?*, Research Project Report (4), Geneva Center for Security Policy (February 2021), p. 3, https://dam.gcsp.ch/files/doc/iran-forward-defence-strategy-en?_gl=1*1njkyd0*_gcl_au*MTM2MjM3NzE3Mi4xNzM1MzIxOTc2*_ga*ODU5NzkyOTQzLjE3MzUzMjE5NzY.*_ga_Z66DSTVXTJ*MTczNTMyMTk3Ni4xLjEuMTczNTMyMjE1Mi4zOS4wLjA.

39 Azizi, *The Concept of "Forward Defence"*, p. 8.

40 See Manuel Almeida, "Iran's 'Forward Defense' Doctrine Has Become a Contradiction in Terms," *Arab News* (April 21, 2018), https://www.arabnews.com/node/1288911.

41 See Hooshmand Mirfakhraei, "The Quest for Power and Respect: A Survey of Iranian Foreign Policy since 1921," *Iran 1400* (October 21, 2020), https://iran1400.org/discover/quest-for-power-iranian-foreign-policy/.

42 Ray Takeyh, "Iran's 'Resistance Economy' Debate," *Expert Brief*, Council on Foreign Relations (April 7, 2016), https://www.cfr.org/expert-brief/irans-resistance-economy-debate. Also see Supreme Leader Ayatollah Ali Khamenei speech at Shrine of Imam Reza, March 21, 2007: https://english.khamenei.ir/news/1609/Leader-s-Speech-at-Imam-Reza-s-a-s-Shrine#axzz2KgI76Gh8.

43 See Supreme Leader Ayatollah Ali Khamenei speech at Shrine of Imam Reza.

44 Jacopo Scita, "China-Iran Relations through the Prism of Sanctions," *Asian Affairs*, Vol. 53, No. 1 (2022), pp. 87–105.

45 The author met with President Raisi both in September of 2022 and 2023.

46 Author's discussion with the late Iranian President Ibrahim Raisi in September of both 2022 and 2023.

47 See Ross Harrison and Alex Vatanka, "The Middle East Might be Moving Toward Stability," *Foreign Policy* (June 26, 2023), https://foreignpolicy.com/2023/06/26/iran-saudi-arabia-china-middle-east-diplomacy/, and Fiona Hill's analysis about the calculation of countries in the Global South, *Lennart Meri Lecture 2023*, https://lmc.icds.ee/lennart-meri-lecture-by-fiona-hill/.

48 See "President Rouhani's Policy of Positive Equilibrium," *Islamic Republic News Agency* (September 12, 2014), https://en.irna.ir/news/2737235/President-Rouhani-s-policy-of-positive-equilibrium.

49 Shireen T. Hunter, *Iran and the World: Continuity in a Revolutionary Decade* (Indiana University Press, 1990), pp. 22–23.

50 See Nikki R. Keddie and Mark J. Gasiorowski (eds.), *Neither East Nor West: Iran, the Soviet Union and the United States* (Yale University Press, 1990), pp. 1–10.

51 See Mark N. Katz, "Iran and Russia," Wilson Center (undated), https://www.wilsoncenter.org/sites/default/files/media/documents/article/Iran%20and%20Russia.pdf.

52 W. Morgan Shuster, *The Strangling of Persia: A Personal Narrative* (Penguin Random House, 1912).

53 Yasuyuki Matsunaga, "Is Iran Seeking Regional Hegemony?," *IranSource*, Atlantic Council (April 12, 2016, https://www.atlanticcouncil.org/blogs/iransource/is-iran-seeking-regional-hegemony/. I had similar discussions with the leadership of the King Faisal Institute in Riyadh, Saudi Arabia and with Ali Shihabi in Washington, DC.

54 Don Oberdorfer, "Soviet Deal with Kuwait Spurred U.S. Ship Role," *The Washington Post* (May 4, 1987). https://www.washingtonpost.com/archive/politics/1987/05/24/soviet-deal-with-kuwait-spurred-us-ship-role/276d225e-90f8-44bd-9b1e-44fb7fed9eab/.

55 Arash Reisinezhad, "Iran's Strategic Loneliness and Non-State Foreign Policy: From Curse of Geography to Geopolitical Predicament," *International Quarterly of Geopolitics*, Vol. 19, No. 69 (January 2023), pp. 269–306.

56 Jerrold D. Green, Frederic Wehrey, and Charles Wolf, Jr., *Understanding Iran* (Rand Corporation, 2009), pp. 33–36.

57 National Foreign Assessment Center, *Iran: Exporting the Revolution*.

58 Akbar Khan and Han Zhaoying, "Iran-Hezbollah Alliance Reconsidered: What Contributes to the Survival of the State-Proxy Alliance?," *Journal of Asian Security and International Affairs*, Vol. 7, No. 1 (2020), p. 102.

59 Website of Sayyid Ali Khamenei (English), "Supreme Leader's Speech in Meeting with Officials and Ambassadors of Islamic Countries" (October 24, 2006), http://english.khamenei.ir//index.php?option=com_content&task=view&id=2017&Itemid=4. Also see Shahram Akbarzadeh, "Proxy Relations: Iran and Hezbollah", in Shahram Akbarzadeh (ed.), *Routledge Handbook of International Relations in the Middle East* (Routledge, 2019), pp. 321–329.

60 Marc R. DeVore, "Exploring the Iran-Hezbollah Relationship: A Case Study of How State Sponsorship Affects Terrorist Group Decision-Making," *Perspectives on Terrorism*, Vol. 6, No. 4/5 (October 2012), pp. 85–107.

61 Richard Burkholder, "Iranian Reactions to September 11," *Gallup* (July 30, 2002), https://news.gallup.com/poll/6508/iranian-reactions-september.aspx.

62 "Iranian President Condemns September 11 Attacks," *CNN* (November 12, 2001), https://edition.cnn.com/2001/WORLD/meast/11/12/khatami.interview.cnna/.

63 Ghumman, "Iran-US Relations in the Post-9/11 Days."

64 "George Bush's Memoirs Reveal How He Considered Attacks on Iran and Syria," *The Guardian* (November 8, 2010), https://www.theguardian.com/world/2010/nov/08/george-bush-memoir-decision-points. Also see George W. Bush, *Decision Points* (Crown Publishers, 2011).

65 Ayatollah Khamenei in Friday Prayers Speech, April 11, 2003, https://farsi.khamenei.ir/speech-content?id=3168.

66 See Javad Heiran-Nia, "Retrospective: U.S. Invasion of Iraq was a Mixed Blessing for Iran," *Stimson* (March 17, 2023), https://www.stimson.org/2023/retrospective-us-invasion-of-iraq-was-a-mixed-blessing-for-iran/.

67 See Seliktar and Rezaei, *Iran, Revolution and Proxy Wars*, chapter 5. Also Borzou Daraghahi, "Badr Brigade: Among Most Consequential Outcomes of the Iran-Iraq War," *IranSource*, Atlantic Council (August 16, 2018), https://www.atlanticcouncil.org/blogs/iransource/badr-brigade-among-most-consequential-outcomes-of-the-iran-iraq-war-2/.

68 I want to thank my good friend Mohsen Milani from the University of South Florida for sensitizing me to the risks Iran took in intervening in Iraq alongside the American presence.

69 See Seliktar and Rezaei, *Iran, Revolution and Proxy Wars*, chapter 5.

70 Jessica Mavaro-Stoller, "Iran's Influence in Iraq: Hegemony Through Powerful Militias," *The Tower* (May 4, 2018), http://www.thetower.org/6224-irans-influence-in-iraq-hegemony-through-powerful-militias/.

71 "Ahmad Chalabi and his Iranian Connection," *Worldview by Stratfor* (February 18, 2004), https://worldview.stratfor.com/article/ahmad-chalabi-and-his-iranian-connection.

72 See Aram Roston, *The Man Who Pushed America to War: The Extraordinary Life, Adventures and Obsessions of Ahmad Chalabi* (Nation Books, 2009).

73 See Seliktar and Rezaei, *Iran, Revolution and Proxy Wars*, chapter 5.

74 Reported by *The Times of London*, "Report: Iran Pays $1000 for Each U.S. Soldier Killed in Afghanistan," *NBC News* (September 5, 2010), https://www.nbcnews.com/id/wbna39014669.

75 Scott Peterson, "How Iran, the Middle East's New Superpower, is Expanding Its Footprint Across the Region—and What it Means," *Christian Science Monitor* (December 17, 2017), https://www.csmonitor.com/World/Middle-East/2017/1217/How-Iran-the-Mideast-s-new-superpower-is-expanding-its-footprint-across-the-region-and-what-it-means.

76 Beston Husen Arif, "Iran's Struggle for Strategic Dominance in a Post-ISIS Iraq," *Asian Affairs*, Vol. 50, No. 3 (2019), pp. 344–363.

77 Conversation with Dr. Naufel Alhassan, Chief of Staff of former Prime Minister Haider Al-Abadi, March 2018, https://www.youtube.com/watch?v=LSrhxcwHrro.

78 Discussions with then Iraqi Ambassador to Washington Fareed Yasseen at the Middle East Institute in 2019: https://www.youtube.com/watch?v=3_ILNyctYz0.

79 Babak Rahimi, "Iran's Declining Influence in Iraq," *The Washington Quarterly*, Vol. 35, No. 1 (Winter 2012), pp. 25–40.

80 Author's interview with former Prime Minister Haidar al-Abadi of Iraq (May 7, 2022), in which we discussed both Saudi Arabia's initiatives and Iranian efforts to subvert.

81 Robert F. Worth, "Effort to Rebrand Arab Spring Backfires in Iran", *The New York Times* (February 2, 2012), https://www.nytimes.com/2012/02/03/world/middleeast/effort-to-rebrand-arab-spring-backfires-in-iran.html.

82 Hassan Ahmadian and Payam Mohseni, "Iran's Syria Strategy: The Evolution of Deterrence," *International Affairs*, Vol. 95, No. 2 (2019), p. 352. Also, Karim Sadjadpour, "Iran's Real Enemy in Syria," *The Atlantic* (April 16, 2018), https://www.theatlantic.com/international/archive/2018/04/iran-syria-israel/558080/.

83 See Ariane M. Tabatabai, *No Conquest, No Defeat: Iran's National Security Strategy* (Oxford University Press, 2020), chapter 6.

84 See Tabatabai, *No Conquest, No Defeat*, chapter 1.

85 See Tabatabai, *No Conquest, No Defeat*, chapter 6.

86 See Seliktar and Rezaei, *Iran, Revolution and Proxy Wars*, chapter 6.

87 Ahmadian and Mohseni, "Iran's Syria Strategy," pp. 341–364.

88 See quote from prominent Iranian cleric about this in Ahmadian and Mohseni, "Iran's Syria Strategy," p. 352.

89 Aymenn Jawad Al-Tamimi, "Shi'i Militias in Iraq and Syria," *Middle East Review of International Affairs*, Vol. 19, No. 1 (Spring 2015), pp. 79–83.

90 Eric E. Mueller and Andrew Radin, "Afghan Refugees are Being Recruited to Join an Iranian Paramilitary," Rand (November 23, 2021), https://www.rand.org/pubs/commentary/2021/11/afghan-refugees-are-being-recruited-to-join-an-iranian.html.

91 Mueller and Radin, "Afghan Refugees are Being Recruited to Join an Iranian Paramilitary."

92 Navvar Saban, "How Iran Used and is Still Using Soft Power in Syria", *MENA Affairs* (November 17, 2021), https://menaaffairs.com/how-iran-used-and-is-still-using-soft-power-in-syria/.

93 Kali Robinson, "Syria is Normalizing Relations with Arab Countries. Who Will Benefit?," *In Brief*, Council on Foreign Relations (May 11, 2023), https://www.cfr.org/in-brief/syria-normalizing-relations-arab-countries-who-will-benefit.

94 T. Johnston, M. Lane, A. Casey, H.J. Williams, A.L. Rhoades, J. Sladden, N. Vest, J.R. Reimer, and R. Haberman, *Could the Houthis be the Next Hezbollah: Iranian Proxy Development in Yemen and the Future of the Houthi Movement* (Rand Corporation, 2020), p. 64, https://www.rand.org/pubs/research_reports/RR2551.html.

95 Michelle Nichols and John Irish, "Iran, Hezbollah Enabled the Houthis' Rise, Says UN Report," *Reuters* (September 26, 2024), https://www.reuters.com/world/middle-east/iran-hezbollah-enabled-houthis-rise-says-un-report-2024-09-26/.

96 Stephen Hughes, "Yemen, Iran's Strategic Naval Expansion, Anti-Access, Area Denial (A2/AD), Part I of III," *Jerusalem Post* (April 28, 2015), https://www.jpost.com/blogs/the-iran-threat/yemen-irans-strategic-naval-expansion-anti-accessarea-denial-a2ad-part-i-of-iii-399400.

97 See Abdolrasool Divsallar, "Introduction," in Abdolrasool Divsallar (ed.), *Struggle for Alliance: Russia and Iran in the Era of War in Ukraine* (IB Tauris, London, 2024).

98 The notion that Washington forced Iran to tilt hard toward Russia and China and that Iran has more leverage than ever before with these eastern countries was covered forcefully in the late President Raisi's comments to my questions about this in September 2022.

99 Maziar Motamedi, "Iran Summons Russian Envoy Over Statement with GCC on Islands," *Al Jazeera* (July 12, 2023), https://www.aljazeera.com/news/2023/7/12/iran-summons-russian-envoy-over-statement-with-gcc-on-islands.

100 See Harrison "After the Gaza War."

101 I engaged with President Raisi in September 2022, Foreign Minister Abdollahian in September 2021 and 2022, and (former) Foreign Minister Javad Zarif in April 2019.

102 For a fleshing out of these ideas, see Ross Harrison, "U.S. Foreign Policy Towards the Middle East: Pumping Air Into a Punctured Tire," Research Paper, Arab Center for Research and Policy Studies, Doha, Qatar (March 7, 2019), https://www.dohainstitute.org/en/Lists/ACRPS-PDFDocumentLibrary/US-Foreign-Policy-Towards-the-Middle-East-Pumping-Air-into-a-Punctured-Tire.pdf.

103 Harrison, "U.S. Foreign Policy Towards the Middle East."

104 von Clausewitz, *On War*, p. 4.

Chapter 7

1 See "The Middle East Pivot to Asia," *Asia House Report* (2023), https://asiahouse.org/research_posts/the-middle-east-pivot-to-asia/.

2 Katherine Harvey, *A Self-Fulfilling Prophesy: The Saudi Struggle for Iraq* (Oxford University Press, 2022). I also met with former Prime Minister al-Abadi in May of 2022.

3   Bruce Riedel and Katherine Harvey, "Why is Saudi Arabia Finally Engaging with Iraq?," *Brookings* (December 4, 2020), https://www.brookings.edu/articles/why-is-saudi-arabia-finally-engaging-with-iraq/.

4   Ismaeel Naar, "Saudi Arabia, Iraq Establish Joint $3 Billion Fund During Kadhimi Visit to Riyadh," *Al Arabiya* (April 1, 2021), https://english.alarabiya.net/News/gulf/2021/04/01/Saudi-Arabia-Iraq-establish-joint-3-billion-fund-during-Kadhimi-visit-to-Riyadh.

5   "Saudi PIF Founds $3 Bln Saudi-Iraqi Investment Co—Company's Acting CEO," *Reuters* (May 25, 2023), https://www.reuters.com/article/markets/saudi-pif-founds-3-bln-saudi-iraqi-investment-co-companys-acting-ceo-idUSS8N374037/.

6   Rayana Alkubali and Waffa Wael, "Saudi Arabia, Iraq Work on Data Center, Annual Economic Forum to Promote Trade," *Arab News* (January 24, 2022), https://arab.news/4kj3w.

7   Jennifer Gnana, "Saudi Arabia, Iraq Sign Agreement to Link Electrical Power Grids," *S&P Global Commodity Insights* (January 22, 2022), https://www.spglobal.com/commodity-insights/en/news-research/latest-news/electric-power/012522-saudi-arabia-iraq-sign-agreement-to-link-electrical-power-grids.

8   See "Inside Story: Saudi Arabia Opens Up to Iraqi Shi'i Shrines," *Amwaj. media* (May 14, 2024), https://amwaj.media/media-monitor/inside-story-saudi-arabia-opens-up-to-iraq-s-shiite-shrines.

9   Giorgio Cafiero, "Analysis: Iran's Influence Prevents Iraq's Arab Reintegration," *Al Jazeera* (March 20, 2023), https://www.aljazeera.com/news/2023/3/20/analysis-irans-influence-prevents-iraqs-arab-reintegration.

10 Several Iraqi politicians indicated this in off-the-record interviews in 2022.

11 Interview with former Iraqi Prime Minister Haidar al-Abadi (May 7, 2022).

12 https://www.vision2030.gov.sa/en.

13 April Longley Alley, "After Assad's Fall, Gulf States See Risks and Rewards in Syria," *Analysis*, United States Institute of Peace (December 17, 2024), https://www.usip.org/publications/2024/12/after-assads-fall-gulf-states-see-risks-and-rewards-syria.

14 Mina Aldroubi, "Mosul Reconstruction Project Nearing Completion, Says Unesco Official," *The National News* (March 14, 2024), https://www.thenationalnews.com/mena/iraq/2024/03/18/mosul-reconstruction-project-nearing-completion-says-unesco-official/#:~:text=The%20UAE%2C%20in%20co%2Doperation,a%20and%20Al%20Tahera%20Churches.

15 *Saudi Arabia: Back to Baghdad*, International Crisis Group, Middle East Report No. 186 (May 22, 2018), https://www.crisisgroup.org/middle-east-north-africa/gulf-and-arabian-peninsula/iraq/186-saudi-arabia-back-baghdad.

16 "Iraq to Host Another Round of Iran-Saudi Arabia Talks," *Reuters* (March 12, 2022), https://www.reuters.com/world/middle-east/iraq-host-another-round-iran-saudi-arabia-talks-ministry-2022-03-12/.

17 See "The Enemy Gets a Vote," Center for Strategic and International Studies (CSIS) (May 16, 2016), https://www.csis.org/analysis/enemy-gets-vote.

18 See Ross Harrison, "After the Gaza War: The Risks of Deterrence and the Chances of Peace," *The National Interest* (November 20, 2023), https://nationalinterest.org/feature/after-gaza-war-risks-deterrence-and-chances-peace-207379?page=0%2C1.

19 John Ghazvinian, *America and Iran: A History, 1720 to the Present* (Alfred A. Knopf, 2021). This is a fair analysis of US-Iran relations and balances out the literature that heaps blame on Iran. But it does represent a critique of American foreign policy toward Iran.

20 Meetings with both the president and foreign minister occurred in 2021 (with foreign minister only) and 2022 (with the president and foreign minister) and 2023 (with the president and foreign minister).

21 "China Seen as Overtaking U.S. as Global Superpower," *Pew Research Center* (July 13, 2011), https://www.pewresearch.org/global/2011/07/13/china-seen-overtaking-us-as-global-superpower/.

22 Simon Theobald, "After U.S. Withdrawal, Iran Embraces China," *East Asia Forum* (June 5, 2018), https://eastasiaforum.org/2018/06/05/after-us-withdrawal-iran-embraces-china/

23 Ross Harrison and Alex Vatanka, "China's Plan to Dominate the Middle East Centers on Iran," *The National Interest* (September 19, 2020), https://nationalinterest.org/feature/china%E2%80%99s-plan-dominate-middle-east-centers-around-iran-169219.

24 For a comparative analysis between the Middle East and Europe and Southeast Asia and the prospects for regional cooperation, see Ross Harrison and Paul Salem, *From Chaos to Cooperation: Toward Regional Order in the Middle East* (Middle East Institute, 2017), particularly chapters 2 and 11. Also see Paul Salem and Ross Harrison, *Escaping the Conflict Trap: Toward Ending Civil Wars in the Middle East*, 2nd edition (IB Tauris, 2023) for pathways out of the civil wars.

25 Tesusaburo Kimura, "Vietnam—Ten Years of Economic Struggle," *Asian Survey*, Vol. 26, No. 10 (October, 1986).

26 Kimura, "Vietnam—Ten Years of Economic Struggle," p. 494.

27 Nguyen Vu Tung, "Vietnam's Membership of ASEAN: A Constructivist Interpretation," *Contemporary Southeast Asia*, Vol. 29, No. 3 (2007), p. 486.

28 Allan E. Goodman, "Vietnam and ASEAN: Who Would Have Thought It Possible," *Asian Survey*, Vol. 36, No. 6 (June 1996), pp. 592–600.

29 Meeting with President Pezeshkian in New York City, September 25, 2024.

30 Farnaz Fassihi, "Elon Musk Met with Iran's U.N. Ambassador, Iranian Officials Say," *The New York Times* (November 14, 2024), https://www.nytimes.com/2024/11/14/world/middleeast/elon-musk-iran-trump.html.
31 For an excellent analysis of what drove Vietnam towards ASEAN and the west, see Goodman, "Vietnam and ASEAN."
32 John J. Mearsheimer and Stephen M. Walt, "The Case for Offshore Balancing," *Foreign Affairs* (July/August 2016), p. 83.
33 See Harrison and Salem, *From Chaos to Cooperation*, chapter 10.
34 See Ross Harrison, "Regionalism in the Middle East: An Impossible Dream?," *Orient* (German Journal for Politics, Economics and Culture of the Middle East, 2018).

BIBLIOGRAPHY

Akbar, Ali, "Iran's Soft Power in Syria After the Syrian Civil War," *Mediterranean Politics*, Vol. 28, No. 2 (2023), pp. 227–249.

Ansari, Ali M., "Iran and the U.S. in the Shadow of 9/11: Persia and the Persian Question Revisited," *Iranian Studies*, Vol. 39, No. 2 (2006), pp. 155–170.

Azizi, Hamidreza, *The Concept of "Forward Defence": How Has the Syrian Crisis Shaped the Evolution of Iran's Military Strategy?*, Research Project Report (4), Geneva Center for Security Policy (February 2021), https://dam.gcsp.ch/files/doc/iran-forward-defence-strategy-en?_gl=1*1njkyd0*_gcl_au*MTM2MjM3NzE3Mi4xNzM1MzIxOTc2*_ga*ODU5NzkyOTQzLjE3MzUzMjE5NzY.*_ga_Z66DSTVXTJ*MTczNTMyMTk3Ni4xLjEuMTczNTMyMjE1Mi4zOS4wLjA.

Beaufre, Andre, *Introduction to Strategy: With Particular Reference to Problems of Defense, Politics, Economics and Diplomacy in the Nuclear Age* (Praeger, 1965).

Betts, Richard K., "Is Strategy an Illusion," *International Security*, Vol. 25, No. 2 (Autumn 2000), pp. 5–50.

Bush, George W., *Decision Points* (Crown Publishers, 2011).

Chubin, Shahram, *Iran's National Security Policy: Intentions, Capabilities, and Impact* (The Carnegie Endowment for International Peace, 1994).

Chubin, Shahram, and Charles Tripp, *Iran and Iraq at War* (Westview Press, 1988).

Clausewitz, Carl von, *On War* (CreateSpace Independent Publishing, 2010).

Cordesman, Anthony H., *Iran and the Changing Military Balance in the Gulf—Net Assessment Indicators*, Full Report," Center for Strategic and International Studies (CSIS) (March 26, 2020), https://www.csis.org/analysis/iran-and-changing-military-balance-gulf-net-assessment-indicators.

Cottam, Richard W., *Nationalism in Iran* (University of Pittsburgh Press, 1964).

Cottam, Richard W., *Foreign Policy Motivation: A General Theory and Case Study* (University of Pittsburgh Press, 1977).

Cottam, Richard, "Iran's Perception of the Superpowers," in Barry M. Rosen (Ed.), *Iran Since the Revolution: Internal Dynamics, Regional Conflicts and the Superpowers* (Columbia University Press, 1985).

Cottam, Richard W., *Iran and the United States: A Cold War Case Study* (University of Pittsburgh Press, 1988).

Crosston, Matthew D., "Cold War and Ayatollah Residues: Syria as a Chessboard for Russia, Iran and the United States," *Strategic Studies Quarterly*, Vol. 8, No. 4 (Winter 2014), pp. 94–111.

Dassa Kaye, Dalia, Alireza Nader, and Parisa Roshan, *Israel and Iran: A Dangerous Rivalry* (Rand Corporation, 2011).

DeVore, Marc R., "Exploring the Iran-Hezbollah Relationship: A Case Study of How State Sponsorship Affects Terrorist Group Decision-Making," *Perspectives on Terrorism*, Vol. 6, No. 4/5 (October 2012), pp. 85–107.

Divsallar, Abdolrasool (ed.), *Struggle for Alliance: Russia and Iran in the Era of War in Ukraine* (IB Tauris, London, 2024).

Eaton, J. G., "The Beauty of Asymmetry: An Examination of the Context and Practice of Asymmetric and Unconventional Warfare from a Western/Centrist Perspective," *Defence Studies*, Vol 2. No. 1 (Spring 2002), pp. 51–82.

Esfandiary, Dina, and Ariane Tabatabai, *Triple Axis: Iran's Relations with Russia and China* (IB Tauris, 2018).

Freeman, Charles W., *Arts of Power: Statecraft and Diplomacy* (United States Institute of Peace Press, 1997).

Gaddis, John Lewis, *On Grand Strategy* (Penguin Press, 2018).

Ghazvinian, John, *America and Iran: A History, 1720 to the Present* (Alfred A. Knopf, 2021).

Ghumman, Kashif Mumtaz, "Iran-US Relations in the Post-9/11 Days: Problems and Prospects," *Strategic Studies*, Vol. 22, No. 3 (2002), pp. 170–186.

Goodarzi, Jubin M., *Syria and Iran: Diplomatic Alliance and Power Politics in the Middle East* (IB Tauris, 2009).

Green, Jerrold D., Frederic Wehrey, and Charles Wolf, Jr., *Understanding Iran* (Rand Corporation, 2009).

Hanway, Jonas, *Revolutions of Persia* (London, 1754).

Harrison, Ross, *Strategic Thinking in 3D: A Guide for National Security, Foreign Policy and Business Professionals* (Potomac Books, 2013).

Harrison, Ross, and Paul Salem, *From Chaos to Cooperation: Toward Regional Order in the Middle East* (Middle East Institute, 2017).

Hunter, Shireen T., *Iran and the World: Continuity in a Revolutionary Decade* (Indiana University Press, 1990).

Hunter, Shireen T., *Arab-Iranian Relations: Dynamics of Conflict and Accommodation* (Rowman & Littlefield, 2019).

Keddie, Nikki R., *Modern Iran: Roots and Results of Revolution* (Yale University Press, 2003).

Keddie, Nikki R., and Mark J. Gasiorowski (eds.), *Neither East Nor West: Iran, the Soviet Union and the United States* (Yale University Press, 1990).

Keynoush, Banafsheh, *Saudi Arabia and Iran: Friends or Foes?* (Palgrave McMillian, 2016).

Kissinger, Henry, *World Order* (Penguin Press, 2014).

Koolaee, E., H. Mousavi, and A. Abedi, "Fluctuations in Iran-Russia Relations During the Past Four Decades," *Iran and the Caucasus*, Vol. 24, No. 2 (2020), pp. 216–232.

Lockhart, L., *The Fall of the Safavi Dynasty and the Afghan Occupation of Persia* (Cambridge University Press, 1958).

Mabon, Simon, *Saudi Arabia and Iran: Soft Power Rivalry in the Middle East* (IB Tauris, 2013).

Maleki, Abbas, *Iran's Foreign Policy from Khatami to Ahmadinejad* (Institute of Strategic Studies Islamabad, 2009).

Mansour, Imad, *Statecraft in the Middle East: Foreign Policy, Domestic Politics and Security* (IB Tauris, 2016).

Mearsheimer, John, *The Tragedy of Great Power Politics* (W. W. Norton, 2001).

Milani, Mohsen M., *Iran's Rise and Rivalry with the US in the Middle East*, (Oneworld Publications, 2025)

Miller, Rory, *Desert Kingdoms to Global Powers: The Rise of the Arab Gulf* (Yale University Press, 2016).

Mousavian, Seyed Hossein, *The Iranian Nuclear Crisis: A Memoir* (Carnegie Endowment for International Peace, 2012).

Nash, Geoffrey, *Re-examining the Cold War in the Middle East: U.S. and British Policy in Iran, Iraq and Egypt* (IB Tauris, 2020).

Nizamuddin, Talat, *The Making of the Present-Day Persian Gulf and the Arabian Peninsula: A Dynamic and Tragic Story of Oil Politics* (Prentice Hall, 1990).

Porter, Gareth, *Manufactured Crisis: The Untold Story of the Iran Nuclear Scare* (Just World Books, 2014).

Rabinovich, Itamar, *The View from Damascus: State, Political Community and Foreign Relations in the Twentieth Century* (Transaction Publishers, 2011).

Rakhal, Saikal, *The Rise and Fall of the Shah: Iran from Autocracy to Religious Rule* (Princeton University Press, 2009).

Ram, Harmish, *The Unseen Power: America and the Middle East* (Praeger, 1991).

Ramazani, Rouhollah K., *Iran's Foreign Policy 1941–1973: A Study of Foreign Policy in Modernizing Nations* (University of Virginia Press, 1975).

Ramazani, R. K., *Iran's Foreign Policy and the Changing World Order* (University of Virginia Press, 1992).

Ramazani, R. K., *Independence Without Freedom: Iran's Foreign Policy* (University of Virginia Press, 2013).

Smith, C., *The Middle East: History, Politics and Diplomacy* (Routledge, 2020).

Sobhani, Sohab C., *The Pragmatic Entente: Israeli-Iranian Relations 1948–1988* (Praeger, 1989).

Taheri, Amir, *Iran and the Arab World: The Political Dimension* (Gulf Centre for Strategic Studies, 1998).

Takeyh, Ray, *Guardians of the Revolution: Iran and the World in the Age of the Ayatollahs* (Oxford University Press, 2009).

Tari, Mohammad, *Iranian Foreign Policy Since 1979: International Relations in the Middle East* (Routledge, 2019).

Tarzi, Amin, *A Strategic Overview of Iran: Past, Present, and Future* (US Marine Corps University Press, 2009).

Tristam, Pierre, *The Arab Uprising: The Unfinished Revolutions of the New Middle East* (Da Capo Press, 2012).

Vatanka, Alex, *Iran and Pakistan: Security, Diplomacy and American Influence* (IB Tauris, 2015).

Vatanka, Alex, *The Battle of the Ayatollahs in Iran: The United States, Foreign Policy, and Political Rivalry Since 1979* (IB Tauris, 2021).

Wright, Robin, *In the Name of God: The Khomeini Decade* (Simon & Schuster, 1989).

Yaphe, Judith, *War and Politics in the Gulf: A New Confrontation with Iraq?* (National Defense University, 2002).

Zabih, Sepehr, *Iran Since the Revolution* (Johns Hopkins University Press, 1982).

INDEX

60 Minutes (television program), 48–49

al-Abadi, Hayder, 190
Abbas, Shah of Persia, 8, 11
Abdullah, King of Saudi Arabia, 125, 190
Abraham Accords (2020), 82–83, 130, 211–212
al-Afghani, Jamal al-Din, 34
Afghanistan, 7, 39, 46, 50, 62
Ahmadinejad, Mahmoud, 83, 128, 200
allies, nonstate. *See* militias, network of
American Israel Public Affairs Committee (AIPAC), 48, 49
Amini, Ali, 22
Amini, Mahsa, 10, 128, 164
Amir-Abdollahian, Hossein, 197
Anglo-Iranian oil company, 35
Anglo-Russian Convention (1907), 17, 56
Anti-Access/Area Denial (A2/AD) capabilities, 79, 133
Arab League conference (Saudi Arabia, 2023), 74, 84
Arab nationalism. *See* nationalism, Arab
Arab Spring and civil wars (2010–)
 economic benefits, 96–97
 militias' role in, 54, 130
 regional strategy and, 52–53, 90, 104, 147–148
 Syria, Iran's strategy in, 171–175
 Yemen, Iran's strategy in, 175–177

Arafat, Yasir, 85, 126
Aramco, Saudi, 2019 attacks on, 88, 115, 151–152, 154–155
Art of War, The (Sun Tzu), 150–155
Artesh (Iran), 123, 132
Assad, Bashar
 collapse of regime, 52, 71, 95, 97, 126
 Iran-Russia support of, 55, 175
Association of Southeast Asian Nations (ASEAN), 206, 208, 210–213
Astana process, 90
Ataturk, Kemal, 19, 89
"axis of evil" (speech), 46, 50, 152, 167
axis of resistance
 China and, 59
 Iran and, 32, 110–111, 131
 Iraq and, 92
 purpose of, 10, 25–26
 Syria and, 95, 97

Bagher Majlesi, Mohammed, 11
Bahrain, 8
Bani-Sadr, Abol Hassan, 37
Beaufre, Andre, 119
Betts, Richard, 119
Biden, Joe, 59
BRICS, 59, 136, 189, 197
Bush, George W., administration
 "axis of evil" speech, 46, 50, 152, 167
 Iran's views of, 49
 role in ME, 69

capabilities, Iranian
  conventional military, 132–134
  economic, 134–137
  hybrid system of, 120–123
  importance of, 119–120
  integrated model, 137–139
  militias, 129–132
  soft power, 123–127, 138–139
Carter Doctrine (US), 87, 156
Cheney, Dick, 49
China
  Iran and, 55, 59–62, 221
  power status, 189–190, 197–198
  role in Asia, 216
  role in ME, 64–65, 199, 216
  third power principle, 21–22
  US, relations with, 59–60, 198–199
Christopher, Warren, 48
Clausewitz, Carl von, 148
Clinton administration, 45, 47, 48–49
cohesion, internal
  external threats and, 9–10, 114
  power projection and, 2, 6, 25
Cold War
  end of, 45–47, 65, 95, 112
  Iran-Iraq War and, 36–41
  Saudi Arabia and, 86
  superpower competition, 27, 33–36, 43, 143
competitive landscape
  denial, Iranian strategy of, 144–148
  dual realities of, 72–73, 74, 77
  global powers, 34–35, 221
  Iranian advantages in, 77–78
  military, conventional, 77, 129–134
concentration principle, 148–149. *See also* strategic doctrines
Conoco (US oil company), 48–49
Constitutional Revolution (1906, Iran), 6, 17–18, 120
containment policy (US)
  Cold War era, 27, 143
  dual containment, 44, 45, 47–49, 50

  Iran and, 53
  Twin Pillars, regional containment, 86
Cottam, Richard, 41–42
coup d'état. *See* Mossadegh, Mohammed, 1953 coup against
cyber warfare, 133

D'Amato, Alfonso, 48
Dehghan, Hossein, 56
deterrence
  Iranian loss of, 204–205, 221
  Israeli loss of, 153
  militias' role in, 71, 107, 113
  strategic depth and, 158
diffusion, strategy of, 148–150, 219–220, 221. *See also* strategic doctrines
diplomacy, conventional Iranian militia strategy *vs.*, 72–75, 199–200, 222–223
  Palestinian issue and, 126–127
  past use of, 144–145
  potential for, 107, 138–139, 158–159
  stereotypes and, 57–58
doctrine. *See* strategic doctrines
dual containment, 45, 47–49. *See also* strategic doctrines
Dzhagaryan, Levan, 56

economic capabilities, Iranian
  constraints on, 92–93, 124, 134–135, 136–137
  development of Iranian, 120
  formal economy, 135
  industrialization and, 20
  potential for growth, 134, 136
economic sanctions, 21, 54–55, 58, 129, 179, 189–190
economic system, dual realities, 64–65, 72–73, 74, 77
Egypt, 28–29, 94
Erdogan, Recep Tayyip, 81, 89–90

Europe
  distrust of, 12–13, 34–35
  third power principle and, 20–21
European Coal and Steel Community (ECSC), 206
European Union (EU), 205–206

failed states
  economic relief, Iranian, 92–93
  militias in, 64, 95, 104, 121, 149–150, 158
  policy toward, Iranian, 72–74, 139, 144–145, 181, 183–189, 219
  reintegration, denial of, 146–147, 157
Faisal, King of Saudi Arabia, 86
Feith, Douglas Jay, 49–50
foreign policy, Iranian
  adaptive nature of, 79–80, 187, 210, 221–222
  balance of threats, 12–13, 44–45
  domestic politics and, 2, 6, 9, 25, 200–201, 204
  drivers, 3, 68, 114, 187, 188
  duality of, 68–69, 71–75, 199–200
  eastward tilt, 137, 197–198, 221–222
  evolution of, 162–163
  future possibilities, 201–203, 217–218, 222–223
  historical roots, 1–6, 11–13, 14–16, 24–26
  independence of, 9, 19–20, 23, 25–26
  leadership, role of, 213–215
  lessons learned, 13, 18–19, 21–22, 23–26
  realpolitik pragmatism, 40, 69–71, 90
  scope of interests, 104–107
  status quo, 203–205
  strategy and, 119–120, 141–144
  west, relations with, 204–205
  worldviews and, 27–31

See also diplomacy, conventional Iranian; militias, network of; strategic doctrines
forward defense strategy
  conventional capabilities, 133–134
  as core doctrine, 69–70
  deterrent power, 80, 113, 156–159
  development of, 40, 164, 220
  weaknesses of, 44
France, 14, 15–16, 34–35

Gaza, conflict in (2023–)
  diffusion strategy, 150
  implications of, 204–205, 214–215
  indirect approach, 151–152
  militias' role in, 71, 78, 100–101, 117, 129, 195
  regional politics and, 116
  strategic implications, 179–180
  Turkish response, 90
  See also October 7, 2023, Hamas attack on Israel
Ghaani, Esmail, 192
Ghotbzadeh, Sadegh, 41–42
global order. *See* great powers; power structures, international
Great Britain
  Anglo-Iranian oil company, 35
  Anglo-Russian Convention, 17, 56
  Egypt, views of, 28–29
  Iran, conflicts with, 14, 15
great powers, 55–64
  China as, 59–62
  foreign policy paradoxes, 196–200
  Iranian policy and, 25–26, 198–199, 203–204, 215–217
  Iranian views of, 33–36, 54–55, 64–65
  Russia as, 55–59
  Vietnam, parallels to, 215–217
  See also power structures, international
gross domestic product (GDP), Iranian, 135–136

Gulf Arab states
   competition with Iran, 125, 148, 192–195, 213
   normalization with Iran, 203, 212
   rival strategies for shaping ME, 188–193
Gulf Cooperation Council (GCC), 87, 129, 191
Gulf War I (1990-1991), 42–45

Hamadan military base (Iran), 5
Hamas. *See* militias, network of; October 7, 2023, Hamas attack on Israel
Haniyeh, Ismail, 78, 82, 83, 116, 130, 214
Hashd al-Sha'bi in Iraq, 53, 92, 146
Hay'at Tahrir al-Sham (HTS), 173, 195
Hezbollah in Lebanon
   Assad regime collapse, 52, 95, 98
   attacks on Israel, 220
   creation of, 40, 146, 165–166
   See also militias, network of
Hormuz, straits of, 37, 88, 115, 133, 138, 154
hostage crisis (1979-1981), 10, 36, 39, 41–42
Houthis in Yemen
   in "axis of resistance," 95
   Iranian support for, 90, 99–100, 104
   Israel, attacks on, 75, 113
   regional strategy, Iranian, 71, 106, 120–121, 130, 146
   Saudi Aramco, attacks on, 150–151, 154, 155
HTS (Hay'at Tahrir al-Sham), 173, 195
Hussein, Saddam, 46, 51, 69–70, 94

identity politics. *See* nationalism, Arab
ideology
   foreign policy, role in, 34–36, 68, 82, 86
   Iran-Iraq War and, 40

Israel, Iranian views of, 116
   limitations of, 13, 208
   nationalism and, 127–129
   realpolitik pragmatism *vs.*, 2, 6, 11–12, 31–32, 69–71
   US, Iranian views of, 39, 57
Incirlik air base (Turkey), 89
Indyk, Martin, 47
Instrument of Support of Trade Exchanges (INSTEX), 16
international political arena. *See* power structures, international
investment, foreign, 93, 125, 193, 213–214
Iran
   centralization, 19–20
   Constitutional Revolution, 6, 17–18
   domestic cohesion, 2, 6, 9–10, 25, 114
   foreign occupation of, 17–18, 21
   hostage crisis, 10, 36, 39, 41–42
   identity, 3–4, 103, 107–110, 116–117, 127–129
   leadership, importance of, 213–215
   legitimacy of government, 23–24, 128, 209
   national security interests, 104–105, 107
   role in world, 110–113
   strategic loneliness, 39, 105, 108
   worldview of, 30–32, 111–112
   See also Persia
Iran-Contra affair (1985), 40
Iranian Revolution (1979)
   1959 coup and, 23–24
   Arab Spring *vs.*, 52
   economic impacts of, 136
   export of, 67–68, 80, 127, 145
   foreign policy, impacts on, 1–2, 36–37
   hostage crisis and, 10
   national will, 127–129
   "neither east, nor west," 16, 25
   religion and, 1, 10–11, 109–110

Iran-Iraq War (1980-1988)
  foreign policy pragmatism, 40–41
  forward defense doctrine, 156–157
  indirect approach strategy, 151
  Israel and, 85
  lessons learned, 13, 39–40, 155, 219–220
  superpower collaboration, 36–38, 112
  worldview, impacts on, 36–41, 146, 163–164
Iraq
  counter-ISIS efforts in, 53–54
  investment in, 93, 125, 193
  Iran, erosion of support for, 124–125
  Iranian views of, 45, 91–94
  Iran-Saudi rival strategies in, 190–193
  Kuwait, invasion of, 42–43, 48
  rail link to Shalamcheh, 114
  Shi'ism in, 51, 92, 125, 147, 191
Iraq, US invasion of (2003), 46, 50–51, 62, 91, 147–148
IRGC (Islamic Revolutionary Guard Corps), 51, 122, 132, 135–136, 146
ISIS (Islamic State in Iraq and Syria)
  Iran-US efforts against, 53–54
  in Iraq, 92, 124, 193
Islam
  symbols of, 4, 6–7, 109–110
  as tool, 35, 39–40
  See also Shi'ism
"Islam of the Law," 11
Islamic Culture and Relations Organization (ICRO), 127
Islamic jurisprudence *(vilayat-e faqih)*, 3, 11, 94
Islamic of Iran Broadcasting (IRIB), 127
Islamic Revolutionary Guard Corps (IRGC, Iran), 51, 122, 132, 135–136, 146
Ismail I, Shah of Persia, 7–10

Israel
  drone attacks on, 99–100, 129, 149, 151
  Iran, 2024 direct military conflict with, 79, 151–152, 153, 220–221
  Iran, possible war with, 137, 204–205
  Iranian views of, 81–85
  militias, degradation of, 18–19, 64, 74, 77–78, 84, 134
  two-state solution, 126–127
  US support for, 62
  See also Gaza, conflict in (2023-)
Israel, Hamas attacks on (2023)
  Abraham Accords and, 212
  Israel's response to, 83, 153, 220–221
  militias, defensive claim of, 75, 158, 195

Joint Comprehensive Plan of Action (JCPOA)
  economic impacts, 134–135
  Iranian negotiating power, 53, 107–108, 150
  Iranian stance on, 40, 114, 200–201
  Israel and, 83
  Russia and, 57
  Saudi Arabia and, 86
  US withdrawal, 47, 58, 62, 197
  US withdrawal, responses to, 12, 16, 24

Karbala (Iraq), 124, 191
Kennedy administration, 22, 23
Khamenei, Ali
  external threat perceptions, 43, 83–84
  on Israel, 81
  9/11 attacks, response to, 50
  political role of, 78, 200–201, 214
  on strategic depth, 157–158
Khamenei, Hadi, 43
Khatami, Mohammed, 13, 50, 83, 87

Khomeini, Ruhollah
    consolidation of power, 9–10, 22, 23, 24
    Islamic symbols, use of, 4, 6–7
    on Palestinian issue, 126
    return from exile, 67–68
    Revolution and, 68, 69, 110, 145
    on Saudi Arabia, 85
    worldviews, 3, 6–7, 33–36, 120
Khorasan (Persia), 7–8
Kurdistan Workers' Party (PKK), 89
Kurds, 22, 90, 145
Kuwait, 37, 42–43, 48

labor market, Iranian, 135
Larijani, Ali, 55–56
Lavrov, Sergey, 57
Lebanon
    civil war in, 146, 165–166
    erosion of support for Iran, 123–124
    Iranian views of, 97–99
    Saudi-Iranian competition in, 146–147
    See also Hezbollah in Lebanon
Linh, Nguyen Van, 213

Marota City project (Syria), 97
maximum pressure campaign (US), 16, 99, 115–116, 135, 154–155
Middle East (ME)
    ASEAN, parallels with, 210–213, 216–217
    balance-of-power politics in, 72, 188
    balance-of-threat notion, 80
    China's role in, 60–61, 65, 88, 199
    great powers' role in, 196–200
    hegemony, competition for, 9–10, 147
    investment landscape, 93, 125, 193, 213–214
    Iranian power projection, 48, 52–53, 97–99
    Iranian role in, 110–113, 116–117, 120–123

Iranian views of, 78–81
power dynamics in, 52, 67–68, 71–78, 100–101
rival strategies for shaping, 75, 188–193
soft power campaigns in, 123–127
status quo in, 49–50, 106, 193–196, 203–205
strong states in, 80–81
superpower collaboration in, 34–35, 36–38
US missteps and struggles in, 51, 54, 61, 91
US role in, 62–63, 76–77, 105, 107, 158
Vietnam, parallels with, 210–213
weak states in, 91–94
militias, network of
    after Oct. 7 attacks, 79–80, 100–101, 116–117, 195
    Arab Spring and, 53–54
    capabilities, integrated, 137–138
    capabilities of, 121, 129–132, 220
    counter-ISIS efforts, 53–54
    creation of, 26, 146
    degradation of, 18–19, 64, 74, 77–78, 84, 134
    deterrent claims of, 71, 107, 113
    diffusion strategy and, 149
    power projection, Iranian, 70–71, 73–74, 80–81
    risks of, 63–64, 71, 75, 112
    role of, 54, 64, 91, 131, 146
Millspaugh, Arthur, 20
missile program, Iranian, 105, 123, 132–134, 137–138, 150, 158–159
Mohammed bin Salman, Crown Prince of Saudi Arabia, 74–75, 190
Montazeri, Hussein-Ali, 37
Mossadegh, Mohammed, 1953 coup against
    foreign policy, impacts on, 14, 35, 57, 110

government legitimacy and, 21, 23–24
Mousavi, Mir Hossein, 89, 128
Mujahedin e-Khalq (MEK), 83, 128
Al-Mustafa International University (Iran), 127

Nader Shah Afshar, Shah of Persia, 11
Najaf (Iraq), 124, 191
Nasrallah, Hassan, 78, 116
Nasser, Gamal Abdel, 22, 94, 96
nationalism, Arab
   British views of, 28–29
   in Egypt, 86
   Iranian views of, 85, 96
   in Iraq, 92, 192
   Shi'i unity *vs.*, 125
   in Syria, 94
nationalism, Iranian, 9, 19–20, 32, 67–68. *See also* Constitutional Revolution (1906, Iran)
"neither east nor west" mantra, 34, 35–36
Netanyahu, Benjamin, 83
Nguyen Van Linh, 213
9/11 attacks, 45–46, 49–52, 62, 166–171
1906 Constitutional Revolution (Iran), 6, 17–18, 120
Nixon administration, 86
Nojeh airbase (Iran), 55–56
Non-Proliferation Treaty (NPT), 84, 108
non-state allies. *See* militias, network of
nuclear deal. *See* Joint Comprehensive Plan of Action (JCPOA)
Nuclear Non-Proliferation Treaty (NPT), 84, 108
nuclear program, Iranian, 104–105, 108, 133, 134, 150, 158–159

October 7, 2023, Hamas attack on Israel
   axis of resistance and, 10, 12
   Iran, Palestinians and, 70, 126
   Iran's responses to, 68, 70–71, 78, 106–107
   Israel's response to, 130–131
   militias, deterrent claims of, 71, 107, 113
   See also Gaza, conflict in (2023–)
oil embargo (1973), 23
oil production and exports, 135–136
Oman, 145
Organization of Petroleum Exporting Countries (OPEC), 86
Oslo Accord (1993), 45, 48
Ottoman Empire, 4, 8, 12

Pahlavi, Mohammed Reza Shah, 21, 22–24, 85–86, 144–145
Pahlavi, Reza Shah, 19–22, 82
Palestinian Islamic Jihad (PIJ) in Gaza, 53, 126, 146
Palestinian issue, 70, 82, 87–88, 126–127, 138–139
Pax Americana, 43–45, 47, 111
People's Mujahedin Organization of Iran (MEK), 89
Persia
   external powers and, 12–13, 14, 56
   identity, Iranian, 108–109
   Qajar era, 7, 14–19
   Safavid era, 6–13
   See also Iran
Persian Gulf, 99, 115, 133–134, 154–155
Petraeus, David, 51
petroleum production and exports, 135–136
Pezeshkian, Masoud
   on China relations, 59, 61
   election of, 128
   on Israel, 82
   reformist platform, 83, 214
   on US relations, 76, 78, 200
power structures, international
   historical themes, 12–13, 15–16, 24

Iran and, 110–113, 157, 196–200
worldview, role of, 27–30
See also great powers
protest movements
   in Iran, 39–40, 110, 128
   in Iraq, 93, 124–125, 192
   soft power, loss of, 123–124, 194
   in Syria, 40, 74, 124
Putin, Vladimir, 58–59, 222

Qajar period (1789-1925), 7, 14–19
Qatar, 80, 81, 90, 124, 188
Quds force (IRCG, Iran), 51, 122, 132, 146
Qutb, Sayyid, 34

Rafsanjani, Akbar Hashemi, 13, 40, 43, 48–49
Raisi, Ibrahim
   election of, 128
   on foreign policy, 58, 76, 78
   on global power shift, 197
   on Israel, 82
regime change
   Arab Spring and, 171
   in Iran, 4, 43, 49, 83–84, 182
   in Iraq, 22, 46, 148–149, 167, 169
   in Syria, 126, 173–175, 201
   US regional goals, 49, 52, 61, 63
regional politics. *See* Middle East (ME)
revolution. *See* Iranian Revolution (1979)
Rouhani, Hassan, 200
Russia
   drones, Iranian, 58, 104–105, 133, 178, 199
   historical conflicts, 5, 14–16, 56–57
   Iranian views of, 55–59, 222
   JCPOA and, 108, 197
   sanctions against, 21, 55, 58
   See also Soviet Union; Ukraine, Russian invasion of (2022); Ukraine War (2022–)

Sadr, Bani, 145
Safavid Dynasty, 6–13
Saleh, Ali Abdullah, 194
Salman, King of Saudi Arabia, 125, 147, 190
sanctions, economic, 21, 54–55, 58, 129, 179, 189–190
Saudi Arabia (SA)
   Abraham Accords and, 212
   Arab League conference in, 74, 84
   competition with Iran, 93, 125, 144, 146–147
   Iranian views of, 85–89
   rapprochement, China's role in, 61, 65, 88, 199
   rapprochement with Iran, 107, 115, 154, 191–192, 193
   strategy for Iraq, 190–193
   US, relations with, 60, 86, 154
Saudi Aramco, attacks on (2019), 88, 115, 151–152, 154–155
Selim, Sultan, 12
September 11, 2001, terrorist attacks (9/11 attacks), 45–46, 49–52, 62, 166–171
Shah Ismail (Ismail I, Shah of Persia), 7–10
Shanghai Cooperation Organization (SCO), 47, 55, 59, 107, 136, 189, 197
Shi'ism
   internal cohesion and, 7–9, 10–12
   in Iraq, 51, 92, 125, 147, 191
   in Syria, 96
   as tool for control, 8, 80, 123–124, 125
Shukr, Fuad, 116, 130
Shuster, Morgan, 18, 56, 120
al-Sinwar, Yahya, 78, 116, 130
al-Sistani, Ali, 92, 94
Soleimani, Qassim
   assassination of, 93, 191–192
   regional policy and, 51, 53, 57

Soviet Union
    Afghanistan, invasion of, 39
    collapse of, 32, 44, 215
    tilt toward Iraq, 37, 38
    See also Russia
straits of Hormuz, 37, 88, 115, 133, 138, 154
strategic depth, Iranian, 87, 96, 106, 157–158
strategic doctrines
    concentration principle, 147–148
    conventional capabilities, 133–134
    denial, strategy of, 144–148
    development of, 5, 143, 156, 182–186
    diffusion, strategy of, 148–150, 219–220, 221
    diplomacy *vs.* militia-based, 68–69, 72–75, 199–200, 222–223
    indigenization doctrine, 159–160
    indirect approach, 150–153
    Iranian views of, 113–116
    Sun Tzu and, 150–155
    third power principle, 5, 18, 20, 21–22, 160–162
    "whole-of-region" view, 52–53, 74
    See also containment policy (US); forward defense strategy
substate militias. *See* militias, network of
Sun Tzu, 150–155, 219
Syria
    post-Assad era, 203
    Astana process, 90
    civil war, 55, 58, 152, 171–175
    Hezbollah and, 95
    Iran, popular opinion of, 40, 74, 125–126
    Iran consulate, 220
    Iranian views of, 94–97

Taeb, Mehdi, 95
Taliban, 50, 152

territories, loss of, 7, 9–10, 14–15, 56
third power principle, 5, 18, 20, 21–22, 160–162
Treaties of Gulistan and Turkmenchay (Iran-Russia), 15, 56
Treaty of Finckenstein (Iran-France), 15
tribes, 20
Trump administration
    impacts on Iranian strategy, 115–116
    maximum pressure campaign, 16, 99, 135, 154–155
    second term, 130, 134, 222
    See also Joint Comprehensive Plan of Action (JCPOA)
Tudeh party (Iran), 37
Turkey, modern, 89–90, 192, 195
Turkey, Ottoman, 4, 8, 12
Twin Pillars policy (US), 86
two-state solution (Israel-Palestinians), 126–127

UAE (United Arab Emirates), 9–10, 80, 94, 177, 204, 211–212
Ukraine, Russian invasion of (2022)
    Iranian strategy, impacts on, 177–179
    Iran-Russia ties since, 5, 21–22, 55, 57–58, 104–105
Ukraine War (2022–)
    drones, Iranian, 58, 104–105, 133, 178, 199
    and ME power dynamics, 75–76
UN Security Council (UNSC), 38, 62
UNESCO, 193
United Kingdom. *See* Great Britain
United Nations (UN), 38, 87
United Nations Security Council (UNSC), 38, 62, 108
United States (US)
    Afghanistan, invasion of, 46, 50, 62
    alliances, regional, 60, 83–84

China, relations with, 198–199
Iranian policymaking, role in, 196–197, 215–216
Iranian views of, 39, 62–64, 76, 79, 105
Iranian worldview, role in, 81, 180–182
Iraq, invasion of, 46, 50–51, 62, 91, 147–148
rapprochement, potential for, 114, 204–205
Saudi Arabia, relations with, 86–87, 88, 193
as unreliable ally, 88, 115, 154–155
worldview of, 32, 76
See also September 11, 2001, terrorist attacks (9/11 attacks); specific names of policies and doctrines

Velayati, Ali, 38
Vietnam, 205–217
global geopolitics, parallels, 215–217
Iran, parallels with, 207–210
leadership, role of, 213–215
regional geopolitics, parallels, 210–213
vilayat-e faqih (Islamic jurisprudence), 3, 11, 94
Vision 2030 (Saudi Arabia), 192, 204

Wallace, Mike, 48
"west-toxification," 8, 25, 39
White Revolution (1963, Iran), 22, 23
Wilson, Woodrow, 18
worldviews
9/11 attacks, 49–52
Cold War era, 33–45
post-Cold War period, 45–47
decisionmaking and, 27–30
Gulf War I, 42–45
hostage crisis, 41–42
Iran-Iraq war and, 36–41
Iran's lens, 30–32, 94–95
Manichaeism, 34, 70

Yemen, 99–100, 175–177

Zarif, Javad, 13, 57, 108, 114, 200
Zoroastrianism, 7, 70